Praise for A.A. Gill

'At his best, Gill shows how real insight into a culture can be gleaned from the manner in which its food is produced, distributed, prepared and consumed' *New Statesman*

'Certainly a book that whets the appetite and an ideal Christmas present for the foodie in your life'
Dublin Evening Herald

'What sets Gill apart from the upper middle-class politically incorrect pontificators is that he's interested in people (even if he doesn't always like them) and writes in a clear, economical, puissant style' *The List*

'His reporting, within the space of a few sentences, can be honest, romantic, awestruck, damning, hilarious but, importantly, never sentimental or patronising' *Time Out*

'Gill is a delightful, funny polemicist. His prose floats like a butterfly and stings like a bee and, just when you least expect it, lands a deft and lethal blow beneath the belt'
Sunday Times

'He entertains like a vicious game show' *Glasgow Herald*

'It annoys, arouses feelings and forces one to confront received opinions. Whether one sides with it or not, one can admire the zest of the writing and applaud its splendid lack of political correctness' Beryl Bainbridge, *Mail on Sunday*

A.A. Gill was born in Edinburgh. He is the author of two novels, *Sap Rising* (1997) and *Starcrossed* (1999), books on two of London's most famous restaurants, The Ivy and Le Caprice, two travel books, *A. A. Gill is Away* and *Previous Convictions*, and *The Angry Island: Hunting the English*. He is the TV and restaurant critic for the *Sunday Times* and is contributing editor to *GQ*, *Vanity Fair* and *Australian Gourmet Traveller* magazines. He lives in London and spends much of his year travelling.

By A.A. Gill

TABLE TALK

Sweet and Sour,
Salt and Bitter

A.A. Gill

PHOENIX

A PHOENIX PAPERBACK

First published in Great Britain in 2007
by Weidenfeld & Nicolson
This paperback edition published in 2008
by Phoenix,
an imprint of Orion Books Ltd,
Orion House, 5 Upper Saint Martin's Lane,
London WC2H 9EA

An Hachette Livre UK company

1 3 5 7 9 10 8 6 4 2

A CIP catalogue record for this book
is available from the British Library.

ISBN 978-0-7538-2441-2

Typeset by Deltatype Ltd, Birkenhead, Merseyside

Printed in Great Britain by Clays Ltd, St Ives plc

The Orion Publishing Group's policy is to use papers
that are natural, renewable and recyclable products
and made from wood grown in sustainable forests.
The logging and manufacturing processes are expected
to conform to the environmental regulations of the
country of origin.

www.orionbooks.co.uk

The Blonde

Contents

Acknowledgements

Behind every mediocre journalist there is a host of exceedingly good editors. A lot of people have edited bits and pieces of this book: notably Lucas Hollweg, my editor on *Style*, who has done a lot more than correct my wayward spelling; Celia Hayley, who is responsible for how this book reads; Alan Samson, Alex Bulford, Carole Green and Lucinda McNeile. I also want to thank my amanuensis Michelle Klepper and agents Grainne Fox and Ed Victor.

Foreword

For most people, the enjoyment is enough; pleasure doesn't need explaining. If you ask why they liked the play, the soup, the view, they'll probably use all-encompassing, evocative words of emotion or volume – it was 'great', 'terrific', 'amazing', 'good', 'very good'. Press them, and more than likely they'll describe what they've seen, done, eaten. 'There was this sensational ballet/novel/lap dancer – it was fantastic.' Analysing why something was moving or entertaining or funny, or wasn't, doesn't improve it. In fact, dissecting things might actually break the spell, tarnish the experience.

There is something odd, something obsessive, something a touch neurotic about wanting to be a critic, wanting to pull the legs off delicate bits of fun. It certainly isn't a necessary part of cultured life. I don't think critics feel things more intensely or on another level. Their knowledge and experience, if they have any, doesn't necessarily make them more sensitive to the all-round enjoyment of a sausage than anyone else is. Indeed, many of us critics look like we enjoy life only occasionally and then grudgingly. But being able to organise, distil, articulate and parse a sausage in the context of aesthetics, taste, morality, history, anthropology and fashion, whilst remembering it is still just a sausage, does give me a separate, academic, rather drily smug satisfaction.

Criticism doesn't improve your experience of culture

– but good assertive, stringent criticism does prevent creativity and craft sinking to their levels of least public resistance and to sycophantic pleasantries. And the review itself may be entertaining and provoking. Criticism at its best elicits a response of 'that's what I think, but I'd never have thought it like that'. The strongest parts of the culture are those that hate their critics the most. Critics criticise so that everybody else can get on with enjoying themselves. We are civilisation's traffic wardens.

Over the decade and a bit that I've been doing it, the Table Talk column in the *Sunday Times* has evolved into being more or less about restaurants and food. It's also more or less about whatever has settled on my retina that week. This collection is a forensic filleting of many of these columns, and as a small sop and grudging gesture of good will to catering, I've taken out nearly all the names of restaurants and just left all the good, fatty, sticky, knobbly, tasty stuff. There are also a couple of things I wrote in a food column for *Tatler* before I lost my critical milk teeth.

Here are answers to some of the questions that I've been asked over the years. I *always* book under a false name, but I *never* wear a disguise. Getting into a wig and a costume and talking in a funny voice to eat dinner is weird and way too self-obsessed. It's the sort of thing they do in America. Yes, sometimes I am recognised and the first thing that happens is that everything gets worse. Particularly the service.

I always pay – always. There is no such thing as a free lunch. I never eat with restaurant PRs, or go to restaurants on the advice or recommendation of press releases. The choice is capricious and random. Sometimes I choose, sometimes my editor – mostly the Blonde chooses. I don't have a favourite restaurant, and I don't have secret restaurants that I don't write about.

And no, not anyone could do it.

Reviewing isn't sophisticated or complicated or particularly onerous, but most people who think they can review find that they can't. Expertise isn't necessarily a help; it can make you talk down to your readers and distances you from their experience. But over the years you do acquire it – I now know a lot about food. Except cheese, which like grammar, I simply cannot retain a single piece of useful information about. I've also worked as a cook, a dishwasher, a waiter and a maître d'. And I can cook.

The problem and the skill is not actually in the food or in having an eye for decor, an ear for the staff or a nose for the wine list (which I rarely mention, because I don't drink). It's in the language.

English, which is so gloriously verbose about so much of life's gay tapestry, is summarily tongue-tied when it comes to describing food and eating. The reasons are partially cultural. It has never been considered polite to talk about food, partly out of necessity, as there hasn't ever been much food that you could be polite about. Food and talking about food was something the French did. It's often pointed out that while the words for farm animals are Anglo-Saxon, their names when they're cooked are Norman – pork for swine, beef for cattle, mutton for sheep – distinguishing who actually did the herding and who did the eating.

But then, many of the words that we do have are swaggered in a Pooterish bourgeois snobbery. I can't write 'moist' or 'succulent' or 'luxuriant' without shivering. Writing about food and the sensation of eating can be as nauseating to read as watching someone eat with their mouth open. So you have to pick your way through the verbiage with care and imagination. You do need to be pretty omnivorous – I've always said that I'd eat anything anyone else ate, as long as it didn't involve a bet, a dare or an initiation ceremony. I'm often asked what the most disgusting thing I've ever eaten is. Buried shark in Iceland, jewel beetles in the Kalahari, fertilised duck eggs in Vietnam, seal blubber with the Eskimos in Greenland and warm blood with the Masai in Tanzania all pale into wholesome yumminess compared with the fast food available on every high street after 11 o'clock at night, or the chilled, dehydrated and microwaved amuse-bouches lurking in petrol stations. My particular interest in dinner really only begins with the food. I'm constantly fascinated by why and how we eat. The movement of ingredients, the history, anthropology, mythology, manners and rituals of food. Dinner is a defining human occasion. We are the only species that ever existed that offers hospitality.

Is my opinion worth any more than anyone else's on the bus? With a modest blush I must say yes. It's also worth more than that of most chefs and restaurateurs – I'm a professional, this is what I do; they're big men, but they're out of condition. Do I ever get bored, blasé, bilious? No, hand on heart, I'm always excited about dinner. I still get that frisson with a new menu. Do I ever eat or order badly on purpose, look for awful food to make good copy? Of course not; despite what most of you think, it's actually no easier to write a bad review than a good one; it's just that you prefer reading the bad ones. So here is a collection of the good bits and some of the very, very bad bits from a decade of dinners.

Finally, people often say, 'Seeing as you know so much, why don't you open a restaurant?' And I always think of Brendan Behan's famous quote about us. 'Critics are like eunuchs in a harem – they know how it's done, they've seen it done every day, but they're unable to do it themselves.' Like so much of Behan's work, that's smart but not quite right. Critics may well be like eunuchs in a harem who know how it's done, having seen it done every day, they just don't fancy having it done to them.

1

APPETITE

The amuse-gueule came, as I knew it would: a crab cake the size of a shirt button that collapsed into vapours at the sight of a fork. A man can feel right foolish chasing a crab's toenail round a plate. It tasted fine, in a homeopathic sort of way.

How about this for a doozie of a starter: cream of haricots blancs and roasted garlic and pan-fried frogs' legs and fricassee of snails and Scottish girolles and ... and ... parsley jus. What, no puppy dogs' tails?

This appalling blind-man's-deli-shoplifting-spree came on a single plate. It was truly, heart-stoppingly, sphincter-shrinkingly, colon-knottingly ghastly. The snails were like the pickings from a hippo's nostril, and the frogs' legs had been boned. How much sublimated commis loathing must go into boning frogs' legs? They tasted like something sour and slimy that had been fished out of a heron's throat. The mushrooms were the malevolent, anaemic growths you find in the corners of musty cellars.

For a main course, I had the assiette of spring lamb. Frankly, it would have been kinder to slap a movement order on this sheep and bury it in a quicklime pit.

My first course was stunning: a lump of duck foie like a grey hot water bottle floating in a bowl of the richest consommé. It was fantastic. I could feel it peristaltically clogging all my tubes. It had a deeply sensual taste and the texture of slipping into a coma. For the main course, I had a daube of beef cheek 'cooked like a

grandmother'. God, if anyone had cooked my grandmother like this I'd have visited more often.

Main courses would have got a Third World airline grounded. My lamb would only have been of gastronomic interest to a man who had never eaten a sheep before. The mushrooms wouldn't have tasted wild if you'd soaked them in Ecstasy and given them guns.

Foie gras terrine with grouse breast and Sauternes jelly. Excellent. The combination of rich foie, gamey grouse and the sweet musk of the Sauternes was impeccable. So why did the cook drizzle truffle oil all over it? Inexcusable. Disgusting. Truffle oil and Sauternes – if you want to get the effect at home, try drinking sweet sherry out of a teenager's well-worn trainer.

Pudding: a jelly that involved Campari and fennel. It was a pretty colour, but tasted exactly as I've always imagined suicide capsules would: fatalistically bitter and fraudulently medicinal.

Christmas dinner: the single most disgusting meal ever invented, with the exception of American thanksgiving, which, though similar, manages to be marginally worse. I seem to have been eating off my buffet knee for a month, every plate a hideous game of gastro-Pelmanism. Right, I've got turkey, two sorts of stuffing, sausage, potato, cranberry, ham, mince pie, stilton, cake, pudding. 'Oh, you haven't got any brandy butter. Where shall I put it?' On the sprouts. Nobody sane or loving could invent Christmas food from scratch.

We chose pea and ham soup and courgette soup, followed by

tarragon chicken and a sort of boeuf bourguignon, 'but it's not actually boeuf bourguignon'. If you had been stuck in a snow hole on Ben Nevis for three days consuming nothing but icicles and your fingernails, then the pea and ham soup might, quite probably, have been very welcome; the courgette, however, would still have been green slop.

Ramadan

At the heart of all religions, there is food. Actually, that reminds me of something a Quaker woodwork teacher once told me. We were looking at the simple cross in chapel and he said quietly (Quakers say everything quietly, with an Eeyore-ish emphasis): 'You know what's at the heart of Christianity?' The Holy Ghost? Love? Redemption? Grace? 'A mortise and tenon joint.' It was an opaquely Delphic pronouncement that still niggles, like a paper cut in the corner of your mouth.

Anyway, I can't think of a religion that doesn't use food as part of its ritual. For Christians, there is obviously the Host (or mein Host, as it's known in German churches): the bread and wine. But there are also pancakes and Easter eggs, simnel cakes and hot cross buns, thousands of European Catholic sweetmeats and tarts (both risen and fallen), and enough marzipan saints to make you sick. Hindus have lentils and chapatis. Judaism has its bitter herbs and Passover lamb. And in Guatemala, I once saw animist offerings of rum and fags.

I have a theory – no more than a guess – that religion and the preparation of food arrived together and grew, temporally and spiritually, hand in hand. Cooking is a profound transformation. It's only a spiritual hop and skip to burning heretics at the stake. And the food that was probably at the heart of nascent religions was your neighbour's heart, liver and thumb muscle (apparently a particularly moreish delicacy). Men with beards posit that the original reason for Leviticus prohibiting pork was that pig and human are indistinguishable when thoroughly barbecued.

In many religions, there is also the absence or denial of

food. Fasting has generally dropped off the Christian calendar. There were once two fast days a week, as well as numerous saints' fast days and Lent, which, when there was less to eat, was far more rigorous than just giving up drink or chocolate or Indian takeaways.

Medieval monks were canny at getting round the 'fish on Friday' thing. They made conies (rabbits) into honorary fish, because they lived in holes, like puffins. And puffins were obviously fish. Look, if angels can dance on the heads of pins, then puffins can be fish, okay?

The most dramatic religious fast is Ramadan, which sounds like a Bill Haley chorus. I took the kids to Oman, not for Ramadan, exactly, but during Ramadan. It's a tricky time to travel in an observant country. All the restaurants are closed. You can't eat in the street. Tourist hotels have secret locked-and-darkened midday dining-rooms. I had to tell the children not to drink in public, while at the same time making sure they drank enough.

I asked my guide, who was fasting, what the point of Ramadan was. I thought it would be the same self-mortification as Christian fasting: to rarefy the ethereal reverie. 'Up to a point,' he replied politely. 'Actually, it's self-restraint. It toughens us up. The Koran says we need to be strong to withstand hardship.' I had forgotten what an earthy and practical religion Islam is. Not drinking from sunrise to sunset when the temperature is in the 40s is properly tough.

We were invited to breakfast with a family of Bedouin. In that rather overpolite, respectful, smiley way that white Westerners have when taking part in other people's rituals, I hissed at the children to behave and only eat with their right hands. 'We know,' they sighed. 'We've done religion and other cultures and bum-wiping.'

The first thing that is eaten is dates. I watched an old man stone his with a magician's sleight of hand. The elegance and delicacy of eating with your hands from a communal plate is beautiful, respectful and amazingly neat, if it's done by neat, respectful and beautiful people. I was left cross-legged in a midden of dripped and spilt food. We drank orange juice and laban, a thin yoghurt. Despite the hunger and thirst, nobody grabbed or rushed or stuffed or chugged or gulped.

It was a thoughtful, timely and surprisingly frugal meal. I envied them the appetite that comes with forbearance and faith. I even considered joining in Ramadan for a weekend, but you can't be a tourist in other people's souls.

We finished with a farinaceous soup that was thick and warm and blandly delicious. 'What is this?' I asked. 'It reminds me of something.' A child was dispatched to the kitchen tent to get the recipe, and came back with a tin of Scott's porridge oats. As the huge and miraculous Arabian night sky rolled out over the cooling desert, not for the first time, I was reminded that we are all connected by more than divides us.

Concert

Took my boy Ali to see Eminem. 'Are you sure?' cautioned other parents. 'It's pretty unpleasant. Urban nihilism. Drugs. Violence. It could get very ugly.' Yes, I'm aware of all that – but I think he's old enough to make up his own mind about Milton Keynes. Anyway, I'll be there to remind him to just say 'No ... tting Hill Gate'. Eminem, by contrast, is a poppety socks.

Now I'm about to do one of those things that annoyed the loons and grandpa vest off me when I was a lad. I'm going to patronise young people's culture. I once had an old in-law who would smile with a manic serenity and say: 'You know, I'm not shocked. You think you're all so clever and on your face.' But it's gay-porn Nazis, I'd say, doing it with cripples in the middle of a christening. 'No, no, I saw far worse than that during the blackout.'

Anyway, Ali and I stood in the bowl of Milton Keynes, shouting 'Fug chew, muddyfugger!' as instructed. It was a bonding moment. I know other fathers take their sons to chalk streams and tie small bits of handmade bellybutton fluff to hooks, but, for my boy and me, the father-son thing is woven by singing 'Two trailer-park girls go round the outside.' I love the pantomime audience-participation stuff. Instead of shouting 'Behind you!' and 'Oh, no, he didn't!' we go 'Yo! Fugger pig!' But what I like best about Eminem – and I'm not sure a lot of the audience quite understood this – is that he is, in fact, the second coming of Gilbert and Sullivan.

Now, I can hear you snorting all over the Home Counties. But bear with me – I'm not coming over all Tom 'Contrary'

Paulin just to get a rise. Eminem sings patter songs: they could be from *The Pirates of Penzance* or, indeed, *Ruddigore*. The Lord High Executioner's little list is plainly proto-rap. Eminem just adds a modern touch of Grand Guignol (a theatrical form that has been sadly and shamefully ignored of late) and auto-testicle clutching, which I've always thought there was far too little of in *The Mikado*.

'What has this to do with food?' I hear you say. Or, more likely, 'Yo! Muddyfugger, wheredy fugdy food, bitch?' Well, I was planning on doing an archly amusing little review of the luncheon bazaar that circles the bowl of Milton Keynes. (By the way, I'm sure I'm not the first to point this out, but was it the civil servants' famed sense of humour that named this place after the two Englishmen who would have loathed it the most?) But they're not paying me enough to put this stuff in my mouth ahead of a four-hour traffic jam. And, anyway, it's the one cuisine that you all know intimately: the caravans of burgers and sausages, pizza and lardy ice cream, and a stand with a sign that was as unequivocal as it was untrue: 'Chinese Food'. Given the enormous changes in gastronomy and our growing sophistication about food, it's amazing that the catering at large, popular events remains doggedly doggy. It's essentially the same as it was when I first came across it in the 1960s, and probably longer ago than that. It's the nastiest food in Europe. That smell of onions sweated in fat and water, then seared on a greasy hotplate, is the abiding scent of the English en masse. I'm sure that's what the crusades smelt like – all the way from Tilbury to Acre.

In Milton Keynes there were 64,000 people, all of whom can now find their way round menus in half a dozen languages and three or four continents, who have watched a thousand hours of cookery on television, who use a wine list, who travel abroad. But this event catering is still all people think they deserve when out having communal fun. The problem with it is that it's still very white food. Indeed, the audience for

Eminem was extraordinarily white. I saw only half a dozen black men, and most of them were on stage. This just added to the *Mikado* nature of the event. It's fusion pop culture: the way Fred Astaire fused with black dancing and Elvis fused with the blues. Fusion is never a 50:50 deal. As heat passes from the hotter to the cooler, so popular culture passes from the black to the white, from the gay to the straight, from the street to the square, from angry to amused. It's social thermodynamics.

I was just trying to remember what it was my dad took me to see when I was ten. It was *Coppelia*, with Robert Helpmann, who resembled Eminem in not a single atom. As I recall, it's the story of a dirty old man who falls in love with a mechanical underage sex doll. And you really imagine that's more suitable than Eminem singing about cleaning out his closet?

Politics

If you get rid of the midden of power control, special plead-
ing, social engineering, fevered dreaming, spiritual zeal, do-
goodery, vanity and dumb-thuggery, then, right at the bottom
of politics, you'll find its original idea, the founding purpose of
governance: it's to feed people, or perhaps to allow folk to eat
their dinner in peace. It doesn't need a manifesto or speeches or
plebiscite or subcommittees or baby-kissing or flesh-pressing
to understand politics, it's just about breakfast.

Of course, breakfast is a complicated deal. Jonathan Swift
wrote a brilliant satire on Tara Palmer-Tomkinson's breakfast,
pointing out that half the globe was involved in supplying the
titbits she'd toy with while sighing over her post. Once you've
decided to have tea instead of coffee, and that you'd like a
spoonful of sugar, you're into funding a navy, fighting wars,
building motorways and the Foreign Office. Making a round
of cheese on toast might appear to be the simplest thing in the
world, but its ramifications lead to the nation state, industrial-
isation, global economics, organised religion, civilisation and
napkin rings.

Sometimes, to coin a phrase, it's worth getting back to
basics, which isn't about tupping your secretary, it's about
the ingredients in a cottage loaf. And while politicians would
like us to think they have a higher calling, their fundamental
purpose is to be butchers' boys and milkmaids' udder-washers
(the cows, not the maids). The language of politics is replete
with gastro metaphors: 'a chicken in every pot', 'let them eat
cake', 'jam today', 'guns or butter', 'a mess of potage', 'tighten-
ing belts', 'skimming off the top', 'gravy train', 'fudge'.

In the corpulent West, food has ceased to be a big political issue, or even a minor one. The problem isn't too little, it's too much. This is by far and away the biggest social change in two thousand years of politics: finally, government has achieved what it was set up to do – feed everyone. Food production, distribution and protection are no longer the state's problem. They are handled by private enterprise and civil servants. Government has virtually nothing to do with it. So we've had a result, we've done the job: why don't politicians just bugger off and get real jobs? That's not a rhetorical question. I mean it. Okay, we could keep a couple part-time, in case of emergencies, like a lifeboat crew.

Politics is probably the last industry that's still wedded to the idea of the power lunch. They still imagine that influence is peddled, arms twisted and backs stabbed over a Dover sole. Predictably, it's the ones with the least power who eat the most courses. What astonishes and depresses me is how badly they eat. If food is their fundamental calling, then at least you'd think they'd know something about it. On the very few occasions I've been privy to the peristalsis of politicians, it has not been an edifying sight. It's not just the mannerless gusto with which they fall on a menu, it's that they have no sense of taste.

Politicians are driven by two contradictory engines – personal greed and public parsimony. So they look at the prices and mention how terribly expensive it all is and that the price of one starter could feed a pensioner in their constituency for a month. And then they go at the carte like Pitt and Napoleon carving up the world. An odd thing I've noticed is that all politicians have a weird affinity with the cheeseboard. I think they like it because it's symbolic – you get to do your own knifework. It's certainly not because they know anything about cheese, but here there are hard choices and soft options, and they imagine that it's over cheese that deals are done.

Who knows? Frankly, who cares? They all live in a carvery

of their own making. But it is dispiriting that the people who are responsible for the well-being of our children eat so gluttonously and so badly. If Westminster were in any other country in Europe, it would be the gastronomic centre of the city, because politicians eat there. Here, it's a lunchtime desert for the same reason.

The yak

Consider the yak. I understand you have a busy and complex life juggling the pressing problems of fiscal probity, ergonomics, soft furnishing, personal hygiene and whether or not to start all over again on DVD, but put that aside for a minute and consider the yak.

As you probably already know, the yak's family tree is as matted as its bottom. It is generally agreed among aficionados and enthusiasts that yaks are members of the family Bovidae, though their precise family relationships are open to some rather snobbish discourse.

Herwart Bohlken, a man whose own name, it must be said, raises a few eyebrows, contends that the yak belongs to the genus *Bos* and the subgenus *Poephagus*, with the caveat that responsible, sedate, tame yaks are *Bos (Poephagus) mutus przheval'skii*, whereas wild, clubbing, dirty-little-stop-out yaks should be sneeringly referred to as *Bos (Poephagus) grunniens Linnaeus*. And, to make matters worse, both have the morals of ungulates and mount each other faster than the household cavalry's musical gallop, producing little *bos* who don't know whether they are *mutus* or *grunniens*.

However, this is not the biggest problem to confront your yak. It's the fact that they're generally, as a rule, looked after, herded and attended by Buddhists. Now, you might quite reasonably assume that, in these days of animal rights, being owned by a Buddhist would be the ruminant equivalent of winning the lottery, because the one central edict, the core belief, of Buddhism (apart from talking and smiling at the same time) is not eating meat.

Ah, but life is not that simple – it is ever thus. The land where Buddhists and yak come together in peace and love has very few vegetables (you're ahead of me), and what there are are eaten by the yaks. So the Buddhists have to eat them, which they don't like (the Buddhists or the yaks). Indeed, they are (the Buddhists), in turn, consumed, if that's not too cynical a word, by guilt. So they've looked for a loophole in the rules to alleviate the heavy weight of moral responsibility and dinner, and have found that, strictly speaking, it's not the eating that's the problem, it's the killing.

Frankly, this isn't fooling anyone, but it makes a Buddhist – if not the yaks – feel a little easier. So what they do, and I hope you're sitting down for this, is take the suckling calves away from their mothers until they starve to death. That, on a technicality, counts as an act of fate. If the yak doesn't have a mother, then they put a leather (yak) bag over its head till it suffocates. Again, technically, no blood was spilt, and running out of oxygen can be seen as, if not an act of God, then just bad luck. The traditional yak-herders' prayer is: 'Buddha, can you spare me a kine?'

(There is a moral here for the bunny-huggers and tofu-munchers among you: if two vegetarians live together in harmony, one will always, inevitably, end up eating the other, and an obsession with kindness leads inexorably to extreme cruelty.) Because of the guilt, yak meat is called black food. Yak milk, on the other hand, because it leaves the cow still standing with a faint sense of relief and erect nipples, is considered good, white food.

Buddhists, who love yaks, adore yak milk above all else. They like it neat, straight up, and they like it in tea, but only after it has been turned into butter. Interestingly, yak milk has a much higher fat content than cow's – as much as 60 per cent higher. Buddhists, who love yaks, even go so far as to say that yak milk is better for infants than human mothers' milk, which they claim makes children stupid, and may well explain why we are like we are or, alternatively, why they are like they are.

Yaks are milked in the traditional way by women squatting at the nether end, heads pressed into furry flanks for support. They have buckets, of course, and hooks worn on chains round their waists, which attach to the bucket to safeguard against accidents. These hooks have, over the years, become decorative symbols of femininity, and are often elaborately decorated in silver with coral and precious stones.

At last, we come to the point. It's the Blonde's birthday soon (don't ask, I don't), and it's nigh on impossible to find something to give her because she's already bought everything conceivable – and a few things that are inconceivable – with my money. But I'm pretty sure she doesn't have a Buddhist yak-milker's silver bucket hook (try saying that ten times), and I have a fancy to give her one. It would be an entertaining and attractive talking point.

'Oh, what's that large silver hook dangling on your groin?'

'Ah, funny you should ask ...'

Vegetarians

Don't you just hate pandas? Whenever I find myself with a surfeit mouthful of unfocused loathing, I remember pandas and it slips down nicely.

For a start, it's their faces, that childish clown's make-up. And then there's the ingratitude. Panda should be a synonym for rudeness. After everything that has been done for them – the money, the diplomatic initiatives, the four-star reception centres – all we have asked in return is that they mate. Hardly onerous work. And will they? Will they heck. They just sit there turning their backs on us, begging, stuffing their mouths, occasionally relaxing on a car tyre. A tyre, may I remind you, that has been paid for by you and me. How many decent English families can afford to have a recreational tyre? Exactly. Pandas are just taking advantage.

This country has an unparalleled record in offering a home to persecuted pandas. We've been welcoming them since before *Blue Peter*. And, heavens, nobody's suggesting that pandas with a real cause – pregnant pandas – should be refused entry. But in all the years, how many babies have they given in return for our soft-touch liberal largesse? None. Zilch. Zero. I think I speak for all decent, right-minded people when I say enough is enough. No more pandas.

It's not just their ingratitude – they're not like us. Barely human. Barely bear. If my daughter ever fell for those big black eyes and came home with a panda, I'd ... I'd ... well, I wouldn't be responsible for my sulk. I'd sulk until my nose dropped off. I'd read the newspaper and hum the Dambusters meaningfully. If they've got problems at home, well I'm sorry.

We've got problems of our own. The truth is, pandas are just sexual tourists. They've brought it on themselves.

You may be wondering what all this has got to do with a restaurant column. Well, let me tell you the shocking truth: the real reason we hate pandas. They're vegetarians. Oh, you knew that already? Ah, but what you don't know is that they've chosen to be vegetarians. Pandas are unique in the non-human mammalian world: they're animals with carnivores' metabolisms, digestive systems and teeth who have, through caprice, self-advertisement and subverted anger at their parents, become vegetarian. Their brinking extinction is nothing to do with predators, human encroachment, ozone, motor cars or online banking. It's because they won't eat their bloody dinners. 'Oh no, just a few bamboo shoots for me, mum. I'm a vegetarian.'

Well, they're going. Oblivion is staring them in the bowel. Let the panda be a grim warning to all those little girls who think they'll be more interesting if they give up meat. It will only end in black-eyed tears. Nobody will want to sleep with you, you'll never have babies, and you'll spend all day playing back-axles with a Pirelli.

Vegetarian cooking is, it need hardly be repeated, unremittingly vile. It's omelette without the Prince, Rachmaninov's Third without a piano, *Casablanca* without Bogart; it's a kiss without tongue, Christmas without presents – an endless faux-flirtatious cook-tease. One of the little professional tricks of food criticism is to look at a dish and ask: 'Are these ingredients presented in a way that does them the most justice? Is this the best these things can achieve?' With vegetarian food, the answer is always no. It could have been left raw, or it could have been a bridesmaid to some big-hearted, taut-bummed hot corpse. There is always something missing. Begins with M, ends with T.

'Ah …' I can hear the frail, ululating voice of a wan and flaccid woman, lying exhausted on a sticky chaise longue. 'You just haven't had good vegetarian food. You should try my mixed-pulse cheesy bake.' Oh, yes I have. I was a vegetarian for a decade. A neat turnaround this. Most children become vegetarians because they hate their parents. My parents sent me to a vegetarian boarding-school because they loved me. There is no variation of vegetable muck brought steaming to the table with the exhortation, 'Tuck in, you'll really adore this,' that I haven't tried. And none of it is remotely as good as the stuff I was designed to consume.

The rules of reviewing vegetarian places are not the same as for real restaurants. For a start, vegetarians are people who don't eat things. This is important. Vegetarians ask waiters if they have anything without meat, they don't ask if there is anything with vegetables. Vegetarian restaurants are judged by what they don't cook. The less they cook the better. A vegetarian waiter could come to your table and say: 'Hi! Let me tell you what's off the menu today. We don't have lamb, pork, beef; we have no chicken or fish.' Vegetarians are people who get pleasure from not eating things, and one must keep all this to the fore when breaking bread with them.

Christmas is a bad time to eat lunch in a city. Restaurants are solid with office parties wearing paper hats and shrieking. The Blonde and I decided to try a vegetarian restaurant because we knew a) that we'd be able to get a table and b) that it would be mercilessly free from conspicuous fun and gratuitous enjoyment.

The first thing you notice is the smell: the round, mushy, slightly acidic odour of sanctimonious worthiness. We queued with a tray at the long counter and surveyed the groaning repast set out to tempt us. Vegetarians aren't big on presentation; everything looks as if they've got a bulimic hippo as a food taster. The thing a diligent critic must have, to be fair to vegetarian lunch, is a gnawing hunger. Peckish won't do: you've got to be famished to pass this on to trusting peristalsis.

To start, we were offered tomato and butter bean chowder (let the abuse of the word 'chowder' go) or butter bean soup.

Now vegetarians endlessly boast about the endless variety of their cuisine to us carnivores. Veggy cookbooks always promise a thousand and one recipes, a million things to do with a peeler. It's all nonsense. There are just two vegetarian dishes: mucky stodge and stodgy muck. Here, in a pre-eminent vegetarian restaurant, was the proof: a choice of butter bean soup or butter bean soup with tomato.

'Oh, I think I'll have the, er, um, decisions decisions, oh, what the hell, make it the butter bean.'

The Blonde had added tomato. They were both ghastly, tepid, thick, mono tastes, puréed pulse without a heatbeat. What followed was without doubt one of the worst meals I have eaten. The money I have most resented spending. It was all made without apparent love or care or talent. Again, it convinced me that the only ingredients vegetarians care about are the ones they won't use.

My Moroccan potato casserole was a textbook dish. You might like to make it at home to insult the neighbours. Here, as far as I could work out, is how it was done. First boil some lumps of potato in water that other vegetables have been boiled in. When they've absorbed their own weight in liquid, stew them with turmeric (a yellow food colouring for people who can't afford saffron), add some raisins and a sprinkling of chilli, leave to sit for an hour, serve from a great height with panache.

The restaurant itself was a clever functional imitation of a Methodist destitutes' drop-in centre. Every surface I touched was sticky; the cutlery, tables, trays and chairs clung to us like lonely drunks. We sat miserably for the ten minutes it took to taste and discard the food. The bus boy removed our piled plates without a murmur; we obviously weren't the first or he didn't care. Valiantly trying to digest, we glumly watched the queue pass along the counter that says yes to life. I noticed that vegetarians are all marked by their extremities. They have double helpings of freeform set-aside hair, which they arrange in exuberant abstract patterns, and their shoes are cunningly cobbled so that, if need be, an extra pair of feet may be inserted. They also all sniff fruitily. Nobody smiled.

I have a theory as to why vegetarians never smile. Go and smile at yourself in the mirror, now count along your teeth. Two from the middle are a pair that are sharper and pointier than the rest; they are your canine or dog teeth, God's proof that you were born to eat meat. Vegetarians don't smile because their mouths give away their true natures, and are a constant reproach and reminder of their unnatural proclivities. So pity the poor vegetarian, and give one a great big grin this Yuletide.

Army

Those rumpty-tumpty army-recruiting commercials on the telly, with their frenetic running, jumping, shouting, shooting, gear-crunching, baddy-whacking, peacekeeping, cool-kit action to a lock'n'load beat, can't show you the full gamut of experience and expertise available in today's rounded military life.

They don't, for instance, advertise the martial skill of sculpting dolphins, lions and Gandalf out of margarine. But margarine-carving is one of the specialist skills you could learn in today's high-spec, hi-tech, leaner, low-cholesterol armed forces.

In fact, I think the army is the only place left that has the desire, patience and aesthetic derring-do to turn Flora into fauna. When I was confronted by a long table of oleaginous, unspreadable, non-dairy, pneumatically naked women, Disney characters and regimental badges all made of fat, in the colour and consistency of dead babies, I was forced to wonder, not for the first time, at the speechless otherness, the camouflage dichotomies and contradictions embodied in the secretive, obsessive, inverted world of the military.

I first heard about the annual Combined Services Culinary Challenge while in Baghdad with Jeremy Clarkson. Our minders naturally thought that the four-door Cliff Michelmore would want to see armoured cars and snatch vehicles and stuff that growled and burped hot metal. And, as a journalistic wife and big Nancy's blouse, I could be fobbed off with a gander round the kitchens. I'm sure if there'd been a crèche on the front line in Basra, I'd have been shown that, too. And, in fact, the truth is, I was far more interested in the kitchens than their silly Tonka tanks.

It is a truism that armies march on their stomachs. The unrelenting Gordian complexity of getting enough calories into an army three times a day so that it can go off and ruin someone else's breakfast would give a hostess trolley heartburn. By their very nature, wars don't happen in places with calm good order, local supplies, roads, clean water, gas and electricity.

And that's just to state the bloody obvious. As most squaddies will tell you, 99 per cent of army life is spent doing very little or trying to avoid doing the pointless and unpleasant things that officers try and make them do while waiting for something real to happen. Boredom is the most incapacitating and insidious military enemy. The canteen and the pit-stop of meal times are a vital high point of interest in a day, a week, a tour that is mostly a colourless wait with low-grade anxiety punctuated by peaks of intense fear and courage.

The prefabricated canteen at the air base in Basra was utilitarian rather than welcoming, with piles of body armour and Bergens by the door, and those terse little written instructions beloved of the regimental mind reminding us to wash our hands, unload our weapons, keep our helmets close, and clean up neatly afterwards.

The food was far better than National Service anecdotage remembers. Chips, chips were no longer as big as battleships, but they still loom large in most squaddies' meals. There are also large bowls of fruit and salad, along with an obligatory roast joint that is so well done it could pat its own back.

The food is a careful compromise between good for you and good to you, and enlivened by regular theme nights. Squaddies don't linger over their plastic plates, but the atmosphere is relaxed and, while not Epicurean, warmly hospitable, in marked contrast with the flickering oil-fired desert outside. It's also a contrast with the Americans' canteen in the green zone, which looks like a bulimic convention – vast marines stuffing down their feelings with an orgy of prefab junk that is an unashamedly sentimental taste of home. Every cliché of cooking and childish comfort, mom and apple pie is on offer. The ice-cream freezer is an altar to back home, handing out communion buckets big enough to hide land mines in. The grunts prop their assault rifles against thick thighs and eat with a contented glazed gloom, inhaling homesickness.

The Brits say, with a quiet, veiled smugness, that while the Americans invest in processed ingredients and technology, they invest in cooks. Every British Army kitchen has a strictly restricted list of ingredients from sugar to Marmite, cornflakes to ketchup. I'm shown things that bubble, the Sri Lankan cooks and the Iraqi dishwasher.

The chef explains that they're using a new oven. He's quietly guarded about it. It's early days. It's a bit complicated. It runs on diesel but needs a constant electricity supply. 'There have been problems,' he says darkly. No hot food at the end of a day can plummet morale to the point of mutiny or suicide. Did he ever use the old Soyer stove? I asked. And he beamed like a ripe melon. Of course. 'That's what we all learn to cook on. It would work anywhere, burn anything. No moving parts, brilliant for baking and roasting, stewing, frying and steaming.' The Soyer stove was invented in the 1850s for the army in the Crimea, and it was still in use during the first Gulf war. It is far and away the longest-serving single piece of military equipment since the bow and arrow, yet it's never mentioned in lists of great designs or inventions that changed the world. The Soyer stove has touched and changed the lives of more people, and indeed the course of more nations, than anything created by Alessi or Le Corbusier.

For years I've been a secret nerdy fan of the Soyer oven. 'I think we can arrange for you to see one, if you'd like,' muttered my ever-helpful minder, which is how, six months later, I end up on a drizzly racetrack in the home counties watching a military cook-off. The annual catering competition is held over three days, each day hosted by one of the services. It's all conducted with a high degree of competitiveness, conducted in the smiley, shouty, oafish, good-natured way that the military reserves for necessary things that it suspects are suspect, soft or poofy.

The addition of a great dose of competition is obviously there to keep the girlie stuff sweatily manly. Competition is, of course, wholly antipathetic to the nature of cooking and eating, which should be collective, mutually helpful and convivial experiences. Still, the hall at Sandown Park, Esher, is full of red-faced young men doing double-time butchery under the beady eyes of white-coated sergeants. It looks like origami bayonet practice on chickens. 'Come on, you 'orrible little pansy. Put some 'atred into it. What would you do if that rack of lamb were trying to rape your sister? Yell when you fillet 'im.'

In a series of field kitchens outside, groups of Royal Marines compete to the death to do something a little nouvelle English, a bit Jamie and Nigella, to field rations. Talking to a team of Special Boat Service commandos about adding a touch of Thai spice to the chicken fricassee is both surreal and touching. The food they make is of an astonishingly high standard, and would be even better if they weren't having a race against each other. I lend a hand with the marking and feel like a snotty quisling.

I should have had the courage to be a conscientious obj-ector.

In the middle of the hall there is a pair of Soyer stoves, and a group of senior officers stands around them looking nonplussed in a can-do fashion. They would so much rather be showing me something lethal with a night sight.

The Soyer stove came about by chance. Alexis Soyer was a working-class, French-born chef who worked at the Reform Club. He invented Cutlets Reform and Reform sauce. He cooked for the great and the good, and in early Victorian

London he became a celebrity. He was an ebullient, inquisitive, loquacious, enthusiastic, sycophantic man, who was both loved and mocked. He held an awkward and newly minted role in the hierarchy of society – a common servant, but also a star.

One evening he went to a restaurant to eat with friends but missed them, and so sat in a private room on his own with a paper, where he read a report from another newly minted star, William Russell, the first foreign correspondent writing from the Crimea. Soyer was so moved by the plight of the soldiers that the next day he went to the War Office and asked to be sent, at his own expense, to help feed the wounded. His celebrity opened doors and cut through the bureaucracy that benighted the whole campaign.

When he got to Scutari, he found the most terrible waste, appalling conditions, negligence, ineptitude and gross inefficiency. The kitchens had relatively good meat, but were incapable of preparing it properly. The joints were served as stiff as leather and as cold as corpses. The orderlies threw away the stock that contained all the nourishment. None of the cooks were trained; they were simply soldiers co-opted to kitchen work.

The army had never trained cooks. With inexhaustible energy, humour and patience, Soyer began to make chefs. He cajoled quartermasters, organised and cleaned the hospital kitchens, wrote recipes and almost immediately began to save lives – not one or two but hundreds and hundreds. He made soup. He stopped the cooks burying the cows' heads, feet and offal. He charmed Florence Nightingale, then turned his attention to the rest of the army.

The British army worked as a rough federation of regiments. Every regiment was semi-autonomous and foraged for itself. Each man was given his own daily ration of bread and meat to prepare as best he could and supplement with whatever he could buy or steal. Armies worked on the tacit acceptance of plunder. It was inefficient and immoral but it was the way the British army had fed itself since before Agincourt. Soyer also visited the French army. They did slightly better with their egalitarian peasant background. Rations were organised by company, and one man would cook for everyone. It might be a different man each day.

Soyer, having run soup kitchens during the famine in Ireland, designed an oven that would feed 250 soldiers. Four would feed a battalion. They could be carried on a cart or a mule, and could run on anything that would burn. They were made to the highest Victorian engineering standards for relatively little, and they completely changed the way the army fed itself, and therefore the army. Soyer's stove saved more lives and brought more comfort than any other bit of kit. After 150 years, the army finally lost most of its Soyer stoves when the *Atlantic Conveyor* was sunk in the south Atlantic during the Falklands conflict. If you want to see one in action, they star at the beginning of the film *Zulu*.

Back at the racetrack, the high point of competitiveness has become international. Military teams from our sometimes friends and occasional allies cook against each other in little wars of attrition. For each team, the natural, national taste of their country emerges. The Americans cook big, with loud flavours, the Hungarians are honest and peasanty, the French are effortfully the best. Far more than flags and anthems, food is the metaphor and symbol of where you come from and what you might choose to die for. The breakfast of armies is the most basic communion with what they're fighting for. Soyer was a foreigner who took to being English with an immigrant enthusiasm. He understood that armies don't just march on their stomachs; they get their camaraderie, bravery and patriotism through them.

His oven, his recipes and his organisation of large kitchens invented institutional catering. The shambles of the Crimea created three transcendent personalities of the early Victorian age: William Russell, who invented modern journalism; Florence Nightingale, who invented modern nursing; and Soyer, who invented the recipe for mass catering. Between them, they were the ingredients for much that was to concern and mobilise the modern world. In the main hall, next to the margarine sculptures, the winner of the inter-forces' canapé competition is displayed. I'm not making this up, or at least I don't think I am. The canapés are real enough: astonishingly delicate, goblin confections of wearying dexterity, neatness and studied ingenuity. Their obsessiveness defies appetite. The man who made them is polite, with that closed blankness that soldiers often assume when talking to suspicious civilians they're not allowed to kill.

The canapés were small acts of internal sabotage. They have no conceivable military purpose. Emergency ration packs are never going to have duck and wilted chicory with a muscatel reduction in a pastry *bateau*. They are insurgent mouthfuls of fey mutiny. For all the shoulder-punching, shouty, gung-ho competitiveness the military tries to impose on food, the real struggle is between the ultimately peaceful, hospitable pacifism of eating and the natural proclivity of armies to kill strangers on empty stomachs.

The inter-services competition is yet another uncomfortable military oxymoron. As the last mess-stewarding competition comes to a sticky end, I went back to have a last look at Soyer's stove, beautiful in its simplicity. It has brought a little warm comfort to mothers' sons in every continent throughout a dozen small conflicts, emergencies, police actions and two world wars. Alexis Soyer, the working-class, generous, romantic chef, died within two years of returning from the Crimea. At his funeral there wasn't a single officer, military representative or official from the government. Well, there wouldn't be, would there?

He stole their plunder.

Organic

Can we just get the organic thing clear? Organic does not mean additive-free; it means some additives and not others. Organic does not mean your food hasn't been washed with chemicals, frozen or kept fresh with gas, or that it has not been flown around the world. Organic does not necessarily mean it is healthier, or will make you live longer; nor does it mean tastier, fresher, or in some way improved. Organically farmed fish is not necessarily better than wild fish. Organically reared animals didn't necessarily live a happier life than non-organic ones – and their death is no less traumatic.

More importantly, organic does not mean that the people who picked, packed, sowed and slaughtered were treated fairly, paid properly, or were free from artificial exploitation. The Chinese workers who drowned in Morecambe Bay were picking organic cockles for a pittance. If you really want to feed the hunger in your conscience, buy Fairtrade.

So what does organic actually mean? Buggered if I know.

It usually means more expensive. Whatever the original good intentions of the organic movement, their good name has been hijacked by supermarkets, bijou delicatessens and agri-processors as a value-added designer label. Organic comes with its own basket of aspiration, snobbery, vanity and fear that retailers on tight margins can exploit. And what I mind most about it is that it has reinvigorated the old class distinction in food.

There is them that has chemical-rich, force-fed battery dinner and us that has decent, healthy, caring lunch. It is the belief that you can buy not only a clear conscience, but a colon that works like the log flume at Alton Towers.

In general, I applaud and agree with many of the aims of environmentally careful producers, but it is time we all admitted that the label 'organic' has been polluted with cynicism, sentiment, sloppy sharp practice and lies to the point where it is intellectually and practically bankrupt. What organic actually means is less than nothing.

And it hasn't made anyone a better cook.

We were at the sort of place that couldn't just have a menu, it must also have a mission statement. It revealed that the café was certified by the Soil Association – though not, unfortunately, by two psychiatrists. Its cushions were organic cotton (which, by the way, is fantastically wasteful of water and land) and were coloured with low-impact dye, which seems to mean Indian indigo – so just the same as your multinational exploitative jeans.

The glasses were recycled, the menus were hemp and the bar was 'made from storm oak that was literally (as opposed to metaphorically?) bowled over in the great storm of 1987'. Why God knocking over a tree should be any more environmentally friendly than doing it with a chainsaw was not explained. Nor was the fact that waiting for extreme meteorology is a lousy way to build furniture. Oh, and the waiters (who are made from reclaimed bits of smiley love and unused facial hair) were dressed in 'PC organic T-shirts'. Ours had FCUK written on his, which is presumably a sort of expletive recycling.

Now the food. Our reversible Brazilian waiter told us that the soup of the day was 'gazpacho made with beetroot'. Ah, you mean borscht? He looked at us with loving, endlessly renewable pity. 'Bores, what's bores?' Well, I could tell you, but borscht is gazpacho made with beetroot. 'Oh really,' he said, as if humouring infants. 'Our one is gazpacho made with beetroot.' It was borscht. Made with beetroot. But without talent.

The lemon and rosemary marinated chicken was a shameful

waste of the life of a chicken. And I simply had to have a natural cola: 'Made organically without any of the nasty chemicals and colouring and stuff.' So water, then? It was gratifyingly vile, insipid, emetic, ersatz; a greenly pointless exercise. The Blonde kicked me hard when I tried to inquire if the bottled water was recycled by the management or whether they got indigenous hunter-gatherers to do it.

Pudding was a pecan pie made with treacle, a flavour that, while being wholly wholesome, cleverly managed to recycle the savour of petrochemical waste. The coffee tasted as if it were made from acorns – literally blown from the tree that made the bar. The restaurant was virtually – and literally – nearly empty. Yet this simple, careless, uninspired, do-gooder's grub took three hours to serve. Time, also, is apparently recycled.

What was most extraordinary, though, about this finger-wagging, holier-than-thou chapel to abstinence wasn't that it was like eating retread compost-grown Moonies, it was that the Blonde and our guinea pig, Marcelle D'Argy Smith, both thought it was wonderful. 'We think it's wonderful,' they both said.

If you didn't know this was Soil Association recommended and a heart-warmingly refried mulch restaurant, you'd hate it, wouldn't you? 'Yes,' said the Blonde with a faraway smile. 'But I do know, and I think it's brilliant. For once, we're eating proper, healthy food. I can feel it doing me good.'

No, you can't.

'Yes, I can.'

No, you just think it's doing you good.

'So what's the difference? I also think that eating here is immeasurably making the world a softer place. It's making poor people laugh out loud. It's putting a wind chime on every doorstep. It's helping small brown babies be born painlessly into caring extended families. It's cloning Nelson Mandela. It's irrigating deserts and hugging rainforests. It's kissing Aids better. It's sending mountain gorillas to university so they can become doctors to cure all the sickness that ever was, using just bits of bark and the juice of an as yet undiscovered fruit. It's growing back female circumcisions, cancelling Third World debt, putting a chicken in every pot (but only if the chicken agrees to it and the pot's handmade). It's giving everyone in Africa a duvet and avocado moisturiser. It's making the whole globe sing and dance in one great magic pop concert, with guest-star humpback whales and liquorice condoms free at the point of delivery. Kumbaya, my Lord, kumbaya.'

Oh, good grief.

All paragraphs and sentences in this review have been recycled from other articles. Words are free from artificial vowels and chemical consonants, and no grammar was harmed in the writing of this column. Dispose with care. Have a nice day. Soft fruit loves you right back.

Dinner parties

(1)

Your shirt is clean, your anecdotes polished, and you've had three glasses of Australian chardonnay and twenty-five Twiglets. On cue, the kitchen door flies open and in a cloud of steam your hostess and your dinner enter like Babette presenting her Feast. Only it's not a feast, it's a small square of supermarket pre-prepared 'fisherman's bake' and four grey mange-touts on a stone-cold plate. It sits there like an unwanted skin graft.

You remember that at home your babysitter is being paid £4 an hour to enjoy a splendid cassoulet. Do you smile cravenly at your hostess and pour compliments on her lazy, undeserving head? No, do what you want to do, what you should do – send it back. Courteously, but firmly, ask for something else, something appetising, something sustaining, something edible, for crying out loud.

Most of us, I know, would rather be caught in flagrante with a farm animal by Jeremy Beadle than murmur even the merest syllable of complaint at a dinner party, but sending your dinner back like a contrary Oliver Twist is not impossible.

I know, I've done it.

We are the only animals in God's creation who share our food with members of our own species to whom we are not related. We are also the only creatures who consider that mozzarella salad (made with the wrong sort of mozzarella), followed swiftly by a fibrous fig, constitutes a dinner party. And it's got to stop. We've got to get militant. We've got to start complaining about being called out after dark on false pretences. Let's get this straight: who's doing who a favour?

The received wisdom is that being a guest is a treat, a

pleasure, even an honour. But just think about it: there are
eight of us who have taken an hour to get ready and taxi across
town in clean shirts with bottles of wine in order to be amusing
and entertaining in someone else's dining-room. I reckon that
when everything's taken into consideration we've spent about
£40 each for the pleasure of tucking into the lentil bake and
Play-Doh brie. That's £320. And what did the hosts spend?
Forty-five minutes and a fiver a head.

There is a kitchen adage that says: 'If the food is the star
of your dinner party then you're inviting the wrong people.'
Let's face it: dinner parties are social events and the company
is the main thing. We've all been to parties where the epigrams
sparkled like spumante, where the gossip was riveting and our
flirtatious neighbours hung on our every word. We could have
been eating carpet tiles for all it mattered. But that's no excuse
for serving food that would make the shadow cabinet seem
interesting by comparison. It is no excuse for a host to be too
busy to shop wisely and cook well. If you're too damn successful to look after your friends, then don't give dinner parties.
Take them to restaurants or hire a chef.

The first time I sent my dinner back at a private party, it
was a filthy lentil stew. It had been made from the wrong,
mushy sort of lentils, with a tin of tomatoes tipped in along
with near-raw onion chunks. Accompanying it was one iceberg
lettuce dressed with vinegar. The succeeding course, a plate of
dead apples and a piece of spongy brie, was already on the
table. I said that I didn't think that I could eat the stew. There
was a silence you could have spread on toast. The women to
the right and left of me edged away and the port merchant on
the other side of the table choked on his Bulgarian retsina.

Then the hostess said: 'It is a bit disgusting, isn't it? I've got
some eggs ...?'

There was a great sigh of relief from the ensemble and we
all trooped into the kitchen and cooked each other omelettes.
It was a huge success. I was a friend, and if a friend can't tell

you that your food is a bilious slop which would be deemed an unnatural punishment in a Turkish jail, who can?

(2)

Ten years ago, I wrote a piece about sending back food at dinner parties. If it isn't any good, I said, ask your hostess to take it away and bring something else. Perfectly reasonable. The article had the desired effect – I haven't been invited to a dinner party since.

We should all know that the great Lucifer will tempt and tease us, not with outright, wanton wickedness, but with a cunning simulacrum of righteousness. And dinner parties are the work of the devil, the dark side of honest supper, twisting the feeding of family and friends to malevolence by snobbery, etiquette, envy and pomp.

The dinner party was the dandruff on the shoulder pads of the evil decade, the 1980s – that explosion of big tits, big hair, big heels and big heads. People threw their elderly relatives into the snow and granny flats became dining-rooms, while they tied up miniature vegetables and sprayed raspberry vinegar like tom cats on the pull.

Perhaps at this point we should nail down what a dinner party is. It's a dinner party when you get dressed up to eat in your own home, and when you lay the table with things you would never use if it were just the two of you: specialist exoskeleton removal implements, butter knives, more glasses than you have hands, napkin rings, silver pheasants, stags or goat-legged blokes humping fat Greek birds. It's a dinner party if you write the names of people you know perfectly well on little Alzheimer's cards and stick them into slots in gilt farm animals or scallop shells. It's a dinner party if you're cooking something for the first time and if you're doing it in high heels. And it's a dinner party if you arrange the food on the plates before serving.

It's not a dinner party if it's a couple of mates joining you for supper, if the kids are there, if you can pour the wine without uttering an adjective, and if the first thing you put on the table is brown sauce, a television remote control, the evening paper or a takeaway box.

In the 1990s, the dinner party seemed to die out, knocked on its silly hard head by tiredness, diets and a jolt of good taste. But I can smell the burning polenta in the wind. Dinner parties didn't die – they just slipped out for a smoke. And they're making a comeback. The e-mails have started to arrive: would I like to come over for something to eat? And then the telltale date – a month and a half away. That's not spontaneous supper, that's gastronomic flashing, social quail torturing. It's the thin end of the truffled brie. Duran Duran are back, Band Aid is back, legwarmers and cowboy boots are back. The hell of retro dinner parties can't be far behind.

Those of you who grew up in the 1990s, eating with your fingers, might think, 'Where's the harm? I could handle it.' But before you can say 'kumquat *brûlée*', you've cancelled the new car and taken the kids out of school, just so you can build a conservatory dining-room and install an oven with an integrated teriyaki grill and ambidextrous rotisserie function. Remember: it's just an innocent canapé today, but it's the misery of beef Wellington tomorrow. The real sin of dinner parties is that they usurp the most basic human goodness of hospitality and succour and turn it into a homunculus of social climbing. But they also confuse two distinct occupations: cooks and chefs. Cooks do it at home for love. Chefs do it in public for money. Dinner parties are karaoke cheffery.

There are proper places for social gatherings over dinner, for offering hospitality. They're specifically designed to fill all your dinner-party needs and treat your 'mine host' fantasies. These places are called restaurants. A restaurant does everything you want from a dinner party, but better and cheaper. Yes, cheaper – if you factor in your time at the rate you're paid at work, or even at the pittance you pay your daily.

So, where to go? Somewhere local, somewhere they know you by name, that serves food that feeds conversation and doesn't overwhelm it. I'm loath to recommend a dining-room to you. If you're old enough to be allowed out at night, you're old enough to find one that suits your tongue, pocket and aspirations.

So that's the recipe for a perfect dinner party: eat in – out.

Picnics

Something odd happens to perfectly good cooks when you take their dining-room walls away. The roof falls in on their cooking. A hostess who wouldn't bat an eye at producing a buffet party for twenty will fly into a panic when it comes to preparing a picnic for six.

Sports days, gymkhanas, concerts, cricket, and tennis all invite us to balance paper plates, eat ants and get wet bottoms. Old Tupperware boxes are being ferreted out of the back of cupboards, Thermos flasks are being gingerly shaken, and those wicker hampers that look so 'right', but weigh a ton and only have enough room for a couple of thinly sliced cucumber sandwiches, are being herniaed into the boots of cars.

A picnic takes twice as long and costs twice as much as a dinner party. It's also a fact that whatever the quantity of food you take, you will come back with more than you left with, and that rubbish will grow to fill the bags allotted to it.

Simplicity is the order of the day for a successful picnic. Remember that eating outside is where eating started. Forks don't belong. Ideally, everything should be hand-held. Nothing should have 'a right way up'. Pies and tarts and delicate cakes are out, unless you're prepared to look like a butler on an assault course. Don't worry about presentation; form follows function. Above all, you don't want to look like a Glyndebourne interval.

Glyndebourne is a seriously odd, nay bizarre, place and the picnics rise to the occasion. Eating outside is where we came in. Picnics were our first hunter-gatherer meals and the tribal fears and memories run deep in our psyches. Corpulent, puffing men lug boxes and tables to find just the right spot. As nobody will sit in the open, so everybody searches for a defensible space. Desmond Morris could write a serious paper on picnics at Glyndebourne. Laid over the primeval fears of eating in the open is the thin tulle of civilisation and snobbery.

The interval picnics are hugely risible. There's a terrific amount of showing off; silver and crystal are humped into fields, along with candelabra and ice buckets, collapsible tables with double-damask cloths and numerous bottles and inappropriate sloppy courses with numberless screw-top sauces, creams and unctions and garnishes. And most bizarrely of all, little pots of cut flowers. Now who on earth thinks of taking a bunch of carnations and a vase on a picnic? 'We're going to eat in a garden, have you got everything?' 'Oh silly me, I nearly forgot the flowers.' If a Martian happened on Glyndebourne, he'd see the rolling chalk downs of Sussex dotted with grazing sheep and then one field with a lot of fat men in clip-on bow ties sitting on infant-school chairs trying to get the backs off lobsters with plastic forks, and he'd probably wonder how many you got to the acre and whether you use them for meat or hides.

Good things for picnics are: cold fowl and joints of meat, simply baked without sauce. Take them whole, and pull bits off when you get there. Salads should also be whole; take baby boiled potatoes, cos lettuce, small tomatoes, asparagus, and oil and vinegar in a jam jar. Hard-boiled eggs are a must.

Now sandwiches. Sandwiches were made for the big outdoors; whatever you do, don't get cute with them. Don't stuff them with mountains of esoteric gear. Peanut butter on Wonderloaf is far nicer than aubergine kumquat and herring on focaccia. Sandwiches are engineering, not cooking; they must have stickability, or when you unpack them they'll look like a badly held bridge hand. For pudding take fruit, not a sloppy, fizzing bowl of exotic fruit cocktail.

And so to drink. Drink from the bottle. Everyone should

have their own, all that fussing with plastic cups or glasses that spend most of their time spilling is a bore. Take black coffee in a Thermos, and sugar lumps in a pocket. If anyone is tasteless enough to want milk, use the sugar lumps to attract a cow. Don't take tables and chairs (the only piece of flat ground is beside the road, and no one will carry them more than five feet from the car); leave the ice bucket at home along with the CD player, the hat that won't stay on in the wind, and little Bond Street linen numbers. Every culture that eats its meals on the floor has a national dress that doesn't have a waistband.

Pubs

Gastropub

Bear with me, I'm going to read you a menu. It may help if you imagine it in the voice of Joyce Grenfell or perhaps Peter Ustinov.

Bruschetta, crostini, chicken with pitta bread and tzatziki, BLT, black pudding with glazed apples, smoked haddock crêpes with vermouth cream, caesar salad, *baba ganoush*, hummus and olive tapenade, mozzarella and tomato, melon and parma ham, beef koftas, skewered chilli and garlic chicken, full English breakfast, tagliatelle with mussels and chilli, parmigiana, penne with chicken and rocket, hamburger, Toulouse sausage with champ, Thai fishcakes with lemon aioli, *roti chana*, sirloin steak, brownies, apple crumble ...

Now that's not the entire menu, but it's most of it. What do you make of it? What can you glean? At face value, a menu is a bill of fare, a list, but it's also a statement of intent, an advertisement, a declaration of taste and sophistication.

A menu tells you what the pretensions of the restaurant are, who it wants to attract and what it wants you to assume about it and, by extension, yourself. So where are we and who are we supposed to be? First, let's look at the practical things. There are, give or take, ten different countries' cuisines represented here, some of them in the same dish. There are more than fifty-one primary ingredients, not counting staples (salt, pepper, oil, vinegar) and they're all relatively cheap.

I wouldn't expect any dish on this list to cost more than about £10.

But – and this is a kitchen tautology – there are a bewildering number of cooking methods implied, some of them quite complicated, and there are other things that have to be made against the clock and served instantly (a full English breakfast is one of the most annoyingly tricky things to get right if you're not making it over and over for breakfast).

So what do we know about this place? Well, it's not called Basta Pasta or the Kentucky Grill or the Bangkok Garden. It might be called Terminal 3. It's international, well-travelled food. Except, if you look carefully, it actually isn't. It's cruise-ship highlights. These are all dishes that have become mid-range menu staples over the past twenty years. It's not rim food or fusion food – it's pick'n'mix deli chill-cabinet food, and if you eat out once a month it will be as familiar as your own sock drawer. This is now what typical English food looks like. This is our national cuisine.

So where are we? Well, it's cheapish, though not necessarily good value. It doesn't expect you to eat three courses. The distinction between starter and main is blurred, as is the demarcation between breakfast, lunch, snack and dinner.

Actually, it's a pub: one of those that don't know whether they want to stay a pub, grow into a bar or be the set for *Cold Feet*. The furniture is a junk hunt round Portobello: 1960s Italian moulded plastic chairs, an Arts and Crafts side table, an oversized 1980s leather lounging sofa, sub-Pugin Gothic revival church chairs, 1970s lamps. In fact, the interior shadows the magpie taste of the menu. It's not so much a look as an *Evening Standard* list of bachelor-pad chic.

It's clear that the menu is making boasts the kitchen can't possibly sustain. This food needs a full brigade and a properly equipped kitchen to make it well. But it's a pub; it has probably just got a galley with one overheated Sloane in a pinny and a porter. I see this so often – a menu that's constructed one dish at a time. An owner asks, 'Can you make fishcakes?' 'Yes.' 'Can you make penne?' 'Yes.' 'Do you know what to do with a black pudding?' 'Yes.' 'Can you do them all at once for thirty covers?' 'No, not conceivably.' It is part of a gastropub chain. And this is chain-gang food – chosen by committee, made by one poor sod.

So, what do you order? Immediately discard anything that takes more than a GCSE in home economics to make. Go for something that's a construction job, but with fail-safe ingredients. So the mozzarella and tomato, though simple, won't be nice. Mozzarella has to be perfect and impeccably sourced or it's like eating a blind whale's eyeball. We're probably best having a sandwich – the BLT – but I'm reviewing, so I go for a couple of things in the middle of the range: a caesar salad, the penne with chicken and rocket, and apple crumble with ice cream.

You know, we're desperate to eat out in this country. And a pub like this offers this menu, heavy with style markers, because it knows that this is what we want; this is how we see ourselves. Last week, I went round a huge Tesco's, open twenty-four hours. It was vast. And it was shocking: canyon after canyon of pre-prepared international food, tubs of ready-made sauces and dipping things. The packaging assumed that the customers were perfectly at home with the world's cuisine, had seen plenty of TV cookery, read lots of magazine mouth-porn. And all of it, every microwaveable, boil-in-the-bag morsel, will have ranged from disappointing to inedible.

People don't cook. And frankly, why should they? If you work all day to make your money, why should you employ yourself as a bad commis chef and dishwasher afterwards? Why not eat out? How nice it would be to go down to the pub, settle into the sofa, share a bottle and have a well made parmigiana with a side salad.

So, so ... so how was it for me? Well, you know how it was for me. It was vile. The caesar salad was a compost of what might once have been aspidistra. The pasta came on a plate that was so hot it burnt the waitress through the dishcloth. It had either been blasted in an industrial microwave or seared in an oven. The pasta had been made ages before and was as soft as old cornflakes. The rocket was a green sludge, the cheese pulsating puddles on top, and the chicken papier mâché. The whole thing cohered into a brimstone lump. The apple crumble was also ancient, the crumble itself a soggy hardcore. The apple was glue. The ice cream tasted of sweet lard. It was, in short, what most of the country gets at home most of the time.

But without the washing-up.

It's all such a crying shame and a desperate waste. And it would be so easy to rectify. But I'm not a consultant. If they can't be bothered to read their own menu, why should I translate it for them?

Pub food

I've spent more time in pubs than in any other public building. More than in restaurants or cinemas, theatres or magistrates' courts, libraries, museums or churches. More than in all of them put together. That's an amazing testimony to the power of the pub – and a savage indictment of my social sophistication.

My abiding memory of pubs is not the Hogarthian jostle, the elbow-nudge and spittle-spray or the claggy dampness that implies every surface is the sickly skin of some giant comatose creature. It isn't the bellowed bollocks, the charmless flirting or the desperate, choking camaraderie with geezers whose surnames I never knew, but whose girlfriends I'd shagged.

No, my abiding memory of pubs is the wide open emptiness, the motes drifting in the cue of sunlight above the pool table, the luke-bile gag of the first rinsing mouthful of beer and the fingered and folded *Daily Mail*s, passed from bacon-smoked hand to redundant hand. ''Ere, you went to boarding-school. What's the capital of Nigeria? Five letters. First letter K ... Bugger. That means w**ker's wrong.'

Some – actually, lots of – people have asked me why I spent so much time in pubs.

The answer is that I was a drunk, and that's where drunks go. But that's only half an answer. One of the few perks of being a full-time professional drunk is that you can do it almost anywhere – benches, emergency stairs in multi-storey car parks, other people's spare rooms. And yet I would assiduously get up every morning and go to a pub, the way my grandfather went to the bank. I was never late and I never took a day off sick. I'd sit and wait till they rang bells and threw me out.

It's the waiting I remember most vividly, waiting for something to happen. The pub was a metaphysical airport lounge and, standing at the bar, I was like those drivers with a passenger's name scribbled on cardboard. I stood there for years with this invisible sign that just said: 'Anyone. Anywhere.' At the core of the Wagnerian despair of your committed drunk, there is a Micawberish glimmer that something will turn up.

It's a long time since I've been to a pub with intent. Like all folk who make, or are forced to make, life-fracturing decisions – the defrocked priest, the refrocked transsexual, the refugee, the divorcee – I'm ambivalent about the rooms I've left behind. Going into a pub is like revisiting the scene of a crime, being both victim and perpetrator. One of the things I hated at the time was any confusion of the pubbiness of pubs; the trendy pretence that the pub might be a family recreation lounge, a French-ish boules park, a part-time disco, a Cuban cocktail bar or, worse – much worse – a restaurant.

Food and pubs go together like frogs and lawnmowers, vampires and tanning salons, mittens and Braille. Pubs don't do food; they offer internal mops and vomit decoration. The idea that the gastropub is the answer to a lack of reasonably priced decent public food in suburban Britain, and the declining fortunes of public houses, is a Tony-ish mule of an idea.

Pub kitchens are invariably tiny and ill equipped to produce much more than a toasted sandwich. The dreams and desires of drinkers and eaters aren't complementary. A drinker needs room to get clumsy, flick fag ends and do Sean Connery impressions, which tends to get in the way of the organic English spotted loin in mustard and balsamic jus. And what about fighting? You can't have a fight in a gastropub. It would be all Hooray Billy Bunter bun-chucking.

We've had a decade of pub restaurants, and they're virtually all horribly splod and tish. But still they come, little upstairs rooms with a couple of tables, a snug made into a kitchen, barmen doubling as waiters. So it was with less than vaunting enthusiasm that I shuffled down to Lambeth to try the latest one. I couldn't even get the Blonde to come. She said she'd see me for real dinner later.

I walked in and discovered it was a pub: a very pubby pub, pubbled with after-work drinkers. The restaurant bit was in an adjoining room. At 6.30pm, it was packed – and I was amazed. The waitress found me a spot on a table with two couples. The kitchen was a cage the size of a Monopoly board, with a pair of cooks running around like the top hat and the iron. The menu was to the point and very good – modern, non-dainty-Rhodes English. It had that distinctive, meaty smell of Fergus Henderson. I think maybe both the hat and the iron trained with him at St John.

I started with a dish that made the whole room go quiet.

The lights went down and a single spot illuminated the bowl in front of me. In the distance, there was a choir singing the Angelus, and I knew, the way you just know, that I was going to love this dish with all my heart for the rest of my life – or its life, whichever was longer. It was a heart-clutchingly thick potato soup, and nestling in it was a slab, a plinth, an altar of pressed foie gras, gently melting. It was properly brilliant. Every descriptive illustration I can think of to make it live for you is so intimately sensual that we can't print it on a Sunday. It was rough'n'toff.

Hoxton

The only way really to describe this food is 'gay'. Gayissimus. Gayomorphic. Spumingly, frothingly queer. It was proudly, poncily, deliciously, lispingly effete. It was Fotherington-Thomas reads Manley Hopkins. It was a Tom of Finland electric toothbrush. It was the Blues and Royals up the Rambert ballet. And finding it in Hoxton was like finding Tom Ford in Millets. Consequently, the place was nakedly empty, except for us and a table of scowly, sneery local conceptual-video poets, who looked like they'd been tricked into doing Doris Day karaoke.

Ex-pub

It was always a small pub, so it comes as no surprise to find it has been transformed into a small restaurant, with a couple of rickety tables outside. Inside it is sort of Belgian motorway-basic. If the owner didn't get the entire contents for under £50 and the paint job thrown in, he was ripped off.

Of course, decor isn't everything. It isn't anything, until you see the menu, which is so unappealing that it makes the walls seem tasteful. Somewhere in this little corner establishment there is a man, a man who has taken the title chef and run with it, gone fiercely in a direction that is his alone. He has seen the serried ranks of his compatriots tramp the predictable road to excellence and said: 'No, no, I shall do something unique and different, and when people mutter my name they shall do so with awe.'

And you know, if I knew his name I would wrap it in all the awe I could muster. He has taken the lowest, most unprepossessing, huddled raw ingredients and with sheer nerve and devil-may-care bravado transformed them into dishes that uncannily replicate the denizens of chill cabinets in discount cash'n'carry stores. This is food worthy of the name pub.

The Blonde and I started our awesome lunch with a mozzarella and tomato salad, the mozzarella imitating a melted swimming cap sprinkled with a green dusting of oregano. It came, as is the modern way, with a small bottle of olive oil which looked like the type chemists used to sell to unblock ears. Then potato skins. Yum! These had apparently been cooked using the rare and delicate method of age instead of heat. They had naturally peeled themselves. And, because we realised this was the sort of place we were unlikely to pass twice in a lifetime, we indulged in a third starter: strips of flayed fowl covered in a sauce of such odoriferous oriental cunning that it defied deconstruction. And, by the look of it, I wouldn't like to hazard how it had been applied. Next, steak Diane. I wasn't asked how I wanted it cooked, presumably because chef has strong and resolute feelings on the matter. 'When I cook a steak, it damn well stays cooked.'

It came with a camouflage of grey-green sauce – shallot, caper, mustard, and did I detect the merest half pint of Worcestershire sauce? Who can tell? After two bites, not I. The Blonde, limpid eyes bulging in anticipation, tucked into a fishcake. They could have tucked a fish into this cake and it would have had difficulty identifying a relative.

And so on to pudding. The Blonde regretfully declined, with a weak wave of her hand. Enough, enough oral excitement for one day. I tremulously asked for the bread and butter pudding. I was not disappointed. You know, I have always wanted to know what hot yellow jelly would taste like, and now I do. And sweet, soggy white sliced, too. Not just dessert, but an education.

And what of our fellow pilgrims? Worshippers in this temple to the new pub gastronomy? Well, when you saw the greasy, pinstriped, lank-haired, wattled-chinned, carelessly loud, lounging gents of redundant leisure, I reckoned that if this chef could half-bake people, these were the half-baked people he'd half-bake.

Nouvelle cuisine

The case for ...

Sitting around a table last week, someone said: 'What is the most depressing thing you can read on a menu?'

'Oh, lightly steamed.'

'No, no, nestling in a basket of root vegetable matchsticks.'

'A warm salad.'

'Wilted mixed leaves.'

'A coulis!'

'Oh yes, coulis, any coulis, all coulis. The only good coulis has a pigtail and humps tea chests on the Shanghai docks.'

There was no end to the things we hated on menus. All the twee language: the succulent, moist, drizzle-drenched, delicate vegetable verbiage, and the hot adjectives promising a slow pulse. All the things we hated, all the little terms of chewable endearment could have come under one heading. What we really hated was nouvelle cuisine.

These are terms associated with that most despised movement of twentieth-century culture, more loathed than 1970s disco dancing, more ridiculed than plywood effect, stack-heeled cowboy boots, responsible for more merciless hilarity than the Turner prize. Nouvelle cuisine is now universally derided. So I'm now about to embark on the most difficult and dangerous paragraph known to restaurant writers. Drum roll, maestro, if you please.

Ladies and gentlemen, a defence of nouvelle cuisine.

It wasn't all bad. Some of it was really very good. Nouvelle cuisine was like Protestantism. It started in a blaze of right-eousness as a reaction to the discredited Catholicism of old, thick, saucy haute cuisine. All that flambéed at your table, stuff-a-truffle-up-his-bum cooking. Nouvelle cuisine had high ideals of honesty, simplicity and respect but, like Protestantism, it descended into factionalism and fervent absolutist splinter groups such as the rigorous and absurd cuisine minceur. The original simplicity was lost in a wave of internecine argument over how many kumquats you could get in a filo pastry basket, and whether crème fraîche really transubstantiated or was just a symbol. And then the health fanatics got hold of it and it became a silly slimming cult – eat out and lose money.

At heart, nouvelle cuisine was sound and worthy, and it changed the way we eat. It made French food more Italian in style, it put ingredients above recipes, and it accented harmonised flavours as opposed to big homogenous single tastes.

Now, I'm as glad as the next trencherperson that we've seen the last of huge plates with an infant carrot, Kenyan black bean and asparagus lying in a gob of pimento purée, but I'm equally glad that we've seen the end of scallops floating in a glutinous mornay sauce, gratinéed with breadcrumbs and cheddar, with piped potato round their shells. There are many roads to foodie heaven, but, as nanny said, they all have to go down the same big red highway. Hideous shoes may come back into fashion, the Turner prize may still be ridiculous, but the most important bit of our culture, the dining table, is seeing something of a renaissance, and we have, in large part, nouvelle cuisine to thank for that.

… and against

The room was small and full and had the bustle of serious intent and the smuggery of missionaries. The menu came in doggerel – that is, five verses of three lines each, each line being a list of ingredients and a cookery term. The waitress, who came a couple of feet behind her smile, asked if we'd eaten here before. 'Well, then, I'd better explain the menu.'

I could feel myself bridle. (Actually, I couldn't – I've no idea what bridling feels like, but I've read that other people do it, so I wanted to have a go.) What's the point of writing a menu and then having to explain it, particularly when it's a clear list? 'Our portions aren't very large …' (I gave up trying to bridle and silently screamed: oh my God, I'm falling through a hole in the space-time continuum, and I'm going to meet Antony Worrall Thompson at the other end) '… so we suggest you choose, say, three dishes each, or have the gastro-digestive people-carrier option.' Just give us the whole menu, I offered. There's seven of us. Go for it. The waitress caught up with her smile. 'Better not,' she said. 'Confuses the kitchen.'

After much toing and froing we ordered. And then, slowly, like the retreat from Moscow, plates started turning up. Sometimes we'd wait half an hour, sometimes only twenty-eight minutes. For a tiny plate of crisp fillet of red mullet, red mullet soup and red pepper *beignet*. Or rump of lamb, *confit* shoulder, turnip *tatin*, lamb vinaigrette, crackling. Or quail, glazed salsify, sauté of *foie gras* and hazelnuts.

Now, I'm not going to knock the size, because, as you know, size isn't everything. But what is everything is rhythm and pleasure. And size doesn't matter in the least if it's absent. I started with the soup of mussels, baby fennel, saffron velouté, crême fraîche, which was award-winningly excellent, but only three mouthfuls. I wanted a bowl, and if not a bowl, I wanted something else as good immediately. A postage stamp of excellent honey-glazed belly pork an episode of *EastEnders* later didn't do it. Dinner was a syncopated tease that just got you going, then buggered off. It was infuriatingly frustrating. For pudding, I ordered the cheeseboard because I was still ravenous.

All the food was fantastically well made and incredibly clever. But instead of loving it, I wanted to punch its taunting little lights out. It reminded me what the insuperable flaw in nouvelle cuisine is. A mode of cooking invented in a kitchen, not a dining-room, it's perfectly, gratifyingly revolutionary if you're a chef, but tastes like a sermon with footnotes if you're a customer. Restaurants don't sell emotion – we bring that with us. What they do is lay a table and offer the means to evoke it. And that's an ingredient that's older than fire and one I've mentioned before and no doubt will again.

What this place didn't offer is hospitality. It made the easy mistake of imagining that what restaurants sell is food.

For a starter, I had a four-layer soup made like a pousse-café cocktail in coloured layers: tomato, leek, avocado and something else. Why? (Waves hands about.) Why do this thing? Where is the point? It looks stupid, it tastes like a mess. Why would I want to eat four cold vegetable soups at once? The Blonde had a plate of mixed fish: smoked salmon, raw salmon, smoked tuna, raw tuna, loads of bits and fishy slabs, vaguely dilled. Succinctly, she nailed it – 'Finnair business class'.

The menu reads like a mantra that dedicated hunger strikers might repeat to each other to help themselves stay on message. Red deer carpaccio with beetroot risotto and hazelnut oil. Pan-seared monkfish tail with an infusion of saffron, cardamom and anise. Oven-roasted pheasant breast with pork knuckle stuffing and hazelnut jus. No, no, stop. I'll starve to death.

Main courses included a leg of lamb cooked in bee's honey (just in case you thought it might be snail honey or 'Hi, honey, I'm home'), which would be noisome to taste unless you happened to have pressed a soldering iron to your tongue for at least half an hour first. Look, I'm not going to go on with this. It was ghastly. The only meagrely pleasurable things were some slices of Turkish-cheese pizza. For cheese on toast, I could have stayed home.

This wasn't dire. It was far worse than that. Our jaunty waitress recommended the sushi roll of salmon and eel, wrapped in avocado. Now that sounds like a bit of catering-college-exam weirdness. But what came had dumped the salmon and added foie gras instead. Eel-flavoured foie gras in a slimy green coat is the sort of thing you need to be very, very drunk to come up with, and on drugs to eat twice.

Tofu stew in some sort of brown, chunky slime was like savoury earwax-flavoured marshmallows floating in Bovril. And there was a new dish, snow-crab legs. What arrived was apparently the dissected crusty exhaust pipe of a Ford Cortina, up which had been inserted some prawn-flavoured cotton wool soaked in mayonnaise. It was a dish that even an octopus would have turned up its beak at.

The ingénue vegetables were midgets and dwarves, boiled so that they held their natural shape only by a collective act of nostalgia. But they were ambrosia compared with the mutton. The colour of a gravedigger's fingernail, it was a mortified curl of muscle from some unknown extremity of ancient ovine. It resisted knife and fork, being mostly translucent, sweaty gristle and greasy fat. It was inedibly disgusting, without question the nastiest ingredient I've been served this year.

A schnitzel ('crumbled protein escalope with sautéd spinach and a creamy wine and watercress sauce') made me gasp out loud. It was histrionically vile, a tough inner sole of undead flavour coated in sticky crumble with a puddle of bin juice.

It devoutly made me wish I had never used the word inedible before, so I could take it out in all its pristine goodness and whack it on this Beelzebub's emission of the night. Worst of all was a 'cheeseburger' – 'our special blend of vegetable protein, herbs and spices on a sesame bun'. This would have counted as an unfair *artificial stimulant in a face-pulling competition. One mouthful had me girning like a toothless pensioner getting his prostate poked.*

A tart of splendidly ripe figs, gingerbread ice cream and tobacco syrup. I promise you, it's pipe tobacco boiled with water and sugar: a sweet sauce that was a perfect finish to a sublime dish. You could feel the nicotine prickle on the back of your throat. Now what sort of moonstruck loon do you have to be to think of boiling pipe tobacco and pouring it over pudding? And to make it not just work, but levitate?

The chef is touched with a lunatic genius, or he's made a pact with the kitchen devil.

2

INGREDIENTS

The Blonde had gravadlax. Everyone should have it once a year, it reminds you not to become blasé about smoked salmon. A plate of thick, slimy fish-flavoured pink flip-flop with an unpleasant sweet taste, it was everything gravadlax ever is, the very mordant soul of fjords.

A lobster bisque ought to be the crowning glory of the potager. And this one was excellent. Silky as a gigolo's compliment and fishy as a chancellor's promise.

The baby back ribs were like eating the evidence in a war-crimes trial. Apparently, they'd been buried in a peat bog for a month. If you tugged a protruding bone it came clean away, leaving a slab of desecrated room-temperature pig.

It all reminded me of dishes that managed to taste of things that weren't food at all, like the inside of new Volvos, or pencil sharpeners, or cab-drivers' pockets. The shellfish custard tasted precisely, exactly like an ashtray. I said: 'This tastes like an ashtray,' and the Blonde said: 'That's a disgusting and sordid simile.' And I said: 'It's not a simile – it really does taste like an ashtray.'

'Oh my God,' she said, tasting it, 'that's a custard ashtray.' Now, making a fishy custard ashtray is very clever. I just don't ever, ever want to eat it again.

The ham was from a black, oak-fed pig, manacled to one of those contraptions that was probably also used to extract a confession and last-minute conversion. It was £14 a plate, so I had another one. This is the best value in London. 'No, no, Don Pedro, eet eez the best value in the known world. We must take this peeg to the jungle and force the natives to worsheep eet on pain of death for the sake of their eternal souls.' Spanish ham is incontestably the best in the world. It has a flavour and texture without parallel. I love York, I adore Parma, but Spain takes the doubloon. It's like chewing a sweaty infanta.

The real prize for 'will they eat it?' jackass catering was the mushroom thing. I must try and make this live for you. The overall ambience of the dish would be a dank dark corner of a fenland cellar. The olive bread was the colour and texture of a short log that had been left sitting in peat water for a year. Split in half, it had been stuffed with a pair of Portobello mushrooms. I would have guessed they were beech-stump fungal goitres. On them were perched two thick rings of tomato, apparently sliced with a comb, and a spatter of chive and onion aioli, which was plainly the by-product of some long-term organic decomposition. Altogether, if I'd been told this thing had been excavated from a Dark Ages pit, I wouldn't have been the slightest bit surprised.

I cut a sliver of bubo 'shroom and edged it between my teeth. It was cold – cold as the grave, a deceased ex-thing. Half a cup of ooze leaked down my gullet, tasting vaguely, but mortifyingly of silt, sump, brack and bilge. (Talk among yourselves for a moment: I can feel the damnable thing slithering upstream.)

Thankfully, I've never been desperate enough to fancy a winkle. I've put some very unpleasant things in my mouth, and winkles

*are right up there. Winkles are bottom-feeders' chewing gum. If
you want to go for the really big mouthful of knicker elastic, then
they'll happily sell you a plate full of whelks. As a general rule of
thumb, don't eat anything that you need a sewing kit for.*

Cabbage

The entry for cabbage in the *Larousse Gastronomique* starts with the heavenly sentence: 'The cabbage seems to have been unknown to the Hebrews. It is not mentioned in the Bible.' I love that – so French. Just the slightest note of disappointment with God; just the merest raised eyebrow and pursued Gallic lip. You can imagine a French chef in confession: 'Bless me Father, for I have sinned – but I'm not the only one: God left cabbages out of the Bible.'

I can still remember my first cabbage, or rather, my first welcome cabbage; my first cabbage that didn't taste like silage boiled in iodine. Pull up a stool and I'll tell you about it.

There are important meals in everyone's life: dinners that are turning points, lunches after which you are a changed man. I can remember every meal that I've ever been dumped over. You sit down full of love, lust and appetite and just after the waiter clears away the starter the object of your desire reaches across and holds your hand in an anodyne sort of way and says 'A.A., I've got something I need to tell you. I love you like a friend … I need more space … I'm seeing your B.F.…' and then, with the immaculate timing that you only get in the best establishments, the waiter returns with a huge plate of cassoulet, chips and a mixed salad. Your stomach turns to curdled milk and the food looks like someone has been sick on your plate; what's more, you don't know whether to brain the bitch with the bottle of claret or to beg and whimper. And then you remember you're picking up the bill as well.

Bad things always happen over dinner and good things always arrive at breakfast, but the most memorable, most precarious

meals are always lunch. When I'm under the number 9 bus and
my life flashes before me, the highlights will be a selection of
lunches, such as the one where I had my first proper cabbage.

It was in Paris. I must have been eighteen and I was there
with my father and brother; I can't remember another time
when it was just the three of us together. Nick was sixteen
and training to be a chef on the Left Bank, and my father and
I had gone across to see how he was settling in. I had been
to Paris before, but this time it felt new and original; it was
early summer and sunny and we were all pleased to be in each
other's company.

Although Paris is a city that my father knew well (he helped
liberate it), it was now occupied by the next generation and
belonged to Nick. He took us around like Christopher Wren
showing off St Paul's. It was a charming reversal of roles. My
father had always dragged us around cities refusing to use a
map and pointing out baroque whatnots with tears in his eyes
while my brother huffed along behind complaining about his
feet and wanting Fanta.

This time Nick strutted off, diving into bars and cafes where
the patron would shake us by the hand and give us tiny, sweet
kirs on the house. Chefs, even very gauche sixteen-year-old
commis, are respected in Paris. Daddy had a list of restaurants
he had personally liberated in 1944 and which he had been
personally liberating two or three times a year ever since. He
suggested a few, but Nick said we should eat Alsatian food
instead – food from Alsace-Lorraine, the department on the
border with Germany that has changed hands once a generation for the last five hundred years.

The restaurant was called the Cochon Noir, the black pig,
and I think it was near the Bastille. It might have been next
to the Opera; anyway, it was cool and beautiful. We could
have gone anywhere, but this was just right. In the entrance
hall was a black piglet wearing a pink ribbon (so French, to
let tomorrow's lunch smell its mummy cooking). We sat at

a corner table and laughed and teased each other and Nick said he would choose, because he wanted to show off, and after a while a huge silver dish was borne unsteadily across the room by a bandy-legged waiter. On it was cabbage, the most divine aromatic mountain of sun-bleached, straw-coloured choucroute. And before you turn up your dainty noses and say 'Ugh, sauerkraut,' let me tell you that this dish had about as much in common with the grey sludge you get in bottles as Juliette Binoche has with Barbara Windsor. On its foothills were base camps of sausages, three or four kinds, and further up were precariously-lodged veal chops, anaemic and milky. Closer to the summit were languid, voluptuous strips of fat pork. Ah, but the very best was at the apex: stuck in the top of the Eiger that was lunch was a split of champagne. The sweating waiter gratefully slid the edifice on to the damask and, taking a deep breath, tapped the neck of the bottle with a knife. The champagne erupted, frothing and sparkling all over the mountain. Such a surprise, such a joy, so right for the mood of the day.

That was a life-changing lunch. I never looked at cabbage in the same way after that. It was a bit like the bit in *Now, Voyager* when Bette Davis steps off the boat transformed from a dowdy frump into the most heavenly woman you have ever seen. That's what cabbage had been before: a frumpy vegetable and boring waste of plate space, with a smell that generations of Englishmen associate with floggings, polish, Latin and buggery.

Cabbage is now an almost universal vegetable. From Reykjavik to Canton, you can walk into the kitchen with a cabbage and the chef will smile. The *Brassica* genus (for that is whence the cabbage comes) has spawned a huge number of exotic cousins: cauliflowers, Brussels sprouts, kohlrabis. The cabbage itself comes in hundreds of shapes and sizes and the ones you are most likely to come across in Europe are the straight-leaved green cabbage (school cabbage), the curly savoy, the hard red (best cooked with vinegar and jam) and the white (for sauerkraut).

Cook cabbage gently in a little water, wine, stock or goose fat. It has tons of vitamins, but most of these are lost in the cooking; not that I care. I'm told it's good for the bowels, but since I'm not particularly interested in mine, I wouldn't know. The hard red and the white need to be cooked for longer than the other varieties. The best way to deal with cabbage is to eat it with butter and fresh black pepper; no, the best way is to poach it in wine and water with a piece of salt pork; then again, perhaps the best way is to cook it slowly with potatoes and sausages while you're out at the pub.

Cabbage, they say, is at the centre of the Russian soul. Just as New York is the Big Apple, Moscow is now the Big Cabbage. A businessman I once met told me it was called that because it has many layers, a hard heart and is full of wind.

Rice

We are all children of the lawn. Among the many things that conjoin and divide us as a species, grass is the most fundamental. We all eat a lot of grass.

You, of course, may not think you eat grass at all. You may be one of those who harrumphs at salads and says: 'Bloody grass. I'm not eating cricket-pitch clippings.' But then, that shows how much you know. Without grass, we're nothing – and would have been for the past ten millennia.

The grass family (Gramineae) is extraordinary. From its largest member, maize, to one of its smallest, teff, grass provides the staple diet of humans. If you believe that you are what you eat, then you're a Flymo bucket. And you can divide the world neatly – indeed, almost exactly – in half between two Gramineae-philes: wheat-eaters and rice-eaters. When Mummy smiled at you in the morning and said: 'Eat up your breakfast, then you'll grow up to be big and strong,' it very much depended on whether your bowl contained Weetabix or boiled rice. If it was wheaty, then the likelihood was she was right: barring accidents, you'll live until your early seventies, have a brace of kids who'll outlive you and die of the diseases of indulgence, having lived a relatively comfortable life.

On the other hand, if it was rice, then Mummy's words were more wishful thinking. You'll grow up, but not as tall, and you'll probably only make it to your early fifties. You'll have more children, but, heart-breakingly, you'll see some of them buried. And it's more likely to be the diseases of neglect and poverty that carry you off.

The wheat world and the rice world are better definitions

of our most fundamental division than the myopically geo-political 'first' and 'third', the mealy-mouthed 'developed' and 'developing', or the plainly geographical north/south. We are far more what we eat than what we vote or what we pray.

But why wheat-eaters should have so comprehensively beaten rice-eaters to the other good things in life is, if not quite a mystery, then an enigma shoved up a conundrum. Rice and wheat began to be cultivated at about the same time, roughly ten thousand years ago: wheat in the golden crescent of the Middle East, rice either in India or northern China, both of whom vie for the credit. The northern Chinese word for rice is dao; the Dravidian Indian word is arisi, from which we glean riso, riz, arroz and rice. Padi is the word for it in South East Asia. Alexander's army brought rice back to the Romans after their invasion of what is now Pakistan. By 1000BC it was being grown in Japan, Persia and Madagascar. But, late again, the Americans didn't get it until an experimental planting in Virginia in 1609 (American Indian wild rice is an indigenous grass, but of a different genus).

Today, rice is grown in 112 countries and accounts for between 35 per cent and 60 per cent of food in Asia. In terms of wholesomeness, rice and wheat are remarkably similar. Wheat has slightly more protein, rice more carbohydrate. For labourers, rice alone is just enough for sustenance.

And herein lies a part of the answer to the enigma-stuffed conundrum: you can feed more people with an acre of rice than an acre of wheat. Population grows to consume the food available, not the other way round. For instance, the huge increase in the population of Ireland occurred with the introduction of potatoes, which fed larger families than cereal crops. And there's a tribe in the arid south of Ethiopia whose population has remained constant for thousands of years, dictated by how much water it is humanly possible to draw from its ancient wells.

So rice will sustain a dense population, but it is also more intensive to grow than wheat. Look at how many people are needed to plant a paddy field compared with a wheat field. It needs elaborate water management; it's high maintenance. Rice may keep a large population just above starvation, but it also needs that population to grow it. Paddy fields become a closed circle of work producing the energy to work.

Wheat, on the other hand, feeds a smaller population, but allows them more space and time to do other things, such as develop a social system and technology that ends up colonising rice-eaters. After breakfast, space and time are everything.

You can never be too thankful that you come from the wheat world. And, personally, I've always been ambivalent about rice, partly because it's the one ingredient that, whatever I do, I can never cook properly (except as rice pudding), but mostly because it's the bland taste of rural indenture. I can't look at a bowl of rice without thinking it has been boiled in tears.

I should have started this the way they start Hollywood film trailers. Have you noticed how they always begin with that man who has had his epiglottis Velcroed, saying: 'In a world without ...'? It's a good phrase, 'In a world without ...' You just add your desired condiment word – 'pity', 'law', 'mercy', 'lavatory paper' – and you're off. For those of you who find writing a pain, I couldn't recommend it more. It gives your most meagre thoughts gravitas, while being suitably vacuous.

So, for instance, if you hate writing thank-you letters, just begin: 'Dear Araminta, in a world without gratitude/spotted Dick/that nice friend of Trevor ...' Students, if you're tearing your hair out trying to compose one of those tricky begging letters home, you could do a lot worse than: 'Dear dad, in a world without generosity/student loans/unplanned pregnancy ...' You should write it on the memo board beside the fridge. 'In a world without cornflakes/light bulbs/milkmen/the 4.15 from Doncaster ...'

Anyway, where was I? In a world without rice, chopsticks would be sticks, sushi would be dead fish and we'd have to throw potatoes at weddings. In fact, east of Zanzibar, it's impossible to imagine a world without rice. It's the grass that created two-thirds of the globe, a staple that is the basis for some of the most elaborate and complex epicurean cultures.

And I've just seen where they end up. If you take the beginning of rice's journey with mankind as bronze-age China, then the furthest reach of its evolutionary tryst is a bijou shop I stumbled across. I've simply got to share it with you.

There were video screens and twinkly pastel plastic takeaway boxes. It was very wowynowy. And the theme ... In a world without taste or irony, the theme was rice pudding. I swear, cold rice pudding in novelty flavours. Oh Pip, what flavours! Pristine bowls of sludgy puppy vomit dyed into a National Trust colour chart by the addition of spicy Indian chai (tea), summer fruits and more.

'You're not going in there,' screamed the Blonde. I've got to. 'No, you don't.' This is what I do. 'Dear God, please. They won't think any worse of you. I won't tell anyone.' Don't you see? A critic has to do what a critic has to do. 'Why can't you just turn around and pretend you didn't see it? What about me? What about us and our life together?' What life would we have? It would always be there between us. You might not mention it tomorrow, or the next day. But one day, you would – the man who turned his back on rice pudding and ran. 'Oh, you're all the same. It's all about your silly pride. Well, go on then. Just don't expect me to wait for you. I won't wipe pudding off your chin. Boo, hoo, hoo.'

I stood in front of the counter and calmly ordered the pineapple and basil. The term 'inedible' is overused – I've seen film of a man eating poodle poo – so I won't say this defied possibility. But two mouthfuls made pooch poop look like a mighty yummy alternative. You know how basil has a slightly medicinal flavour? Well, with pineapple, it spookily imitates that smell of Swiss industrial lavatory disinfectant. The rice was thick and slimy and could have been what gave the sperm whale its Christian name. I can't begin to reconstruct the process by which someone became convinced that this concept was a good idea or even on nodding terms with something that had once met a good idea. My best guess is that it's the creation of a coven of bulimics who wanted something reversible: one dish you could eat three times a day.

Fish

Fish and chips

Whitby is one of my favourite towns, a Victorian huddle of propriety that sits on a purposeful harbour, under the ruined abbey. It was home to Captain Cook's *Endeavour* and also *Dracula*. This is where Bram Stoker saw the shipwreck that inspired the start of the story. Up on the cliffs, there's a Bram Stoker memorial bench where youngsters go to give each other memorable love bites.

Alum was mined here, and jet, the geological remains of monkey-puzzle trees, which was used to make the funereal jewellery made fashionable by Albert's Great Exhibition and Victoria's glum forty-year mourning for him. Whitby was one of only a handful of British towns shelled in the first world war. The imperial German high-seas fleet steamed up in 1914.

Now the fishing boats have taken a beating and been reduced to a couple of smacks. Nobody can remember what alum is for, and none of us mourns anything with brooches. Only drunks want to swim in the North Sea, and the trippers' trade has been replaced by the undead Goths, hordes of them, swaying on uncertain heels. There is something touchingly, peculiarly English about the posy of Captain Cook, Dracula, jet, styptic pencils, Huns and Goths.

Whitby has one other thing that makes it a joy and a place of pilgrimage – the best fish and chips in the world. Well, the best in my world. Fish and chips is one of those dishes that are generally better remembered than eaten. It's a totem of Englishness, a thing that is more than mere dinner and rather less than actual food. Battered fish leaves Continentals cod-eyed with repulsion. Indeed, almost all of it is a horrible torture for both the consumed and the consumer. But here, it is sublime, transcendent. The nice lady asked if I'd like cod or haddock. That was always the shibboleth for north or south. Haddock is up here, cod down there. 'Haddock, please.'

A thick fillet was dipped in batter and fried. Here there's nothing soggily waiting. It's all made to order. I had a cup of tea in a Styrofoam cup, brewed from a tea bag that tasted of brown. The vinegar was malt, the ketchup caged in small packets, the mushy peas dyed green. Everything else was as you'd expect from anywhere in England. Except for the fish, which came, eight minutes later, blisteringly hot. The batter had been immolated into a filigree of stalagmites and fans of coral. I broke off a corner. The fish smoked and glistened translucent white.

What do you fry it in, I asked. 'Beef dripping.' Just dripping? 'Only dripping.' I doused it in vinegar, sprinkled it with salt and went and sat on the harbour wall, where Cook took out the *Endeavour* early one morning and the haddock had landed in the dawn. It was stupendous. The chips were pale and crisp, hot and floury. The batter crunched. Beef dripping is everything, in terms of both chemistry and gastronomy. Only animal fat burns hot enough to seal the batter instantly into this light coat. Inside, the fish doesn't fry – it steams itself in its own hermetic juiciness.

Fish and chips is a silent meal. You shouldn't talk and eat. It is a race against falling temperature. You need to be perfectly concentrated, constantly blowing and sucking, wolfing with bared teeth and flared nostrils. But even lukewarm, chips fried in dripping have a delicious, sweet, meaty tang. The faint, fugitive flavour of the bull is the subtle ingredient that makes this perfect.

That seems a nicely British combination: beefy batter, vinegar and the sea.

Fishing

If you live long enough to wear rubber boots, someone is sure to make you fish. It doesn't matter how far from water you live; there will be a momentary lapse in concentration, you'll find yourself next to a coast or river and, before you can say 'Get off, you smelly pervert', you'll have some bloke's rod in your hand and he'll be whispering 'Easy does it, it's all in the wrist' into your frozen ear. It doesn't even have to be a drown-able amount of water. A trickle, a puddle, is enough to spawn proselytising piscatores. Short of becoming a born-again Kalahari Bushman, it's virtually impossible to avoid dabbling in untroubled waters.

I have been teased into attempting to fish on five continents, and the closest it came to being fun was in South America – shooting doves in the morning in Argentina, then sticking them on hooks and throwing them into a river in the afternoon, and pulling up piranhas. Piranhas are the young Tories of the fish world – collectively vicious, singly idle cowards. They don't fight on the line; they just hang, supine, grinning with grim gnashers. And, like all Tories, they're repellently inedible. The only real sport is the deep-tissue manicure of trying to retrieve your hook from their Lecter-like gobs. But then, of course, you employ a local communist to do that.

Catching tiger fish on the Sand River, in Tanzania, also had its moments. You stand on the banks of a river that boasts the highest density of crocodiles in Africa, which adds a certain piquancy to the process. There is bait at both ends of the line.

In principle, the sort of fishing that sounds most fun is big game: you, on a boat, with some mates in bikinis. You don't have to touch a stick until something is hanging off it. And you're fishing for things that really are worth catching. The reality, though, is noisy, smelly, boring and vomitory. Well, it was up until last week. I was in the Caribbean and was again induced to try fishing with my children (not actually with them, but in their company). I rather loved it. No, in truth, it was shriekingly exciting. Because this time, there was something that had always been missing before – fish.

First, it was the sight of Flora and Ali catching their first proper fish: tuna, yellow jack and the astonishing *jolie laide* dolphinfish. And then there was catching one myself. When I heard the line squeal, and clumsily stuck the bucking rod into the socket between my legs, I had that feeling of dry, expectant terror that I haven't felt for years. I recognised it with a Proustian horror. It was stage fright. People were whooping, my children were imploring, and I was about to take part in a performance that could well leave me looking utterly foolish.

But there was another feeling – a rarer, more basically primal one. For want of a better word, it was 'connectedness'. Down there, something large and lithe and alien was attached, via this thin line, to me. And it hooked something far back in my head, at the base of the cortex, in the dark, damp, airless basement of my hungry synapses; something from our generic past. This tug could have been anything. Down there be monsters. Just last week, two dozen new fish were discovered off New Zealand: bizarre, original and spectacular. And that was New Zealand, the test card of countries.

So here's my Ahab/Jonah moment. Perhaps this throb I feel is a leviathan, a mermaid, Poseidon. Actually, what it feels like is a brick privy. Old game-fishing hands will tell you that a 60lb yellowfin tuna is minute, a midget, barely bait, an anchovy's girlfriend. They lie. Fishermen lie about the size of their sprats, and they denigrate my Moby Dick. Getting it up was like winding a caravan up a hundred yards of cliff while sitting on a seesaw. The screaming urge to let go was cacophonous, but the gruff, adjective-free, stumpy sentences of Hemingway were pounding in my temples, and I just had to see it through to the gaff. Slicing the toro out of its twitching gut, it didn't taste like sushi – it tasted of sweat and salt and acid adrenaline. It tasted of ancient victories.

Bouillabaisse

Last night, I went to a restaurant that only serves one thing:
bouillabaisse. This is one of those dishes that has mythological
culinary status. Cassoulet is another. And salad dressing. And
the Bloody Mary.

The orthodoxy of their preparation can make or break
friendships, and I have actually seen chefs come to shoving
and slapping over the correct recipe. The problem, and the
joy, of bouillabaisse is that it has so many moving parts: do
you put chilli in the *rouille*? Do you add Gruyère? Are there
potatoes? My feeling has always been that potatoes make it a
bourride and that tomato purée is de trop. But the one thing I
hope we're all agreed on is that it must contain that indigenous
Mediterranean fish, the rascasse.

This restaurant sells hundreds of gallons of the stuff for five
months of the year, and you can barely get a table – so this
is probably as close to a Vatican encyclical as we're going to
get. And they serve the intense fish broth separately from the
fish, which includes rascasse, rouget, langouste and tiny little
crabs. The *rouille* has vicious garlic, psychopathic chilli and
sweet-talking saffron. There's no cheese at all, which I think
is probably correct; save the Gruyère for your French onion.
Controversially, they offer waxy yellow potatoes for you to
add separately. I must say, the whole performance is pretty
sensational.

Bouillabaisse is still, for me, geographically specific. I can
only eat it here in the south of France. Anywhere else, it just
makes me sad.

Oysters

The four seasons are dead. Have been for a good number of
seasons now. All that is left of them is an annoyingly moreish bit of Vivaldi that is played in Cotswold second-hand

bookshops. Yet we all conspire to believe that our lives are governed by seed time and harvest. You sniff the air on the long ploughman's walk between patio and Volvo and say: 'Ah, a crisp autumnal morn.' As if that had anything to do with life or the price of eggs.

'Lovely weather we're having for the time of year,' you cheerily say down the telephone from your double-glazed office to some other double-glazed office.

Most of us don't spend more than ten minutes a day without a roof and some sort of artificial temperature over us. The only time the seasons make any difference is when we are abroad. But we like to keep up the pretence, pretend that somehow we're in touch with and beholden to the orbit of the spheres. 'Red sky at night, junior school's alight.'

Food is where we feel most firmly connected. 'The first asparagus of summer,' you smile like a sophisticated Phil Archer contemplating a spear that has been grown under plastic in Brazil. 'Oh, you can't beat the new-season lamb,' you murmur knowledgeably over a leg of immature sheep that has been prematurely conceived and stall-fed on sugar beet in Lincolnshire. To all intents and foodie purposes, there are only two seasons, Christmas and not Christmas. Whatever you may think in the organic cottage-style wholemeal cosiness of your kitchen-cum-nonjudgmental-dining-area, this is a good thing. The whole march of agrarian history has been a half-famished marathon to overcome the tyranny of the seasons. Seasonal eating actually means getting lettuce three times a day for a month and then not seeing it again for nine months. Until 200 years ago, a significant proportion of the population starved for three or four months at a time, the months we think of as so delightfully bosky British – late spring and early summer.

No, the nostalgia for the seasons is the province of those who have fridges and tin-openers and accounts at delicatessens. It's in September that we are lulled into a faux Victorian seasonability by marketing men. The good things of the wild beckon. We've had grouse for a couple of weeks and partridge are about to start. Then various duck, deer and pheasant. The first of September is a red-letter day. September has an 'r' and we've been r-less for four months.

The one piece of food lore that everyone knows is that you eat oysters with an 'r'. Which is another way of saying you don't eat them in the summer. Although, of course, you can, you can eat the long thin Portuguese oysters that taste of tears and iodine. They are cheap and farmed all year. The round or native or belon oyster is the one that arrives with the 'r'. These are the ones that are worth waiting for. So come last Sunday, it was off to have oysters for lunch.

Just before we get to lunch, let me tell you something interesting about oysters. They are a good measure of the efficiency of the Roman transport system. In middens throughout the interior of Britain you find oyster shells, which means the Romans must have been able to carry them very speedily. Unless, of course, they used the empty ones as lavatory paper. Which is unlikely and silly.

We were sat in a booth. I beamed and ordered three dozen finest natives. The waiter looked shifty.

'Three dozen?'

Three dozen. My friend can't eat them.

'We're a bit short of oysters. I can do you nine and nine and six.'

Shucks. Would you believe it, the first day of the traditional oyster season and the traditional oyster restaurant can't lay its hands on three dozen of the things. It wasn't as if they were overwhelmed by demand. All the time we were there, there were only five other customers in the place – Americans deciding on whether to go and see *Oliver!* or *Riverdance*.

Anyway, the twenty-four oysters came and were two dozen perfect mouthfuls. Every year I'm astonished at the miraculous power in the taste of native oysters. They are such a long, deep, complex flavour. A note of summer holiday, a bit of unmade bed, a touch medicinal, but also amoral and decadent. Psychologists say oysters are considered aphrodisiac because they mimic the texture and consistency of sexual organs. All I can say is they must have no sense of taste.

Whale

How fresh do you like your fish? Day after it's caught? Same day? Only eat stuff you grabbed yourself like an otter, still flapping? Fish and fresh go together like things and stuff.

Well, how do you fancy fish caught in 1989? The best and most interesting fresh fish I've eaten recently was eleven years old. It was whale – and before you reach for the pedant key on your computers, I know that, technically, whales aren't fish – like I know that, technically, Christopher Biggins isn't a big girl or, indeed, a whale. But for the sake of keeping terra firma and life simple, whales are fish. If they want to make separate breathing arrangements, that's up to them.

The whale I ate was a fin whale, the second-biggest animate thing in the world, if you don't count John Prescott's self-delusion. The last one was harpooned in 1989 in the North Atlantic and some bright monger decided to sell it to the Japanese, stuffed it in containers and shipped it to Tokyo. On the way, a scavenging troop of blubber-hugging sniffer-ecologists chained themselves to the big fish and the monger thought, 'Sod this, Ahab,' and sent it back to Iceland, where it has been deep frozen ever since. A wonderful chef called Ulfar Eysteinsson has been slicing little bits off and serving them in his restaurant, Hja Ulfari, which means The Two Overcoats and also The Two Frenchmen. Why the Icelandic for overcoat should be the same as Frenchman, I can't imagine – except, I suppose, that when you shudder they're both all over you.

Whale is wonderful meat. I started with sushi – as good as any tuna or salmon, dark and rich – then steak *au poivre*. You can treat the meat pretty much like beef, but whale steak has a much finer grain, hardly any fat and a big elegant flavour, like two Samoan fullbacks waltzing naked in cream and cognac.

Whale has another unique property. The meat on its tummy has no blood supply, so if it lands heavily and cuts itself, it doesn't bleed. This is meat, not fat, and is perfectly white and very mild, with a silky texture. What can you say? One fish that produces both steak and veal at the same time. Call me Ishmael, but I think we should eat a lot more whale.

I know there will be some of you blubbering: 'Ooh, ooh, poor whaleypeople things. They've got brains bigger than Mary Archer; they suckle their children; they read Penguin Classics and speak fax; and they're best friends with dolphins, who everyone knows are the most intelligent, sensitive, cultured and spiritual things in the universe.' Well, just forget it. Whales are big fish, that's all. Sumo sardines. And they commit genocide on krill. Yes, you never think of krill, do you? They may be small, but krill have got rights, too. They're only human.

For all you armchair ecowarriors, the kicker is that whale is possibly the healthiest meat in the world: free-range, wild and mostly fat-free; no additives, chemicals or pesticides. And it's full of all those things you buy as gelatine-coated supplements from the health-food shop. Just think: stuff that's good for you and tastes good – and nobody has yet managed to develop a whale allergy.

We don't need to kill a lot. Perhaps half a dozen a year. Okay, say twenty. No, make that fifty. Give the cod and sea bass a rest. Let's get those harpoons smokin'. There's a lot of little fellas out there in the cold who'll thank you.

I was in Iceland for the Stinky Food Festival. This is a jocular tourist-board name for a lot of very weird grub – such as seal flipper, which comes on a plate looking distressingly like a frostbitten Ranulph Fiennes hand. It's singed and pick-led in vinegar and tastes rubbery-fatty-fishy and thoroughly unpleasant. And cod stomach, stuffed with cod liver, which is surprisingly good – a cross between fish pâté and fish sausage. Smoked puffin tastes like fey tarred grouse. Mountain oysters are sheep's testicles and are like ... well, like having testicles in your mouth. (Most of you will know what I mean, and the rest of you are lying.) Dried catfish is a thinner, tougher, yellower version of bacalao and isn't a catfish as we know it, but the fearsome saltwater wolf fish. Smoked lamb's head is variously subtle in a muttony sort of way. I asked what it was smoked over, as there's no wood on Iceland. Dried sheep dung, as it happens; it adds that daggy *je ne sais quoi*. Perhaps most delicious and interesting were lamb spare ribs preserved in whey. I've never heard of anyone saving food in this by-product of cheese, but it was very good and softly sour.

All this may sound like a bit of a dare-you joke, but beneath your well-fed metropolitan smirk, it's not funny at all. Stuck out in the North Atlantic, for hundreds of years Iceland was dependent on Norwegian and Danish ships that often wouldn't – or couldn't – sail for months on end. Indigenous natural ingredients are as sparsely meagre as anywhere on earth. Imperative and invention meant that anything and everything edible had to be utilised.

This food isn't disgusting or amusing. It's a salutary reminder that food is, first and foremost, life. It's a measure of the value and tenacity of humanity and its remarkable achievements. On Christmas Eve, when the rest of Europe is busting the larder, the Icelanders share a dinner of rotten skate. I mean really rotten – the stench of ammonia makes your hair gag. They do it to remind themselves of a shared heritage of hardship and stoic purpose. Sometimes the odour of the sanctity of life isn't quite what you think it will be.

Durian

Bali is a funny old place. Botanically, it's the far end of Asia. Swim off its southern tip and your next footstep will be on Australasia. It's also a Hindu island stuck in a predominantly Muslim country (indeed, the only Hindu spot outside the sub-continent). It's a quietly beguiling place, built on Escher-like steps of paddy and prayers. Bali is an ethereal mantra-jam of praying, a silent, imploring cacophony. The place is knee-deep in offerings.

It is difficult to see what they're praying for. Everything ticks over in a stuffed glut of religiosity. Perhaps they are asking for something decent to eat, because, frankly, Indonesian food ain't great – just *nasi goreng* and odd bits of tough chicken, butchered blindfold with a cleaver. But then there is wonderful fruit: mangoes, rambutans, mangosteens, and a strange and beautiful thing I know as a snake fruit. It has brown skin that looks like scales with, inside, the texture of a waxy apple and a perfumed flavour not unlike guava.

And then there is the mighty, devious, dark Gollum of the forest: the durian. Durians look like spiky melons. They're a relative of the jackfruit and grow as buboes, high up on trees. When ripe, they fall with a brain-splattering thud. The durian is possibly the oddest of all God's little gastronomic tests. Originally from Malaya, it's now farmed all over the Far East, where it is not just loved, it's addictively adored. Durian stalls dot the roadside, yet it is illegal to carry them on public transport and many airlines refuse to take them as cargo.

You can tell you're in the presence of a durian from twenty feet. They smell. No, they stink. No, stink is just too small a word for what a durian exudes. They have the most exotically complex and psychologically confused life cycle of any vegetable, and rely on fooling carnivores to spread their seed. So they give off the odour of rotting flesh. It's the scent of corruption, a whiff of the charnel house, a gag from a hot grave. If Stephen King books smelt, they'd smell of durian.

Inside, the flesh is marmoreally slimy, some say silky. Personally, I think it's like lost babies who have been drowned in baths of whey. The flesh clings to the stones like putrefying muscle. You have to suck and nibble. Few Westerners manage that twice.

The actual flavour is one of the most complex and difficult I have ever come across. It's one of those tastes that we consider grown-up, like truffles or anchovies, olives or oysters, tastes that teeter on the edge of disgusting and are rites of passage to acquire. For most Europeans, the durian is way over the edge, in the Vale of Vile. It has been likened by horrified travellers to civet cat, sewage, stale vomit, onions, cheese, used surgical swabs, fruit-eating bat pee and brown sherry. The best I can come up with is that it's sort of like camembert, garlic and faint wine gums, with a roof-of-the-mouth whiff of ancient gnawed dog bone. The actual taste is a discordant descant of the smell. It's not sweet or savoury or acid or juicy, but it lingers for hours like the manifestation of avarice, corrupt indulgence and suppurating decadence.

Now, through true professional vanity, I hate not being able to eat and understand the pleasure in things that others eat, and this was my third confrontation with the durian. I managed two mouthfuls before recoiling, and I'm just getting a glimpse of the possibility of perhaps nearly, just about, enduring it. But to do so might mean stepping over an invisible line into a world I'm not spiritually equipped for. Filipinos, Malays and Indonesians happily turn durian into ice cream, sweets and cakes. They eat it with salt, or stewed with sugar, or pickled with vinegar. It defies categorisation and nothing so marks the yawning gulf between hot East and cool West as this strange, misbegotten Caliban food – a vegetable that thinks it's a cadaver.

Afterwards, still with the savour lingering, I had a Somerset Maugham moment, a mawkish cafard. Coming from my chilly, Protestant, northern fastness, I had a childish suspicion that the durian might actually be properly evil.

Blood and beluga

We have been away in Tanzania and, ever mindful of my responsibility to put outré things in my mouth on your behalf, I asked my guide to show me the local cuisine. 'Are you sure?' he replied. 'We are in the land of the Masai.' Sweetheart, I said, I have eaten in Islington and Cheshire: Masai tea holds no terror for me.

The Masai, as I'm sure you know, are got up as extras from *Star Trek*. Tall, shaven, with an austere, arrogant beauty, they wear red tartan togas and a jangling confection of keyrings, Christmas ornaments and padlocks slotted into holes in their heads. They also carry elegantly vicious lion spears, which, of course, means that the waiter is always right and the customer invariably wrong.

As they are traditional herdsmen, their cattle are their wealth, and they're loath to spend capital by killing them, preferring to live off interest. Which poses a problem: how do you have your cow and eat it? I was taken to a boma – a kraal of circular huts and cattle pens within a stockade – and introduced to a very distinguished chap who looked like a black, gay Rob Roy and who spoke surprisingly precise English. He was surrounded by a giddy collection of resplendent wives who easily fell into miming beauty hints with the Blonde.

My host asked if I'd like to go straight in to dinner and led me to a dining-room-cum-byre, a minimal space made of deeply fashionable African hardwood and furnished with cow-hide and ankle-deep dung. The main course was being held head and tail by a couple of sommeliers. It was a small light cow, a sort of Masai moovel cuisine, simply prepared with a tourniquet round its neck. The chef then stepped forward with a bow and an arrow with a blunt tip (this is not something you can learn from Delia). He fired at a bulging vein and missed. After a couple more goes, a spurt of blood arced out of the neck. Dextrously, he caught the flow in a gourd. After half a pint, he started whisking vigorously with a stick to stop it clotting. The cow had a finger of dung applied to the wound and retired back to the larder, having made not a sound or shown any sign of discomfort. My host generously handed me the vase. Don't you usually mix this with milk, I inquired. 'Sometimes,' he said, 'but connoisseurs take it neat.'

Now the thing about a gourd is that it's bulbous at the bottom, tapering to the lip, and I wasn't quite sure whether the entire contents would tidal-wave over my face and down the Ralph Lauren safari suit. So I approached it gingerly. The first thing you notice is the smell (the gourds, by the way, are cleaned with urine): a sultry, damp, furry, sleepy, animal nidor that's almost too solid to go up your nose. And then the blood itself: sluggish and surprisingly thick, like double cream. And warm – deliciously, comfortingly warm, with what food technologists call 'coatability'. It insinuates like a sly french kiss. And the taste? Fabulous. The best, freshest, softest steak: subtle and smooth, with less tannin and iron than I expected. Not at all like sucking a cut finger.

I drained the pot. 'Ugh' I can hear you saying, because everyone I've told has said, 'Ugh, how could you?' Well, I got back home to an argument about whether it was okay to feed assorted poo to cattle if it had been boiled first. Now, tell me please, who's more disgusting: a society that keeps happy, outward-bound cattle, never killing them, treating them like members of the family and taking a symbiotic, painless sustenance from them, or us, the most gluttonous, overfed, spoilt continent in the world, splenetic with rage, boycotting cynically manky carcasses? May the 'Ugh' stick in your throat and choke you.

I handed back the gourd and the chief said: 'You know, this isn't my day job. I also teach English at the local school.' Oh really, what's your favourite book? *'Tom Sawyer.'* Oh, isn't it fabulous? Don't you just worship Mark Twain? 'Have you read any James Hadley Chase?' And here was one of those gratifying moments that happen occasionally when you travel. The two of us about as different as is possible to conceive suddenly joined as close as books on a shelf. The joy of journeying is not seeing what divides us but discovering how much joins us. Travel is not broadening the mind, it's narrowing the gap.

After we got back, I'm rather embarrassed to say, I went to a caviar restaurant. I don't need much of an excuse to eat caviar and it was my friend Lucy's birthday: it seemed like a treat. We also took Eric Fellner, the film producer who made *Notting Hill* and *Four Weddings*. He rose brilliantly to the occasion by bidding millions of pounds for a book he hasn't read over the phone to Los Angeles. Oh, and Jeremy Clarkson gate-crashed and brought a socialist – as a joke.

The thing about caviar is, you can't muck about with little bits of it. You've got to have a lot, or none at all. Personally, I like it best with a baked potato, where you have to play hunt the potato.

So we ate a lot of caviar and tried all the different sizes. As ever, I prefer the ossetra. We spooned and hummed and cogitated, and Jeremy and Eric kept up the tone by comparing the size of their Ferraris. And the socialist pointed out that there wasn't anything like this in Dalston, as if that were one of Dalston's strong points. When I say a lot, I don't mean a huge lot. We didn't leave any. We weren't flicking it. It was a sufficiency. And we passed on pudding, because you don't really want anything sweet after caviar.

I got the bill and the chaps broke off their mutual motor masturbation to chirp: 'This is on the paper, isn't it?'

I unfolded it and blushed. I rarely blush. But we'd managed to consume £1,600 of fish eggs. And because they're both richer than the Russian mafia, I made them split it. The joke is that all the cook had to do was bake some potatoes and open some tins. Didn't even need a bow and arrow.

'Worth it?' is a fruitless question. Worth it for a jolly evening and Lucy's birthday? Of course. Worth it for caviar, one of the top five tastes in the world? Yes. Is the restaurant a rip-off? No. They're charming, their product is impeccable and the prices are printed on the menu.

But worth it, in the scheme of things? Well, it would buy an awful lot of blood.

Pomegranate

I have a very strong memory of the first time I ate pomegranates. It was my second year at boarding-school, and I was twelve. It was the same year I went to my first dance and bought my first pop record (*Sgt Pepper's Lonely Hearts Club Band*), read *From Russia with Love* and had my first kiss from a girl who closed her eyes and smelt of Johnson's Baby Shampoo and warm winceyette. She played the 'Moonlight Sonata' on the black Bösendorfer in the chilly music room, then leant across and kissed me. I caught a faint opalescent glimmer of her breasts down the front of her nightie. I think she imagined that you should kiss someone after playing Beethoven, and I just happened to be there. I can't hear that piece now without missing the feeling of lips on mine during the silence at the end. Unfortunately, I wasn't there for Rachmaninov.

The day after that kiss was Saturday, and I took my half-crown to the local town as usual, but instead of squandering it on fish' n' chips or a Wimpy, I bought a pomegranate. I really don't know why, as I didn't know what they were. I was at a vegetarian boarding-school, so gastronomy was a long way down the list of important things. I do remember being starving at the time, but then a pomegranate isn't what you go for when you're hungry. I'd like to think it was a sympathetic memory of the glimpsed bosom, but perhaps it was because I was unhappy. Homesickness is the worst thing in the world when you're twelve.

The pomegranate was as alien to dormitories – and bells, farting boys, wet socks and the flat, dun-coloured, damp East Anglia that I was stuck in – as it was possible to get.

A beautiful russet and rose ball, a comfortable weight in the palm of the hand, it seemed to promise exotic sunshine, distant dusty mountains and warm earth. I took it back to my room and cut it open with my going-to-school penknife, to discover I'd bought a treasure box of beautifully packed precious beads, more delicate and mysterious than anything the ghastly dining-room had to offer. I had no idea how you ate a pomegranate, and eventually decided to use a straightened safety pin, spiking each perfect seed and rolling it around my tongue as though it were a sweet-tart tear. It whiled away a miserable afternoon. Every Saturday during the autumn term, I'd buy a pomegranate and eat it, a seed at a time, huddled on the school playing-fields watching the house XI kick their opponents' shins.

The flavour of pomegranate is ineffably sad. It's the taste of mourning, of grief mixed with happy memory. I couldn't have picked a better metaphor for how I felt about being away from home, about the girl who kissed me, about my life and body changing from boy to young man. I'd like to say that I understood all this, that I realised that the fruit was a symbolic catharsis, an allegory, but I didn't. I did, however, learn that nice things given when you're unhappy can make you sadder, and that the flavour of sweetness counterpoints bitter-salt sourness.

The pomegranate was a symbol of life long before I got hold of one at school. Persephone, Demeter's beautiful daughter, was kidnapped by Pluto and forced to be his bride in the dark Underworld. She mourned for the green, living world above, and was told that she could return to her mother, so long as she hadn't eaten anything in Hades. But she had eaten six pomegranate seeds. So for six months of the year, Persephone had to remain with Pluto in Hades as a Queen of the Dead, while the earth mourned, and for the remaining six months she returned to her mother and the world bloomed. She also fell in love with Adonis, but that's another story.

The pomegranate grows wild in Asia Minor, and was cultivated by the ancient Egyptians and Greeks about 3,000 years ago. But I'm not sure how they ate it; as far as we know the Greeks didn't eat fruit with meat – it was kept for symposia where wine was drunk. Considering pomegranates have been around for such a long time, recipes for them are few and far between. I've just been leafing through my cookery books and the Greek and Middle Eastern ones often leave them out altogether. Perhaps they've always just been a symbol of sex.

If you want to cook with pomegranates, you need to remove the seeds with a small spoon and avoid the sour-tasting intricate membrane. If you want the juice, simply press the seeds through a sieve. I can hardly ever eat them: they make me sad. Still, the best way to do so is one seed at a time, when the fields are bare and bleak and you think spring will never come. Taste the subtle, ancient flavour and remember Persephone, ruling over the dead as she counted the days before she could return to the sunlight and the green shoots appeared again.

Fondue

The good fairy that visited my natal crib must have had a busy day. I came too late for the more exotic and useful blessings that had been bestowed on the little mites who screamed into the world ahead of me. To them, she had given skill with ball, the fellowship of numbers, minds that could unknit Gordian philosophy, and the sexual prowess of a kayak ploughing the rapids.

As she peered into my converted Tesco box ('Bananas. This way up!'), there was precious little left in her gossamer Kelly bag. 'Oh dear,' she said, 'this misshapen little thing must make his way earthbound without benefit of goblin luck. Ah, but look, I have one favour left. It's not much, but perchance he'll find it useful.'

And so it was that the only supernatural gift I have ever had is the uncanny ability to determine how long a couple have been married by looking at their kitchen. Not, on the face of it, a talent that has much mileage, but a talent nonetheless.

It has been pointed out by those who are, frankly, envious of my gift that it might be easier simply to ask either of the people involved. Couples don't tend to be secretive about the years they've put up with each other. Like unfit competitors in a marathon, they puff: 'Six down and only twenty to go. And it's all for charity.' But the easier way is not always the most aesthetic or elegant. So, I could look at your kitchen and the telltale Le Creuset pot would whisper that you sent out your wedding list in the late 1960s, that magical time when stews became casseroles. The Le Creuset would have to have been orange, of course. Green or blue were bought by your mother from Peter Jones when you got your first flat.

An asparagus steamer would place your vow of monogamy in the mid-1970s, after which we had the terracotta years: tagines and Spanish chafing dishes that smell of sardines. The 1980s saw the ridiculous and ungainly wok, which was used as a hunchback frying pan, and stacking vegetable steamers. In the 1990s, you were all wedded to Alessi – the retro-ludicrous kettle with the bird whistle and that spaceship lemon squeezer that was better at drilling holes in your worktop than squeezing lemons.

Kitchens are all archaeology: you never throw anything away. Things lie in sticky strata at the back of cupboards. I bet most of you have equipment that your grandmother used – and there's comfort, if not gastronomy, in that. My own kitchen, of course, is a veritable tar pit of marriage misguidance, stretching from the invention of the fork to those fabulously complex bottle openers that look like they ought to clip on to missile launchers.

Before Elizabeth David, nuptial gifts were not for cooking, but presentation. Newlywed pride was all in the dining-room: electroplated Georgian-style cream jugs and table mats showing the Cries of London. The wedding present that marked the move of showing-off from dining-room to kitchen, from hostess to cook, was the fondue set.

I could write a thesis on the pivotal cultural importance of the fondue set, but I won't. It was a talisman and inanimate pathfinder of almost everything we consider contemporary. This simple cast-iron pot with its meths burner and barbed forks stood on the cusp between two societies: one that looked back to the Edwardians for its instructions, and another that looked forward to a new, clean, abstract Elizabethan age.

The fondue set lived in the dining-room, but it was also of the kitchen, and it blew away the serving hatch, that grim checkpoint between the means of production and consumption. Indeed, it demolished the whole wall to reveal the multi-purpose kitchen-dining-room. The fondue set broke down the formality of placement and silver service, and, unless you were there, you can't imagine how daring it was. How many sleepless hours the fondue set induced in young wives. And how deep the worried tuts from new husbands, who suggested that, though entertaining was, of course, her territory, it was his boss – and wouldn't they be better off with dependable cutlets and his mother's steamed pudding?

Fondue provoked nervous titters and bluff jokes from guests. In the early 1960s, it was as close as most English people got to an orgy. The strange, dangerous odour that emanated from its witch's cauldron wasn't just Blue Nun, meths and boiling cheddar pretending to be Emmental, it was the illusive, corrupting whiff of anticipation, emancipation and contraception. It was blue jeans. It was ripping up the carpet and pushing the beds together. It was shower attachments and spin-dryers. It was divorce and atheism, films with breasts and novels with sex. It was spice racks and marijuana, package deals, knitted ties, and lashings and lashings of suntan cream.

If it hadn't been for one teeny-weeny, hardly-worth-mentioning little fault, today there might well be a fondue set on the flag. Fondue might be our national dish, and Terence Conran would be claiming to have invented it. Sadly, fondue tasted like hot baby poo. And so the future caught up with it, the bowl became first a joke and then an egg boiler, and fondue was relegated to a risible, provincial, bubbly, stringy totem maypole of naff.

Right, well, given all that, you can imagine my astonishment when I saw fondue on the menu of a restaurant in Shepherd's Bush. This was about to be a madeleine moment.

I braced myself.

With a catch in the throat, we ordered fondue all round. The waitress took our orders individually, so we had to say 'fondue' four times. And it struck me that the most pitiful definition of loneliness must be fondue for one.

It came in the distantly remembered pot with the awkward, tongue-worrying forks and the little bowls of duck-pond bread. Haltingly, as if trying to remember a poem from long ago, I pronged a gobbet and dipped. The Blonde dipped hers at the same time and, deep in the pustular, boiling dairy fat, our tridents collided. I felt a frisson, a spark of electricity from the deep. Our eyes met, and I was whisked away to that time before sex, before Sunday magazines, before life in technicolor. Lasciviously, I withdrew my prong. My bread was lost in Davy Jones's Swiss-cheese locker. That was the other fault with fondue.

I tried again, and this time pulled up a cheesey whatsit. And as I popped it into my mouth, alert for the Proustian recall, something else that I'd forgotten tugged at a corner of my mind ...

Aaaaaaaaaaaagh! Shit! Hot, hot, hot!

Almonds

I was on the march. Not your march. My march was bigger than your march. My peace march could have beaten up your peace march. I thought: 'Half the world's going to be marching. Hyde Park's going to be freezing. And there's going to be Ken Livingstone and George Galloway. And there's bound to be Harold Pinter. So why not go somewhere where we can protest and sightsee at the same time – somewhere with decent coffee and sunshine and pretty people?' You may call this shallow, effete, dilettante opportunism. I call it fusion diplomacy.

And so we went to Rome and stayed at the Hotel de Russie, which was incredibly comfortable and convenient for joining three million Romans on a guided tour. They said it was three million, but I reckon it was probably more like four if you counted the folk who were there by proxy on the other end of mobile phones. The Italians haven't really got the hang of communal chanting, they just all shout into their Nokias. 'I'm on the march! No, on the march! We're stuck under an aqueduct! I don't know when I'll be home! I'll call! What are we having for dinner?' It was very chic. The banners were all co-ordinated. 'This year we'll mostly be waving 1960s retro flags with Peace written on them' – or 'Pax' for the culturally ironic. I was next to a girl carrying a solitary Basque flag. Sorry, love, get to the back of a very long queue.

Rome, of course, is the perfect place to muse on imperial aggression. Everywhere you look, there are columns and arches covered in elegant murder, beautiful pillage and aesthetic massacres. These are the very avenues down which Roman generals held their triumphs. Behind them was a man who whispered: 'You are not a god.' Now, here we were on a march that was larger than the entire population of classical Rome, all shouting, 'Bush thinks he's God Almighty. Basta!' into their mobile phones.

I should have been thinking peaceful thoughts as I marched, but I wasn't. I was thinking about almonds. I was thinking about almonds because of the columnist Barbara Amiel. Now I like Barbara. Actually, I rather fancy Babs. But I'd have to kill her afterwards. Her politics make me combust with rage. She has written that Iraq is a new country, drawn on a colonial whim, as if that in itself made it disposable, ersatz. Oooh, aaargh, gnash gnash.

Ur, ancient Iraq, is the oldest state in the world, the first country. It existed before the end of the ice age. The fertile crescent that runs between the Tigris and the Euphrates was where farming was invented, the first place where more than 200 people could live together. It was the beginning of civilisation, because they grew food. And one of the first things cultivated were almonds.

Now, consider the almond. It's one of the great mysteries of human consumption. The fruit, from the same genus as apricots and cherries, is only edible when unripe. The stone is the nut. And here's the miraculous bit. You know when you get a bitter almond, how deeply unpleasant that is? Well, that's the natural flavour of almonds – they're poisonous with prussic acid. The sweet almond is a mistake, a very occasional genetic cock-up. So, how did they manage to grow them? You might get one sweet almond in a blue moon on a bitter almond tree, but it would take years of selective breeding to get sweet almond trees. And if, by chance, you did come across a sweet one, you couldn't plant it, because you'd already have eaten it. You work it out.

Almonds are a magical ingredient. They have found their way into all European and Asian cooking. They can be both sweet and savoury. They were hugely important to medieval and Renaissance banquets, and are still the sweet devotion at the heart of all our festivals: simnel cake at Easter, the French *galette des rois* at Epiphany, German stollen, English Christmas and wedding cakes. In Iraq, they celebrate with *lowzina*, a triangular almond sweetmeat flavoured with rose-water and cardamom, and decorated with gold leaf.

If you think you can taste a hint of a prussic parable here, you're right. We're all connected by the gossamer web of shy pleasures and shared joy. The triumph of civilisation has always been to find the one sweet nut in the bag of bitter ones.

And, boy, are we suffering a lot of bitter nuts at the moment.

PS: Most of the world's almonds are now grown in America.

Roses

Two events drastically changed the way we eat and what we eat today. What were they? Hands up. What altered our eating habits more than refrigeration, canning and preservatives (which are merely ways of storing food more efficiently)? One was the discovery of the New World. As a result of this, the number of ingredients found in most kitchens – food that would become staples, not just exotic spices – doubled in a hundred years. The other, which caused the biggest change in northern European food, came about long before that – the Crusades.

There is nothing like invading someone's country and killing loads of the natives to give you an appetite. Apart from syphilis and enough bits of wood from the true cross to build a fair-sized barn, the Crusaders brought back all sorts of things for the wife's kitchen. At the time, of course, this might not have seemed much of a recompense.

Picture the scene.

'Hi, honey; I'm home!'

'What bloody time do you call this?'

'Well, I said I might be late.'

'Late? Late? You pop out for a bit of a Crusade and I don't hear hide nor hair for twelve years. Not even a postcard.'

'Sorry, love, but I did bring you a present.'

'This had better be good.'

'Here, what do you think of that, then?'

'What's it called?'

'It's called an "orange", and look, here's another one. A "lemon".'

'Well, what do you do with a lemon when it's at home? I'm not wearing it. And what about those?'

'You eat them.'

'They look like shrivelled testicles.'

'No, sweetpea, they're "dates".'

'I'm not putting that in my mouth.'

'But what about this?'

'It's a twig.'

'No, dear, it's "cinnamon".'

'What am I supposed to do with that? No, don't tell me. I'm supposed to eat it.'

'Okay, okay, here's another twig.'

'A spiky twig.'

'It is now, my love, but in the summer it'll have the most beautiful flowers you've ever seen. It's called a "rose".'

'Well, I don't care what you call it. By any other name, it's a stick. Let's get this straight. You disappear God knows where for twelve years and bring me back some wrinkled Arab gonads and two twigs.'

'There, there … They're the mysteries of the East, angel.'

'I'll give you mysteries of the East … Where's the bloody key to my chastity belt? And if you're expecting dinner, you can just go boil a twig.'

The flavours that the Crusaders brought back to the sleepy shires revolutionised British cooking. You may not have noticed, but our indigenous food is very long on spices. We mix far more dried and ground spice with both sweet and savoury food than, say, the French, who tend towards herbs for flavour. The Crusaders, being particularly religious, used the spices to give thanks at religious festivals, so we get cinnamon and allspice in hot cross buns, and the whole lot with the Arabic dried fruit at Christmas.

Roses were one of the most successful immigrants – so successful, in fact, that we tend to think of them now as being indigenous ('an English rose'). The Arabs valued them very highly. Their concept of heaven is a garden, and they cultivated flowers for meditation and leisure for hundreds of years. The Crusaders returned with the flowers and the idea of a heavenly garden. It fitted in with a Christian Eden. Roses were used a lot in cooking right up until the middle of the last century, when their elusive fragrant flavour was submerged in the French fashion of haute cuisine.

You can cook with roses in two ways. You can frost the petals with sugar, which is a bit Fanny and Johnny, or you can use rosewater. Now I'm sure you're familiar with rosewater in the boudoir and the bathroom. It's a rather grannyish smell, lovely on handkerchiefs and cleavage. Well, it tastes good, too. Rosewater has a weird, fugitive flavour. It's deceptively pervasive and quite unlike anything else. Everything else that's cooked with it immediately tastes old-fashioned and bosky. It goes with the slow ticking of clocks, the humming of the evening bees, and the distant bleating of chalk-downy sheep.

It comes as a surprise when you're in an Arab country (where rosewater is used a lot), recognise the flavour and are wafted back into childhood. A sweetmeat in the Marrakesh souk can drop your memory back into a childhood handkerchief drawer.

Rosewater is one of those flavours that I use passionately in everything for six months and then don't touch again for two years. There's something sad and tearful about it, reminiscent of faded summers, absent friends, and the slow ticking of clocks.

White Park, a breed of beef I've never eaten before and had always assumed was purely ornamental, was really excellent: softly chewy, with that strong distinctive almost corrupt flavour of proper beef, like eating an old roué uncle. If you've only had supermarket beef – or don't have uncles – it may come as a shock.

I ordered a lasagne. There's only so much you can do for lasagne in the looks department. The only garnish that would improve it would be a power cut. And you have to go gingerly. It can be like emptying Vesuvius into your mouth, turning your tongue into a Pompeian pumice mummy. I needn't have been such a scaredy-cat; you could have stirred this one with a peeled baby. It was lukewarm on the fringes and refreshingly cold in the middle.

Have you ever considered the symbolism of the wedding cake? Here you have a large, darkly mysterious fruitcake dressed in pristine white like the bride. The groom grabs a special knife – sometimes a sword, no less – and with his new wife's hand on its hilt, stabs it, giggling over how difficult it is to pierce. I'm sorry, but you don't have to have taken O-level myths and legends to surmise that they've just performed a metaphoric sex act in front of their octogenarian aunts. Just for the chronically literal, they save the top layer for a christening.

The chicken broth was boisterous, but had that slightly ossified flavour from being boiled too hard, a bit as if it had been made out of George Hamilton's ears. Scottish smoked salmon filled with poached salmon was too monotonously huge: nicely made, but a bit like eating a soggy pink scatter cushion.

The Blonde asked the waiter about the sea bass.

'It's a fish,' he said.

He seemed proud of this nugget of knowledge. He beamed and said it again, in case we hadn't absorbed the full import. Although lacking in elegance and erring on the concise, 'it is a fish' is the fairest thing I can think of saying about this bass.

The chicken had been flame-roasted to the point where it should have been served by a priest in a garden of remembrance.

Roast monkfish, tart of ceps and Alsace bacon was chewy – just chewy – and certainly no reason to leave your own bed, where you can chew your own fingernails with more enjoyment.

Soufflé Suisse: a difficult dish that always feels a bit Edwardian and normally comes the size of an inflated crème brûlée. What arrived was hot egg with napalm cheese, twenty storeys high. It was the Dirk Diggler of soufflés. The waitress ascended in one of those machines they clean street lights with to pour extra cheesy sauce into the volcanic hole of its summit and dust it with a kilo of paprika. It was delicious, but you had to eat it quickly. If it collapsed, it could kill you and the table next to you. I have no hesitation in saying it was the best Swiss soufflé in the world. It almost was a world.

My editor hit the high spot of the meal with his mussels cooked in Tuborg beer (accept no substitutes) and chillies. These groyne feeders had been poached so long, they had shrivelled to look like nothing so much as a get-to-know-your-clitoris aid. The taste and smell were gagging in quite a complex way. There was a hint of derelict fridge and a top note of boiled tripe. 'You know,' he said, cautiously, his cheeks filling like a mime doing Louis Armstrong, 'you know how they say oysters have that wonderful savour of the sea? Well, these taste exactly like the Thames. High tide at the Isle of Dogs, I'd hazard.'

I had a small disagreement with the waitress about the Blonde's game sausage. What's your game, I asked charmingly. 'Venison, boar and pheasant.' Pheasant's out of season, I smiled. 'No, it's not.' Well, it sort of is. 'No,' she replied, with spirited bellicosity and a balletic non sequitur, 'the only thing that had to be killed was the boar and the venison.' I realised I was staring over the precipice of one of those conversations that has the potential to escalate into three managers, a cook with a cleaver, phone calls to the Guinness Book of Records *and a sleepless night where you pace the room saying 'what you don't understand is ...' to the wallpaper. So I nodded my head and stepped back from the brink. Anyway, the sausage was dry and granular as game sausages – whoever's in them, dead or alive – invariably are.*

3

RESTAURANTS

Menus ought to be plain. They ought to be simple and straightforward and informative. So what's Tataki of Iki Jimi Yellowtail when it's at home? They have stolen Tataki. I, Iki Jimi Yellowtail, swear vengeance. We shall wipe the pale face from the land of the buffalo. And try getting your gums around Garrotxa. Is Garrotxa: 1) a weeping boil on the thigh of a llama? 2)a short-bladed adze used by Portuguese wheelwrights; or 3) a waterproof hat with earflaps made out of pressed biscuits? 'Oh I don't know Frank, I think they're all bluffs. We'll go for the weeping boil.' Well, you're probably right because that's what it tastes like.

Service was from the J.R.R. Tolkien school of butlering: everything was an interminable journey and a saga.

The customers were mostly young, tungsten-faced mag hags with terrifyingly geometric haircuts, high heels for boyfriends and tightly wrapped buttocks with no VPL, all discussing features through gritted lipstick.

There were two other men who lurked, apparently somehow connected to the room, in a Samuel Beckettish sort of way. One of them turned out to be the Is Everything All Right? Monitor. 'Is everything all right?' he asked twice a course, and each time I broke off my complex but compellingly moving monologue to say a curt yes. But he kept returning. I think perhaps he was having

doubts, that the question wasn't about the food on my plate but the play of some graver metaphysical imbalance. Perhaps he was questioning the weft of life and broader spiritual horizons of a man whose existence is measured solely by asking strangers 'Is everything all right?' My correct answer, of course, should have been: 'No, your life is a meaningless, echoing husk of desiccated self-loathing, but the risotto's lovely.' But that would have been a lie. The caballo nero and treviso risotto wasn't. It was too wet. And my starter portion was so mountainous that it could have pebble-dashed a lighthouse.

It was not an impressive building: a two-storey redbrick house on a main road. The guide book said it was best to arrive in the day time so that you could get the benefit of the gardens, bridges, sluice gates, weir, lily pond, etc. Frankly, sluice gates have never been my big thing. I would suggest arriving on a moonless night with the headlights off.

The first thing you notice – it would be difficult to miss – is a man carving turnips into chrysanthemums, a calling that shames God. If only He'd taken a couple more days over the world, I'm sure He'd have got round to creating Transformer roots, though not even God could have thought of carving an anatomically perfect Mickey Mouse or mermaid from a watermelon. 'Watermelon,' said the carver helpfully, in case we doubted the evidence of our bulging eyes.

At lunch, it's full of women in the sorts of hats that they make you put through X-ray machines at airports, and international art dealers who specialise in biblical martyrdoms. For dinner, it's slidey Euro business merchants with tiny, shiny tasselled feet and girls whose hair is grown out of season under polythene, and who don't smile unless they are in a jeweller's.

The basement was a nightclub, which, viewed from the top of the stairs, has all the elegance and excitement of a long-distance meat container full of assorted refugees.

The food was a smiley Happy Meal compared with the service, which was attentive to the point where I felt we were being groomed like a Catholic priest's hard drive.

Pizza Express

Richard Curtis hates me. He also wrote *Four Weddings and a Funeral*, *Blackadder* and loads of other stuff. As far as I can tell I've never actually met Richard Curtis, but I know he hates me because kind, informative people keep telling me. I'm introduced to complete strangers and they say: 'Oh, you're the chap Richard Curtis hates. Do you know Richard? What a charming man. So talented.'

I'm beginning to think that being hated by Richard Curtis is my most endearing quality. A couple of weeks ago, the Blonde shouted from the kitchen: 'Hey, it's Richard Curtis on *Desert Island Discs*. You know, the one who hates you.' And the man did, indeed, sound utterly charming and talented. His choice of music could have been mine; except, of course, if it had been mine, he'd have hated it. But what was really impressive was his luxury. He chose the Notting Hill Pizza Express. Now that's inspired. That's why he's feted as the new Geoffrey Chaucer with Jeffrey Archer's bank balance, while sadly, with me, it's the other way round.

What could possibly be more brilliant than to take Pizza Express to a desert island – and the Notting Hill one at that? I mean, that desert island must be the A-list party of the century by now: all those celebrities wandering around with their endless luxury paper and pencils and cases of champagne and moisturiser and a hundred bloody grand pianos and nowhere to go for lunch.

And Richard turns up with a Pizza Express. He's gonna clean up.

After a bit, the citizens of Notting Hill are going to say: 'I must have a margarita. Cabbie, take me there. I don't care how much it costs.' And then they'll see all that top-of-the-range celebrity and they'll want to move to the island. Property prices for split-level grand pianos will soar and Sue Lawley will have to start recording the programme from there and it will be called *Wrap Up Warm British Isles Discs*. And Richard will appear as a guest and bring the Notting Hill Pizza Express home with him in time to write *Four Prenuptial Agreements and a Papal Annulment*. And probably the *Bishop of Dibley*. Brilliant.

It's been some time since I went to a Pizza Express. It's one of those places that's comforting to know is there just in case you come over all faint with desire for pizza balls. The Blonde and I went and had lunch. We shared a mozzarella salad. I had the Four Seasons. She had the Neapolitan. Chocolate cake and ice cream. Coffee, water and a glass of wine. And the bill came to ... my, that's very reasonable.

You may be asking, 'Why is he reviewing Pizza Express? We already know what Pizza Express is like. It's like Pizza Express, only slower.' But that's precisely the point. Most of you do know what Pizza Express is like, whereas only a very few of you will ever go to all the other restaurants I eat in. Pizza Express is one of a handful of cultural experiences that are truly pan-national. It belongs to no particular class or social group: from Buddhist dukes to Methodist lesbian dustmen, everyone has been to Pizza Express. You all know what I'm talking about, which is a rare relief. It wouldn't be the case if I said: 'Well, you all know that good bit in the second act of *Parsifal*'; or 'Do you remember the way Elizabeth Hurley squeezes your thigh under the table?' You see, we live in fragmented times. There is no shared culture. Everyone constructs their own personal scrapbook of belief and experience from bits and pieces snatched from the groaning conveyor belt that is the smorgasbord of civilisation. So, not to put too fine a point on it, Pizza Express is a sort of gastronomic post-modern version of the *Morecambe and Wise Christmas Special*.

We've all been there and done that.

There is another reason I've been nudged to write about this chain. I bumped into Peter Boizot the other day. We meet every year or so, usually in dinner jackets. Peter invented Pizza Express (and it's a civic shame that he hasn't been made Lord Boizot of Venice by now). I would say he was the culinary 1960s version of Richard Curtis, except that he's pleased to see me. I'm a great admirer of Peter's, not just because he invented the Express, but because he has an unerring eye for spotting quality and the coming thing. He gave me my first job, at the back end of the 1960s, running the only one-man Pizza Express, called Pizza to Go.

It was my first experience of catering. More shockingly, it was my first experience of work. I was on a steep learning curve, although not as steep as the customers, who were mostly *Guardian* journalists. The ovens took about half an hour to heat up and I was forever forgetting to turn them on; I had to serve raw dough with cold tomato on top and tell the stupid, liberal hacks that they ate their pizza rare in Sicily. In fact, so many things went wrong that I invented a chef called Mario, who never appeared. I'd apologise to the customer for some ghastliness on their plate, then march out the back and scream at an empty room, replying to myself in a whining, high-pitched Italian accent. People used to ask after Mario. One kindly old regular bought him a Valentine card. I told her he was a poof.

Some weeks, I took so little money that, through sheer guilt, I put half my wages back in the till. Needless to say, Pizza to Go went shortly after I left. In fact, I think I can claim to be responsible for the only failure in a chain that now numbers several hundred, including outposts in Cairo and Delhi.

What's amazing about Pizza Express is not that it has been successful, but that nobody has managed to copy it successfully. Formulaic chain restaurants are still universally nasty, the economies of size breeding the culture of contempt. Quality is aimed squarely at 'this is what we can get away with', and customers are just another problem way down the list of problems.

Pizza Express has managed to produce a chain that somehow remains subtly branded, but also unique in different locations. Only Hannibal Lecter would conceivably have a favourite Café Rouge or All Bar One, but everyone has a favourite Pizza Express. The bottom line is product: the pizzas are good. They seem to have shrunk slightly since the last time I was here, but perhaps I've just grown up. The menu has changed very little in thirty years. It's a model of clarity, helpfully telling you that all the tips go directly to the staff, if the staff can ever be bothered to come over and collect them. They are still just as slow and smilingly gormless as we all were in the 1960s. The puddings are still horrid, the ice cream a sort of un-egged industrial sludge, and 25p of every Veneziana sold is still donated to the Venice in Peril fund, which now stands at a staggering £700,000. You could fill in the Grand Canal with that many pizzas – and it would make Venice smell better.

The blindingly obvious reason for Pizza Express's continuing pre-eminence in the fast-food market is that it sells you exactly what you want at a wholly equitable price: a fresh, one-course meal in a bright, clean modern room. There is a simple pleasure in the fact that nobody's ripped off, everyone's happy, you get your pizza, they make a million. And although the food is Italian, there's something utterly English about it all. The other customers were a complete mix of Londoners: kids on their way to the park, crumbly couples eating with each other's teeth, students sipping cold coffee and rolling toothpick fags, drop-dead au pairs reading last week's foreign papers. It struck me that Pizza Expresses are really olde English tea shops serving Italian food, and staffed by halfwits, which is about as good as the olde English tea shop could ever hope for.

But there is also another reason for their continued success. It's something more ephemeral. As I sat down behind that familiar marble table, it all swam back to me: the girls I'd brought here as a priapic pauper, the rows over late-night crusts and gassy Peroni beer, the intense arguments when I was a student about whether you'd rather sleep with George Orwell or Jean-Paul Sartre, all the plans, the time-wasting, the hurried pre-cinema American Hots. My life has crisscrossed these small tables.

I'm fond of these places, not just because they do what they're supposed to, but because they have followed me round, marking the years. And as I've got older, Pizza Express has stayed the same.

I have an investment here. It's more than lunch and dinner. I spend my life reviewing places that will be gone and hardly missed in a year or two. As restaurants become more like theatre runs, our acquaintances or our passionate flings, Pizza Express has stuck around to be an old friend – and you can forgive old friends their tardiness.

And I like Pizza Express because it doesn't hate me. When Richard Curtis gets the Notting Hill branch to his desert island, I'm afraid he'll find me sitting at a table in the corner: Yoo-hoo, Richard, over here!

Country pubs

What is it with dirty jokes and country hostelries? I'm talking about those 'fine dining' pubs, where 'Dennis and Fiona welcome discerning travellers to relax, revive, savour and marvel in an atmosphere of timeless rustic elegance. No children, no smoking, no proles' overalls. Dogs by prior arrangement – but not those silly yapping poofs' merkins that city folk have instead of neighbours.' In short, the sort of place that makes you fervently wish it were possible to order up bulldozers like minicabs.

Why is it that these places invariably have smutty cartoons in the men's lavatory? The public bits are smeared with brown-nosing labradors, wafting woodcock and Georgian huntsmen. But when you go to the loo, there's some bit of blokey juvenilia involving a bad drawing of big breasts, a shooting double entendre and talking foxes. What I particularly hate about this crapper comedy is the assumption of inclusion, the idea that all men collect at the urinals to tell the one about the midget and the nun. The prudish, leering hypocrisy of these men-only gags is an endearing staple of country hospitality and I don't want to be implicated in it when I've got my flies undone.

I mention all this because the cartoon in the bog at the last country pub I ate in is so obviously a big attraction. I know this because, while I was there, a local man came in showing around a visitor and said he'd once brought the good lady wife in so that she could enjoy the sophisticated joke – while he stood guard at the door, naturally.

I suppose I'm going to have to describe it to you now (and I apologise for spoiling the village's only punch line). There's a rough cartoon of a group of Welsh miners in the changing-room after work. They're all naked and all black – Dylan Thomas black, black with coal dust. All except one of them, who has a white willy. His mate's saying, 'I see Llewellyn went home for his lunch.' Geddit?

Okay, pick yourself up. Wipe away the tears of mirth. Yes, I know, miners don't go home for their lunch because they're a mile underground and I also know that they'd only get their bits sooty if they were mining naked. But it's not my cartoon – and anyway, I don't have a sense of humour.

It was an unimpressive building, set back behind one of those pub gardens that are supposed to be evocative of Edwardian husbandry, but actually reek of easy maintenance. The first space in the car park was ostentatiously marked out for a horse, with a bucket that's for either oats, dung or me to throw up in. Inside, it was the usual confusion of levels and spaces that don't know what they're for. There wasn't a dining-room as such, just tables strewn about in the charmless rooms and corridors.

The Blonde and I were meeting Michael Gambon and Philippa Hart here on the way to Wales. We were sat at a sticky round table that could have been a Braille menu. I squinted at the fare on a distant blackboard. Just as I was making up my mind, I was offered another paper menu; and as I transferred my choice to that, a third, notelet menu arrived. Why, I asked, are there three menus? 'There's the *blackboard*,' said the waitress in a tone of dinner-lady's rich irritation, 'and the *à la carte* and this is the *specials*.' Yes, I understand that, but why are there three of them? 'There's the blackboard ...' she started again. Okay, okay.

Actually, the à la carte was a bit of a treasure, not for the food, but for the open letter from our hosts on the back. I dearly wish I could print this in full. It is a huggable evocation of the steely, smiling non-hospitality that is such a feature of eating out in rural England. Here is an amuse-oreille: 'We are very aware that children's attention span can be short-lived, especially in an adult environment, but we ask that noisy toys be left at home and that they do not run within the building or climb trees, our gate or garden ... Our staff carry hot and heavy plates which could be dangerous when dropped ... We are delighted to introduce a new idea for dining this summer: picnic rugs. These can be hired from the bar for a small cash charge of £2, are for use on the front lawns and are ideal for those of you who enjoy a traditional enjoyment of our summers ... Please don't feed Harry, our springer spaniel ... Please don't use mobile phones within the building.' Heaven. Utter heaven.

The place was full of whispering old folk, the itinerant retired who traipse the B roads of Britain, eking out the unforgiving days and squatting in places like this because they have nothing else to do. The food is the sort of careless English fare that owes more to daytime TV and women's magazines than any particular county, and for which Gary Rhodes has much to answer.

Michael and I started with individually baked pies of Keene's cheddar and onion. As we cut them open, a viscous gruel of curdled liquid ran out. It was like lancing a boil. 'Christ, what's that?' said Gambon. It wasn't cheese and I don't think it was onion. Perhaps the pies had been cooked in the dishwasher. They looked nicer than they tasted.

For main course, I ventured the locally smoked gammon with two free-range fried eggs. This was an even more repellent and pointless sacrifice of pig. Local doesn't necessarily mean good, improved or better. It just means you're living next to someone who doesn't know what he's doing and couldn't cure a hangnail. The meat was biltong tough and saltier than a fat bloke's cycling shorts, and the beef dripping the chips were fried in tasted as if it was also used to make candles.

It was replete with everything that makes eating out in the muddy bits of England such a hideous torment. It was pretentious, twee and seemingly run for the convenience of the management. The food we ate was risibly bad, the atmosphere smilingly inhospitable, the decor a sordid cliché of rural nostalgia, puppy porn and green-welly fascism – and they charge you two quid to sit on the ground outside. It is not just everything I despise and loathe in lunch, but everything that embarrasses and depresses me about tweedy Albion.

Stick this up in the gents.

Chefs

This week, I had my annual lunch with my oldest friend, Chris. We've known each other since before solids (he still has a problem with solids). After all these years, it's strange to see how things have panned out. Here am I, your urbane, debonair, louche charmer – sort of the Sergeant Troy of the home economics pages – and there he is, turned, or perhaps grown, into your gnarly, mossy, purple-cheeked Gabriel Oak of the commuter belt.

He talks with that clip-clop rural rhythm, like a very old donkey pulling a very heavy cart along a very windy road. He spoke lovingly, yet pointlessly, of his old-fashioned, hollow-stemmed wheat field, all girt about with corn cockles (no, I don't know, either, but I don't expect you can eat them, so I didn't ask).

In the middle of a soft whiffle through the joys and tribulations of gang rape among barbaries, their aftercare and maintenance (I think it was ducks, but it might have been neighbours in waxed jackets), he paused mid-flow, or what passes for flow, and said, as if noticing his surroundings for the first time: 'Where do they all come from?' He said it in the manner of one who has just woken from a profound coma to find himself propelled into the distant future, dressed as a white rabbit in a self-service Venusian brothel. 'Where do they all come from?'

Restaurants? I offered hesitantly, for we were sitting in the middle of one. 'Yes, no, not restaurants. I know where they come from. They come from dead newsagents and fishmongers and haberdashers and bicycle-repair shops and those places that sold wicks for oil lamps and sensible soap that didn't have biology in it and those circular nylon brushes on bamboo poles for getting cobwebs off pelmets.'

Ah, that's what those were for. I've often wondered. 'No, it's cooks. Where have all the cooks come from? I mean, ten years ago you couldn't get more than four decent meals between here and Inverness. Now look at it.' He regarded his plate as if the boned quail were a spread-eagled Venusian lovely. 'Is someone intensively rearing them?' Quail? 'No, chefs.'

Now this isn't such a daft question, given that questions are all relative, of course. Compared with 'What do you do with a circular nylon brush on a bamboo pole?' this one isn't so left-field. In fact, I've been wondering about it myself for some time.

Take a chef, any chef, and consider him.

What does he need to know? Well, he needs to know physics, chemistry, biology, thermodynamics, engineering, prestidigitation and basic surgery. Whereas a doctor only has to know surgery on one species, a cook has to have a working knowledge of a couple of dozen: mammal, avian, and piscatorial, not counting assorted bivalves, crustaceans and things with exoskeletons.

And then there are vegetables. And fruit. And herbs and spices. And minerals and distillations. And oils. And gelatine. And enough recipes to make a lawyer's library look like an under-five's reading shelf. And he needs to know 'How do you do?' in three or four languages, plus a lexicon of technical terms. All of this before he's even a good chef.

To be a good chef, he needs artistry, design, imagination – oh, and I haven't mentioned taste. He has to have taste, in both senses. Now consider that anyone who wants to be a chef will, *ipso facto*, have an IQ on a par with that of a radish, the ambition of lard and the social skills of squid ink, and it's a blessed miracle that there are any chefs at all. A restaurant with twelve tables (about the smallest that's viable) needs at least three. A restaurant with thirty or forty must have dozens. Good grief, that means there are hundreds of thousands of chefs within walking distance of where I'm sitting.

It's a terrifying thought: all those knives in the hands of dexterous, sociopathic imbeciles.

'Mummy, where do chefs come from?'

'Under gooseberry bushes, dear.'

We have, in this country, a couple of hundred art schools, each pumping out graduates like petrochemical waste. We produce roughly (very roughly) one international artist every two hundred years.

There are maybe three or four catering colleges, but we've got more chefs than traffic wardens, with the same jolly, happy-go-lucky temperament. The traditional training for chefs is to start in a kitchen the day after they leave school. Then, if they have the grit, the aptitude and a high pain threshold, eight or nine years later they might make it to sous-chef. This can't be happening now. So where do all the chefs come from?

The answer to this gristly conundrum may shock you. They aren't chefs. Those blokes you see hanging round the bins in checked trousers and boils, sucking furtive Rothmans, they're just pretending to be chefs. They're imitating chefs. They'll cook your dinner, but they're not cooks.

There are perhaps a meagre couple of hundred true chefs in this country. The rest are semi-skilled artificers: collators, assemblers. Just as the skilled craftsmen of heavy industry have been replaced by pick-a-stick operatives, so chef skills are now being done by outworkers. Meat and fish are delivered, boned and prepared. Vegetables and salad are washed and peeled. I know of one large catering wholesaler who delivers ingredients on three skill levels, from competent to Irish barman. Look at any modern menu and see how many dishes are simply compiled rather than made.

Out of this artlessness, this craftlessness, has grown a new style of restaurant that makes a virtue of semi-skill. They go big on sourcing. They hunt to the ends of the earth for the very finest olives, anchovies and mole cheese rolled in sand. They have odd bread and Moluccan celery. This is catering as butterfly-collecting.

Perhaps I'm being too hard. Perhaps what you all want is a perfectly nice table where you can have a perfectly nice cup of coffee and a perfectly nice bit of cheese while you're reading *Marie Claire*. I just wish this wasn't the way urban catering was going – where an epicurean is someone who knows 12 different types of caper and 127 goat's cheeses.

Beware of restaurant menus that are dotted with odd names, and where the ingredients come with a home town. It probably means that nobody in the kitchen knows how to chop an onion.

Waiters

Esprit d'escalier. Such a useful expression. Literally, wit from the staircase. It's all those neat pithy Dorothy Parker things you think of when it's too late, when the conversation's over. I spend half my life redubbing arguments in my head, most of them with waiters. I leave a restaurant and the Blonde says: 'You're pensive. Penny for them?' and I say, shut up, I'm tearing a strip off the maître d' and it's just getting to the good bit where he breaks down in tears and begs my forgiveness.

The trouble with waiters is that the conversations are all the wrong way round. They ought to be telling you things but you always end up telling them stuff. It starts off badly. They get in first with: 'What do you want?' and your mind goes completely blank. Christ, what do I want? God knows. World peace and universal love and understanding. To be tied to the bed by a weather girl. Perhaps just a caesar salad.

If you ever do try and prise information out of a waiter, it's like interviewing enemy airmen. 'I'm sorry, under the Geneva Menu Convention I'm only obliged to tell you my name and tonight's specials. Hi, I'm Tony and tonight we have a very nice spleen soup with a garnish of finely chopped toenails. For a main course there's fillet of Yellow Pages. The fish is walrus.'

Waiters, in general, are remarkably badly informed about what it is they are selling, but they always manage to make you feel like the dummy.

This is all rather to the fore at the moment. I just had a particularly obtuse exchange with a waiter. 'The special tonight is venison.' 'Great, what sort of venison?' 'It's the fillet, sir.' 'No, where does it come from?' 'From our specialist supplier,

sir.' 'No, you don't understand, what sort of venison is it?'
Now he's only grinning from the nose down and he says in
a voice that implies it's me who's thick: 'It's a deer, sir. They
are wild animals. They look a bit like elegant cows.' I know
what bloody venison is. What was the deer called? 'You want
to know the name of the deer?' The French accent became
thicker, and he looked round to see if the rest of the restaurant
was aware that there was a man here asking for a date with a
dead ruminant. Yes, I want its name. No, I mean I want to
know what its family name is. 'You want me to ask the chef?'
This was said with the barely camouflaged threat that, 'if I go
into the kitchen you may not see me again for some time and
does it really matter anyway?' Well, yes it does, it could be red
or fallow or roe or muntjac or sika. Does it slough its horns
annually? Because if it doesn't, it's a ruddy antelope and, while
we're at it, matey, it matters because you're going to charge me
£21 for 125grams of the stuff. In fact, while we're on the subject,
I'm about to invest somewhere in the region of £150 and an
evening of my guests' and my time in your establishment, so
I'll ask the questions.

I didn't say that last bit, not out loud anyway. To be fair
to the waiter, he wasn't that bad. He just didn't know, and
that probably wasn't his fault. Chefs never explain anything to
waiters. They think they're a lower form of life with less intellect
and fewer uses than polenta. Tell me, what other business is
there where the manufacturer has a need-to-know relationship
with its sales force? Then again, what other product do you buy
for so much and ask so little about? Dinner for four can cost as
much as a stereo, and you'd certainly cross-question the staff
about that. Anyway, the deer was roe and it was a buck. The
chef didn't tell me it was a bloke. I could tell. It had that odd
tang buck gets when it's rutting. It's some sort of secretion.
Not unpleasant, but discernible.

If the menu had just said horny male roe it would have saved
us all a lot of time.

The room itself looked like the worst type of ostentatious Mediterranean yacht; not a farthing had been spent unobtrusively. It's a style that used to be facetiously titled Louis Farouk, a gaudy design Esperanto 1920s Odeon-style urns next to Georgian architraves, Spanish-style still-life murals looking down on an unaccountably Ikea-like hostess trolley. The food and the decor constituted an exact period re-creation of the early 1980s conspicuous consumption, and they had done it well. Thatcher, the early years, lived all over again for me. Every other table had some Gordon Gekko wannabe with a polished chestnut, no-sex date.

As I looked down the tables, all the suits seemed to be made from the same dark-blue worsted. There was a lot of loud table-hopping and cork-popping, a lot of very pleased to be here, very pleased to be me, very pleased you can see me here being me.

All in all, the waiters earned their tip. My *esprit d'escalier* is probably nursery rhymes compared with a waiter's.

Bills

Why don't more people do runners? Maybe they do, but they are so fast I don't see them. I bet most people do them from the cheapest places. I bet the average bill that is run from is less than £10. It's ever thus. Default on a £100 debt and you're in trouble. Default on a £100m debt and the bank's in trouble.

Seriously, why don't more people do runners from expensive restaurants? Tip: thoughtfully walk outside to answer your mobile and never return. (A lawyer writes: only try this at home.) Given the quality and service offered by so many London restaurants, combined with their prices, I'm astonished more people don't simply refuse to pay.

I was reminded of this because of Kim, an old friend who I hadn't seen for, God, it must be eighteen years. 'Doesn't time …?' Yes, I know, beat the crap out of you. 'Do you remember when you taught us all how to do a legal runner?' My, I'd forgotten all about that. It was years and years ago. We were all poorer than church mice – we'd have eaten a church mouse if we'd had the cash to buy one. I discovered from a defrocked lawyer in a pub (some misunderstanding about a widow, the will and a time-share in Andalusia) that a meal in a restaurant is a private contract. What you can do when presented with a bill is simply refuse to pay.

But here is the nicety. Attempting to avoid payment is fraud, and that's criminal.

So what you have to do is leave your real name and a bona fide address (your lawyer's or mother-in-law's is best), then offer what you consider to be the actual value of the raw ingredients. As a rule of thumb, in an expensive restaurant, this is about one-quarter or one-third of the menu price. For spag napolitana, it's about 20p.

Minus service, of course. You don't want to pay that. You must, though, pay the full price for wine, unless you reckon there was something wrong with it.

Having done all that, they have to let you go or call the police. Plod will tell the maître d' what I've just told you: it's a civil matter and there is no prima facie evidence of fraud. The restaurant can sue you for the difference.

Three words of warning here. One: you need a skin like a rhino. On the scale of bourgeois embarrassment, having a stand-up row about the bill comes just underneath having your phone ring the theme from *Bonanza* in the last act of *King Lear*.

Two: if they do sue you, courts take a dim view if they think you're trying it on. But remember, the contract isn't just for the food; they're charging you for the entire experience. If your evening has been made miserable by the atmosphere, the noise, the draught, the smell from the bogs (or the waiter), then you have a reasonable case.

And three: don't try this in the same restaurant twice. In fact, don't plan on going back unless you have the skin of a herd of rhinos and a taste for the sort of outré comestibles you're more likely to find in a gastro-urinary textbook than a cookery book.

Kim laughed: 'Ha, ha, ha. I remember you told us that and then you got arrested.'

Well, yes. But not for not paying the bill. I got arrested for calling a policeman 'Darling'. It was very late and I was very, very drunk. And because I happened to be on my hands and knees pretending to be Glenda Jackson, they thought they could charge me twice. 'I know my rights!' I shouted in Elizabeth I's voice from underneath the banquette. So they called the police. Helpfully, and still in character, I explained the law to the constable, inadvertently referring to him as Dear

Heart and Luvvie. He charged the restaurant with serving drinks after hours and, as my vindicated foot hit the pavement, arrested me for being drunk in a public place. I begged to be allowed to try on the handcuffs. He said I wasn't running anywhere and held my hand all the way to Earls Court police station.

Everyone should spend at least one night locked in a police station. 'Tell the magistrate you're sorry,' said the kindly copper. Sorry? I wouldn't have missed it for the world.

The point of all this is that you're not revolting enough. I have a sense that, while prices continue to hyperventilate, the quality of cooking and service you're getting is sloppy, inconsistent and careless. People are left at the bar, or hurried out without pudding. And what you do is grumble. In the end, the word of mouth damages the restaurant, but they don't know why. I can't tell you how many times I've heard waiters huff: 'Well, we've never had any complaints before.'

The modern, sophisticated packaging of restaurants makes customers feel that it's uncool to complain, as if it showed you, like – duh! – cared. But a restaurant isn't a teenage boyfriend, it's a service. Shrugging and saying 'Whatever' in a bored voice isn't putting it in its place. If you don't like it and if it's not what was promised, don't pay. Don't be cool, be magnificent. And if they go to the mat, offer to return the goods there and then.

I took a friend out to dinner at a smart London restaurant the other day. 'You know,' said James Baker, my guest, 'the service wasn't like this last time I was here. They do treat you differently.' Well, of course they do. I'm the restaurant critic of the *Sunday Times*. But what you should ask is: was the service bad without me? No. And look around. Are people having to unzip their flies to attract the waiters' attention? Are glasses empty? Is anyone eating their guest? No.

It was, however, expensive. I asked for the bill and then realised I'd forgotten my wallet. For the briefest nanosecond,

I considered legging it. Look, I said, this is terribly embarrassing, but somehow I've come out without ... The waiter beamed: no problem. Couldn't matter less.

James gave me a very old-fashioned look. 'Unto those that have shall be given.' I feebly said they'd do it for anyone. 'Whatever.'

Rainforest Café

There is nothing new about themed restaurants. In fact, show me a restaurant that isn't. Ever since the first public dining-room, restaurateurs have been asking, 'What shall we make it look like?' The difference recently has been that, whereas the set used to complement the food, now the food is an adjunct to the marketing – or 'the experience' as it is invariably called.

Lunch is now an experience, like seeing a road accident, losing your virginity or the weather forecast: 'The Midlands will experience intermittent showers and Gill will experience chicken in a basket.' I hate experiences because, by Disney definition, it makes me a passive rubbernecker in my own life. Eating is a proactive pleasure, not a gawping, cud-chewing exercise with moving walkways, animated dummies and scripted experience facilitators.

For the experience of the Rainforest Café, I have to thank Nick Bloody Allott. 'Let's take the children to the Rainforest Café,' he said. 'This Saturday,' he said.

And I, in a forgetful moment of weakness, said: 'Fine.'

The last time Nick suggested an outing, I spent an hour and a half being dribbled on by bungee-jumping Argentinians. Ominously, he was told we couldn't book. So we turned up with six assorted children under thirteen and five grown-ups. The rainforest has come to Shaftesbury Avenue in the middle of 'Where the hell are we?' tourist London. You enter not a restaurant, but a shop full of the stuffed, cute tat that turns children into manic lottery winners and parents into Gradgrinds.

The point – the unique selling point – of the Rainforest Café is that it is supposed to transmit some of the awe and splendour of a primeval, tropical boskiness to kiddies, along with a dose of Greenpeaceish guilt and finger-wagging responsibility. What is truly splendidly, awe-inspiringly, jaw-unhingingly spectacular about it is the ozone-warming cynicism, not to mention the humid irony, of putting a hundred oilwells-worth of petrochemical-derivative Day-Glo animals, sweat shirts, shampoo and baseball caps at grab level.

The centre of this pristine natural environment is a bank of tills manned by smiley friends of Sting who, instead of CDs in their lips, have radio mikes, just like presidential bodyguards. The room is covered in wholly non-authentic plastic foliage and giant butterflies.

There are two sad-looking, real-feather macaws and an animated plastic alligator in a puddle. Tourists throw coins at it, and I can think of no better allegory for the whole environmental movement than chucking money at a rubber lizard.

We could have a table in an hour. Now, if it had just been adults, I would have gone round the corner for the authentic dim-sum experience in Chinatown. But children anchor you. They had gone native. The Blonde, who won't put off any experience longer than it takes her to kick off her shoes, said: 'Look, I know you never do this, but ...' And she called a manager and, in stentorian tones, informed him he had in his establishment A. A. Gill, the restaurant critic of the *Sunday Times* – readers: 4,000,027, gastronauts to a man. '*The* A. A. Gill,' she added, with pantomimic subtlety. I tried to look like a puce velour iguana.

There was a lot of flurrying and whispering into headsets. 'Ah well, of course, in that case, the wait will only be sixty minutes.' The poor girl returned looking like an endangered species. So we waited for an hour in the airport shop from hell.

At this point I should introduce you to Tracy Tree. I stood under Tracy Tree shouting: 'You can't have a really sweet, soft, three-foot seal. Seals don't live in rainforests.' And Tracy

Tree spoke soothingly to me. 'Hello, I'm Tracy Tree,' she said. Which raised the possibility of all the trees in South America having Essex girl names. I imagined David Attenborough fighting his way through the canopy, saying: 'And here is Sharon Tree and Dawn Tree and Lee Tree and Dion Tree.'

Tracy was one of the Babes in the Wood. She had big, rolling eyes and a rubber mouth and a voice like a Tampax advertisement. She asked me to hold up a plastic bag and imagine it was a dinosaur. She said if we weren't careful, when I grew up all her little friends would be extinct. A possibility to be devoutly wished for. After fifty-five minutes of this, I was promising to introduce her to Charlie Chainsaw and Freddie Flamethrower.

Oh, I forgot to mention – they underlined the cancelled-Torremolinos-flight Gatwick experience by giving you a passport to wait with. This document bore the name of Mr Orang Utan, and inside was a lot of fascinating information about Maya the 'regal' jaguar and Cha Cha the practical-joking frog and all their little friends. And there were the five Es of the rainforest, none of which, unfortunately, were illegal substances, but included E for employees, 'who are provided with opportunities to succeed and grow', and E for earning, 'which it is our responsibility to earn as a return on investment'. This place is a rare and precious thing – a restaurant that could make you sick before you've eaten.

Finally, over the Tannoy came the call of the wild. A thousand tourists looked up. 'Will Mr Orang Utan and his party of eleven please come to the elephant? Your adventure is about to begin.'

Mr Orang Utan shuffled his clan with head-bobbing embarrassment into the basement.

The restaurant itself is a stygian, arboreal dungeon that looks like the garden-furniture department of Harrods. Under the evergreen swag, dusty fake fur gorillas frot and jerk obscenely and roll their eyes. Bizarrely, there is a fountain representing

Atlas holding a neon Rainforest Café sign. If, inadvertently, I have made this sound the remotest bit exciting, adventurous or an experience worth anticipating, please ignore me.

The menu is, almost comfortingly, exactly the same as every other theme restaurant menu on the planet. It's hamburger and pasta caught between a Hard Rock and a hard place. World junk food, given new names: Rumble in the Jungle (caesar salad), the African Wind (chicken salad), Mojo Bones (ribs). And, as with all theme restaurants, this is fast food delivered interminably slowly. We didn't get anything for an hour. Then the children were fed and finished before the adults started, so they were bored and, like small aboriginals, wanted to move on to the tundra, savanna, mud-flat or Piccadilly-amusement-arcade adventure experience.

The service, naturally, was charming, like being fed by a well-rehearsed Moonie. Every half-hour, the cellar went dark and a tropical rainstorm flashed and rumbled above the noise of the Gipsy Kings and customers desperately trying to attract a waiter. It came as a bit of a shock, especially to the under-threes, who were all traumatised into regurgitation and fits of hysteria and had to be carried out in sobbing lines.

Oh, and, of course, it seems hardly necessary to point out that the food was utterly disgusting. It is expensive, too; even with five children's portions and £20 taken off for the wait. It is about here that I should sit up, lower my voice and say it's money donated to Friends of the Earth or the Body Shop or someone who would save a thousand trees and keep a family of hunter-gatherers in dental floss and aftershave for a year. But I won't – and don't you dare send any money to the rainforest. Without a rainforest, this place couldn't exist. I am going to make it my life's work to stamp out this sort of thing, even if it means setting fire to Indonesia, Papua New Guinea and all of South America.

The funny thing is, though, that if you have been to a real rainforest, you will know that they are dank, dark, boring, smelly, fetid, uncomfortable places where everything stings and you are lunch. Inadvertently, it is exactly the right metaphor for this place.

When Flora and Ali grow up, I will be able to take them to the high places and show them the deep, lush, vigorous vistas of cynical exploitation and marketing, heavy with burgers and twelve varieties of shake, fat of rib and boneless breast. They will hear the timeless ringing of tills and the Gipsy Kings, and see the great herds of wide-eyed branded merchandise, and the copyrights and trademarks will flit and flock numberless to man.

And I will be able to say: 'My children, all this is yours, as far as the eye can see. I bequeath it. You can take your axe of irony and your chainsaw of black humour, and hack and slash and burn without ceasing, because it is bigger than the world itself. It is your birthright – a theme without end.'

The Dome

I haven't finished with it yet. With the Dome. It's the worst place in the world. They couldn't have made it any more horrible if they'd built it in Pontypridd. There's far more to say about the Dome than there is to do in it.

The fox flap, for instance. Did you hear about the fox flap? No? Well, it has one. I'm not making this up. The Dome has a small door for foxes. In fact, foxes are the only thing that can get into the Dome without queuing. How depressingly, cringeingly, screamingly, raiment-rentingly, predictably New Labour is that? Apparently, when they started building the place, they discovered a family of foxes on the site (single-parent vixen, cubs out of control, taking and driving away cats, chickens, etc.), so they built them a door. Any day now, it will be a stipulation for every new house. Undoubtedly Chequers has half a dozen.

Equally predictably, the Dome is a fox-free zone, and having sampled the catering, I can see why. There are some things even foxes won't eat. If you were thinking of celebrating all that's best of British, the amazing turnaround in our cuisine might have struck you as being sort of important. You'd have imagined that someone at the Dome would have put their hand up and said: 'Please miss, why don't we use the Dome to show off the best of British cooking?' Considering that London has more Michelin-starred restaurants than any European city except Paris, it's sort of obvious, isn't it? So what do you get? What's on offer? Europe's biggest McDonald's.

Here's a gap ( ) for you and I to wave our palms at heaven and speechlessly make like a goldfish. It's beyond language.

The rest of the catering facilities are what you'd expect to find in a mainline rail terminus: juice bars, cloned coffee bars and sandwich shops, and a Yo! Sushi stuck in a corner as an afterthought.

There are two restaurants supposed to cater for those of us with an appetite for fine dining: one provincial-looking seafood bar and, above it, a British restaurant called Acclaim!

Let's just pause for a moment and roll that name round our tongues. Acclaim! How utterly, spinningly Domeish. Get your congratulations in first. Pat your own back, chuck yourself under the chin, give yourself a big tip. Pass the sputum cup, nurse.

Acclaim! has apparently been designed by a bored trainee scaffolder. It's a sort of opensided mezzanine-floor affair with a view of dull Tetrapak sideshows. When the Blonde and I approached the desk at about one o'clock, the restaurant was two-thirds empty. One harassed girl was trying to deal with people waiting and settle half a dozen credit-card bills at the same time.

As we hung around, something that has never happened in all my years of restaurant reviewing happened. A furious man stormed out and said: 'Don't go in there. If you're waiting to eat, don't. It takes hours. Everything comes in the wrong order. They're rude. It's disgusting.' And then, you know what? It happened again. Another man, completely unconnected to the first, buttonholed the Blonde. She doesn't actually have a buttonhole, but he transfixed her where her buttonhole might have been if she'd had one, and ranted about how awfully rude, useless, etc., the staff were, and that under no circs was she to accept a menu from these people. Dragging his eye away from her domed, phantom buttonhole, he caught sight of me. A flicker of recognition brought a thin, humourless, malevolent grin to his lips and he did a simply marvellous about-turn, without losing an iota of vehemence. 'No, go in. Go. Eat. Eat. You must go. Go now. Please.'

A maître d'appeared out of nowhere and interposed himself, asking if we had booked. Well, no, principally because the Dome has only been open for two days and nobody knows you're here. 'Ah well.' He gave me that practised, I'm-so-sorry-you-sad-dung-person look. 'I'm afraid we're full.' No, you're mistaken, I kindly pointed out, I can see empty tables stretching to infinity. 'They're all booked.' Really? 'Yes.' Really and truly? 'Yes, yes.' Okay, so when will there be a table available? 'Oh dear, not for a long, long time. Anyway, you have too many things to see.' I do? 'Yes, perhaps another day.' You think I'm going to come back to this godforsaken place? When can you give me a table? 'Ah,' he said, thinking of a number and doubling it. 'Not for at least thirty minutes.' Done.

Did I mention he was French? Well, you probably gathered. An English restaurant called Acclaim! in the big national-boast Dome, and they get a French major-domo.

Half an hour later, the Blonde and I are sitting in a virtually empty restaurant watching the queue for McDonald's. To give Acclaim! its due, they did try and pretend it was full. The waitress was always serving invisible people in the far distance, and the kitchen make-believed it had to get through a dozen orders before starting on ours.

The menu was short. Not short enough. Not short enough by 100 per cent. It is fabulously annoying. There were little signs at the bottom, saying: 'All dishes may contain traces of nuts or seeds.' Seeds? Why seeds? (I'm typing in falsetto.) When was the last time you heard someone say: 'Hold the seeds'? And then there was the V symbol: 'Suitable for vegetarians.' And they put it next to a dish that's called 'Chef's Vegetarian Dish of the Day', just so you can be doubly sure the vegetarian dish is suitable for vegetarians. Ah, but it's not next to the cheeseboard, under which is written 'Suitable for vegetarians'. Well, don't they think (falsetto again) that vegetarians already know they can eat cheese? 'Aw, am I allowed cheese? I can't remember. Does Gouda have a soul?'

But there's nothing saying you can't smoke, because – durr, stupid – it's obvious that you won't be allowed to smoke. It's not even worth mentioning.

I watched the Blonde get her first course, a neat *timbale* of salmon hash, beet-cured salmon and sweet dill dressing (what's beet-cured salmon, please?). Her pretty face was a picture of serene expectation. Then, a moment later, it was as if she were sitting still, but her head were travelling at Mach three. She let out a small, strangulated mew and coughed: 'Cat food.' What, it's like cat food? 'No, it is cat food. It's Rory Bremner beetthingied salmon doing such a good impression of cat food, it's uncanny.'

My terrine of brawn started by being a tautology. Brawn is already a terrine. But that's academic nit-picking, because this wasn't brawn anyway. It was a pig that had been beaten into a brick with a hammer, with a hot black-pudding salad that was silly, and piccalilli that was yellow – the sort of yellow that makes you say: 'If you ever buy me a tie that colour, I'll sleep with your sister.'

By this time, my irritation levels were so high, I was virtually levitating. Main course: salmon fish and chips. Look (as Tony says), look, I already know salmon is a fish. I already know it's not an umbrella or the little plastic thing on the end of shoelaces. Salmon fish and chips is a really, really stupid idea. It came, traditionally, with mushy peas – except they were pureed garden peas, not marrowfat – and a tower of chips, presumably designed by a committee in charge of the Chewing Zone. The salmon fish was poached, but the batter had been drizzled onto a hotplate to make a zingy pattern, then laid on top.

At this point, the blood pressure in my head went critical and I blacked out. When I came to, I had 300-degree peripheral vision and the Blonde had her hand over my mouth, whispering: 'Please stop shouting.' In the muffled distance, I heard someone familiar yell: 'This is the stupidest thing in the stupidest place in the world. This is so stupid that in a stupid contest it would be disqualified for taking the piss. Cooking salmon with batter is deeply stupid. But cooking the salmon and the batter separately because they don't go together is so stupid it ...' And I felt myself slipping away again.

Luckily, the Dome's nice PR girl (what's the worst job in the world? I bet she just goes home and sits in the bath and cries and cries) came panting up. 'Oh, I thought I might find you here. I've been trying to phone them all morning, to warn them you might pop in. How is everything?'

It's, it's, it's ...

'Unbelievable,' interjected the Blonde.

'Oh good.'

Health

Now, you can look at health food two ways: like this, or like this. You either think that health food, irrespective of taste or aesthetics, is anything that allows you to go on boring people well into triple figures; or you think that health food is stuff that will get you to 8.30pm fit enough to be able to eat a solid dinner. I am of the second persuasion, which will come as no surprise. When the Blonde led me to the door of a bright, home-made little café – one of a crop of places called things like Crush, Squash, Press, Throttle and Eviscerate – on Kensington High Street, I must admit I came this close to tendering my resignation. I will put most things in my mouth, but this goes too far.

It was self-service, so we joined the back of what looked like the unlucky placebo group from a chronic acne test. Why is it that people who spend all their time thinking about their bodies are so damn unappetising? And why is it that everyone you see on a bicycle looks like they're pedalling to their own funerals?

Anyway, what these places serve isn't food, it's medicine: quack medicine with the quack removed. This isn't a café, it's an alternative witch-doctor's chemist. Along the walls, like a born-again church, are shelves of help-yourself bulletins that have been photocopied from the Internet. It's no wonder people are turning to pornography if this stuff is the alternative. There are tracts such as Update on the Health Benefits of Soya Fibre, The Great Vitamin Debate (between whom, where?) and, my favourite, Echinacea In-Depth. You really couldn't make that up. I wish I had enough space to quote at length (at considerable length).

Here's just the opening paragraph from the deathless, probably literally, Echiwhatsit In-Depth: 'If you ever get a chance to play word association with a herbalist, try "Colds" and "Flu". Most likely, the response will be "Echinacea".' Word association with a herbalist – I ask you. Long car journeys with these people must be simply hysterical.

The menu is utterly original in that it's made up of collections of things that nobody else in ten thousand years of continuous experiment has considered putting together and actually swallowing. Most of it is some generic stuff called Smoothies. They have individual names such as Marathon Powerboost, Melon Madness and Strawberry Fields, and are pulped fruit and veg suspended in non-fat yoghurt. Added to this is an extra Boost, another collection of things with specific guttish properties.

I went for a Power Girl Smoothie: pineapple, two sorts of melon and banana, with an extra female Boost (nagging, dithering and a three-figure telephone bill). Gingerly, I approached the straw. If I grew bosoms, I'd never have to go out again. But damn it, you have to be a woman already to get the full benefit. In fact, you have to be Linda Lovelace to get the turgid stuff up the straw. Reluctantly, giving up on my dreams of sexual self-sufficiency, I tried a soup: 'All natural, no artificial ingredients.' Taste, skill and subtlety are obviously artificial ingredients. This was warm Body Shop anti-dandruff shampoo with a hefty boost of fried garlic. So that got left.

Next, the vegetarian wraps. God alone knows what the inventor of this peculiarly noisome assault was thinking of. What I thought of was orang-utan nappies: a parcel of limp tortilla filled to the brim with about a stone of hummus and some tomato and spinach. Now imagine trying to eat a soggy plop of bean mush that weighs more than your head, insecurely bundled in a damp diaper. So I didn't do that either.

What about a snack? There was a bewildering variety of energy bars that looked like a big-game tracker's identification test. I tried one that promised hemp. Fruit-bat biggies is my most conservative description. The hemp had no discernible effect. Do you have any with heroin? I could probably eat the wrap after one of those.

But that's not the end. Oh dear me, no.

I've saved the best for last. Drum roll, please: fresh wheatgrass juice. Now, I know I've often said other things are the worst thing I've ever eaten, and like the boy who cried wolf, I'm now paying for it and you won't believe me. But PLEASE, PLEASE BELIEVE ME – this is the worst thing I've ever put in my mouth. They have innocent turfs of grass on the counter. To all of us who aren't David Bellamy, which is most of us, it looks like perfectly ordinary roll-me-over grass. Oh, but it's not. They say it does all sorts of fabulous things to you and they have a machine that mulches it up, emitting a few livid bile drops of the precious juice into a plastic shot glass. To be fair, they do warn you that if you gulp you might pass out or have fits or turn into the Hulk, so they suggest sipping – which, in retrospect, reminded me of the choice given to seventeenth-century Turkish adulterers: they could either have their testicles squashed between silk cushions or hammered between bricks.

I went for the bricks. I gulped. Oh my God, oh my God. The taste – flavour is too flimsy a word – the taste grows inside your head until your ears start to retch. It's kraken-wake pus. It's like nothing on earth, but just as an exercise, try to imagine a sheep with gingivitis that has lived solely on old curry tins and cigar butts sneezing cud into your mouth. That's a mere soupçon of the truly vile verdant 3-D horror of wheatgrass juice. It induced my first-ever oscular nightmare.

The Blonde, of course, loved it all to death and talked with great enthusiasm, depth and detail about the toilet fun she was ardently expecting in eight or nine hours' time. Lovely.

This juice-bar idea comes from California (naturally), and it seems to me that in their obsessive zeal for immortality, they've missed out one central, indeed vital, fact. We as a species need to eat, not just to stay healthy, but to stay alive. So we go to great lengths to make food look, smell and taste appetising, so that by simple association we will want to do it again. This stuff, frankly, truly, could only be of interest to those of you training to be animal rights martyrs.

Jabberwocky

We were in a very modern restaurant in Soho. Call me cynical (I like to think I'm prematurely wise), but I just knew the food was going to be mix'n'match crossword-puzzle Rim stuff. And it was going to have to try very, very hard to be liked. The menu came and, sure enough ...

Now, I've been searching for some time for a word that encapsulates this sort of food. And as I scanned the lines of dishes, it came to me. This is jabberwocky food: 'Today's special is brillig in slithy toves. We have gyre and gimble in the wabe, mimsy are our borogroves and mome raths will take fifteen minutes to outgribe.'

What, I asked nicely, is zhug? The quail came spiced with it. 'Zhug,' the waitress smiled sweetly, 'is what the quail comes spiced with.' And? I prompted. 'It's a spice,' she grinned helpfully. And finally: 'Would you like me to ask the chef?' That would be kind. Now, hands up all of you who know what zhug is. Exactly. What is the point of having a menu if you need the Rosetta stone to translate it? As it happens, I do know that kimchi is Korean pickled cabbage and can guess that Shanghai choi is probably a relative of bok choi or pak choi, that Andalus aubergine is an eggplant with a passport, wasabi is Japanese horseradish and that tom yam soup is made neither with yam nor by Tom. But that's only because I do this for a living. I'm still at a loss as to what ponzu sauce is. And it's not as if this is a foreign menu written in a real foreign language that would be understandable, if not comprehensible. It's a made-up patois, a gastro gibber that nobody speaks. Soho has always been full of people who talk drivel, but this is stupid and patronising and serves to give the food a phoney, sophisticated international gloss.

'Zhug is a type of coriander,' said the returning waitress helpfully. So why couldn't the menu have said that? Never mind, I'll have it. The quail was jointed and well cooked and accompanied by a hill of couscous. The zhug was shrivelled black bits in some sort of sauce. As a first course, this was a non-starter.

Language and the naming of things are important. Everything grows into its name. These ingredients weren't talking to each other, weren't on first-name terms. It's the perennial problem with jabberwocky food: you get a babel of small, hot, unexpected flavours that are supposed to hit it off like *Blind Date* contestants, and usually end up like *Blind Date* contestants, saying they never want to see each other again. This type of cooking is knife-edge, hit-or-miss. It can only work if based on superlative taste and a solid classical background, like Bruno Loubet's. If it's just free association and enthusiasm, it doesn't. It really, really doesn't.

I'm not going to go through the whole of dinner, because although it was all different, it was fundamentally all the same. You get to the end knowing that you've chewed, but not knowing whether you've eaten. Well, okay, let me just introduce you to a pudding. This is where the most extreme flights of fondant fancy occur.

Mango and peppermint *marquise* with macadamia nut crackling, a plate with a skin graft of jelly, a tennis ball of cream-flavoured cream and a biscuit. The prosthetic-coloured jelly had the oddest hint of flavour. What is this? 'Melted Barbie heads,' said the girl sitting next to me.

Precisely. That's exactly what it is. Which Barbie do you think? 'Ah, tricky. Skiing Barbie, or perhaps Baywatch Barbie.'

And you know, I think she was right.

Jabberwocky's revenge

There's this book – *Fish* – by James Delingpole, about a mad food critic. We sane food critics laughed – it was a funny book. But that's not why we laughed. We laughed because the premise was a critic who reviewed fictitious restaurants, which then started actually appearing. Oh, how absurd, we chortled, how risibly *X-Files*. But then, just to prove that fact has no imagination but merely plagiarises remaindered fiction, it has gone and happened.

Once, I invented not a restaurant, but a style of cooking. Actually, I didn't invent it – I just identified it: jabberwocky food. And then – gor lummy, Mrs Bridges, here's a caution and no mistake – someone faxed me a menu with Jabberwocky Surprise on it. My God, what have I done? What have I created? Not just a jabberwocky, but a surprise jabberwocky.

How do you fancy pine-smoked reindeer carpaccio; triptych of squid; coconut, gold-leaf and *foie gras* soup; beluga tin with blinis and chutney; black-ink hen terrine; or goat essence with Irish moss soup? And that's just for starters.

The reindeer carpaccio tasted like goblin. Tarred goblin. *Foie gras* soup is a totally disgusting idea: fatty liver soup, sweet with coconut, with a beaten toffee paper floating in it. Caviar with chutney: I couldn't, just couldn't. The hen terrine was a puréed, grey, cold, damp, vaguely animal brick that would have made the staunchest liberal an avian racist. Goat essence soup – the essence of this goat was that it had lived entirely on onions. This was thin, chilli-hot onion soup with that faint aroma of hairball. Oh, and I forgot to mention the amuse-bouches: crispy Mexican worms (grubs, actually) on a tomato cracker.

For main course, they'd like to tempt you with seaweed, porcini and hemp risotto with coriander mayonnaise. Hemp risotto: that's dope or rope. Either way, I passed; I just had to have the Jabberwocky Surprise. It turned out to be a nasty green chicken curry with rice moulded into a floor tile that came on a glass plate so fingered and greasy that it could have been a Hendon Police Academy forensic exam. As side dishes, we could have had One More Basket – don't ask; I didn't – or a Heather Caesar. This I did inquire into. What's a heather caesar? 'It's a classic caesar salad.' What's the heather bit? 'I don't know. The chef just likes the name.' I passed on the honeyed Hungarian chilli pig with tiger nut pesto.

All the dishes had a pervasive and ornery contrariness in their preparation and came decorated, wrapped up and served in as many awkward and unlikely plates, shells, husks, shards, tins, boxes and sewn leaves as a gay Egyptian mortician could dream of. This wasn't eating dinner – it was Russian roulette. You never knew if the next mouthful would blow your head off. It was breaking down in the middle of the ghost train and having to walk back. It was a game of chicken played with real chickens. It was discovering that Imelda Marcos was really Barbara Cartland. And it was utterly, utterly horrific in a compulsively fascinating way. Everything that's sad, bad and irrational in modern cooking was taken to its ultimate, doomsday, Dr Strangelove scenario.

For pudding, I asked for the chocolate scorpions, giving the waitress the best line of the evening – 'I'm afraid the scorpions have run out.' I asked for the bill. It came on an abacus. 'Here's the bill on an abacus,' said the waitress. 'If you can't read it ...'

£145 for three!

She took my shriek of astonishment for arithmetical boasting. 'Oh, how do you know that?' It says so on the abacus. 'Usually people can't read it.' Yeah, well, lucky them.

'Come on, Dr Frankenstein,' said the Blonde, 'let this be a lesson to you. Remember what mummy said: it's the little things you make up that come back to haunt you.'

I'm sorry. I'm so, so sorry.

Egyptian

The menu promised authentic Egyptian cuisine. Opening a restaurant that actually boasts Egyptian food sounds like a dare that got out of hand. There are many wonderful things about Egypt, but none of them is gastronomic. An Egyptian restaurant belongs on the same street as a Fijian ballet school, a Ukrainian tailor and a Nigerian interior decorator.

Which is why I went for the prawn cocktail. It was the starter from the mummy's tomb. It is best described as belly-buttons in fake tan. We also sampled the falafel, the Middle Eastern broad-bean patty – they were so old they had grown an exoskeleton and could have been the last thing Cleopatra ever saw – and Wings of Fire chicken wings from mutant hens: small, hairy, wizened things in a tomato sauce that managed to be both insipid and powerful enough to clear U-bends.

I should also mention that to get the authentic ambience, they played 1970s pop music to the otherwise desolately empty room. I particularly enjoyed a cover version of the old Serge Gainsbourg and Jane Birkin classic, 'Je t'aime', which sounded splendidly as if a proctologist was examining a distressed Middle Eastern lady, who gaspingly repeated 'the pain, the pain'.

Now, I've eaten a lot of bad food and, generally, the way you tell it's bad is because it's like something you've eaten before that was well made, so your taste memory has something to compare it with – a yardstick of awfulness. But what came next shot the restaurant into a league all of its own: two dishes that bore not even a passing resemblance to anything I've ever tasted. In fact, the only thing I could compare them with was each other, and seeing as they were both equally unpleasant, it was difficult to tell if they were really bad, or just inventively, playfully Egyptian. *Molakia* sounds like something from the Book of Revelation with three heads and brazen scales, but it is, according to the menu, the delicious green *molakia* leaves cooked in lamb stock with cubes of lamb, ground coriander and garlic. Kebab *halla* ought to have an exclamation mark after it and, again, according to the menu, it is lamb cubes cooked with onions and spices served in a brown sauce. Both were offered in what is best described as dog bowls and came, on first sight, as Stygian opaque soups with a thin film of liverish oil and a deceptive steaming calm on their limpid surfaces, as if some unspeakable dread lurked beneath. The *molakia* sported what I thought looked like a sort of green algae and smelt so pungent that it might have revived coma victims. It was a smell that started as stewed garlic, but had underneath it more complex notes, whispers and traces of timeless ancient amoral places. Like Proust's madeleine, it reminded me of something I couldn't put my finger on. And then I remembered: it was the wheezing breath of an ancient ochre-toothed Moroccan jellaba dealer who once coughed over me.

The brown sauce in which our *halla* modestly hid was a subtler concoction. In fact, brown is the only word I could apply to it with any certainty: it looked brown, it smelt brown, it was the embodiment, the synthesis of all blind, inert, wet brown things. Gingerly, we fished in the goo and, once in a while, came up with a nugget of glistening, opalescent lamb fat with a stringy fringe of flesh attached. These we set on plates where they dribbled and congealed. When the primeval soup gave up no more, they sat there like things you might find between a camel's toes.

With bulging eye and ragged breath, uttering a short prayer, I popped a morsel in my mouth. It was everything it promised to be. The flavour didn't so much explode as seep. It crawled into every crevice and cavity, drifted along tubes and tunnels till I sensed I could actually taste it behind my eyeballs. It hung like marsh gas on autumn fens: anonymously animal, yet faintly chemical, puckish and feral, teasing and mad.

Later, I lay in bed, my thrice-brushed and gargled mouth still pulsating to the distant lustre of the great green *molakia* leaf. The night was full of bestial dreams, of fevered sweats and winding sheets, of mad, toothless grins and shrieks, of hacking coughs and the thrumming ecstasy of 'the pain, the pain'.

Nostalgia

Nostalgia is an equal-opportunity infection. You can, and indeed do, get nostalgic about absolutely anything: 1930s housework, having bombs dropped on your head, marching up and down Northumbria dressed in a metal miniskirt shouting 'Veni, vidi, vici.' Nostalgia is retrospective plastic surgery. Depression housework is lovely, as long as you don't have to do it. Like banging your head against the wall, the Blitz was lovely, once it stopped. Pretending to be a Roman legionary is ... well, that's just frothingly bonkers at any time.

Food is not immune to nostalgia. Restaurants are always playing the 'Whatever happened to?' game, bringing back dishes that have associations – because taste is something that happens in your head and not, as you might imagine, on your tongue. What you like has as much to do with your expectations and memories as with the chef. So, if a menu can offer you something that comes with a resonance, a nuance, a Proustian soggy biccy of lustful youth, then so much the better. All of us are prone to the reverie, the stirring of the synapses that a really artificial prawn cocktail or a tin of warm Spam can inspire.

Which is why, against all my better judgment, I went to a restaurant that promised 1970s retro food. I took Jo, one of the few friends from my dissipated days whom I can still recognise, and Mr and Mrs Johnny Standing. Johnny's an actor laddie of the first water, a thesp who calls his toothbrush luvvie and kisses his underpants on both cheeks. To all of them, I owe a sincere and public apology. The Blonde, of course, is a professional. This sort of evening goes with the boyfriend. But if it happens too often, it undoubtedly will go with the boyfriend.

There were two menus: one for bar snacks, the other for knife-and-fork eating, although the cutlery might be better employed fending the stuff off. We started with some memory-lane bits off the snack menu: a fishfinger sandwich, a plate of home-made pork scratchings, battered saveloy, chips with curry sauce.

The scratchings were deep-fried bellybuttons: not plump, tender, free-range baby bellybuttons, but crusty, saggy, old men's wrinkly, unloved and unlicked umbilicals, boiled in oil until they were a perfect crunchy yet viscous noisomeness. My, I thought, they'll never outdo that. Then a bite of the fishfinger sandwich lurched me to even greater heights of gastro-mayhem. The soft, yet faintly stale, sliced white, with a seeping sludge of ketchup that cleverly mimicked week-old Gallipoli bandage, shyly hid a brace of fish coffins fried in an oil that tasted like it had never seen field or tree, but had done a lifetime's Stygian service in some hellish engine. Oh, that was something.

But the best was still to come. Battered saveloy, a thing that only specialist medical staff handle, with rubber gloves. One bite of its fluorescent pink flesh whisked, nay clouted, me back through the years. Jo and I stared at each other with exclamation-mark eyes that stared inwards, mouths akimbo, tongues desperately, vainly attempting to repel the gristle. We were teenagers again.

It was 1972. Oh happy, carefree, raucous youth. Oh swerving, snorkelled, baggy-bladdered youth. The pubs have shut and we're standing – just – on the neon-slick pavement outside the Acropolis kebab-and-chip shop being operatically sick. And here we are again, having a fight outside the Bosphorus late-night diner, and then being country-and-western sick. In a musical series of Dolby sound, bifocal images, my Russian-salad days splattered and slurped into the gutter of after-hours regurgitation. Now, I haven't actually been sick for twenty years, but it's amazing how fresh and strong the memory was. Who would have thought a simple motherless mongrel sausage could do that?

The Blonde handed me something under the table. It was a warm, full napkin. 'I've never had to do that before,' she choked. The Standings delicately gave me theirs: a herring gull's school lunch. Oh, but we weren't finished yet. We'd barely started. Next: Dublin Bay prawn cocktail, which – point of order – wasn't. You may think that, by this time, nit-picking about piscine nomenclature is like picking up litter on the first day of the Somme, but Dublin Bay prawns are what we know as langoustine – or scampi. These were those little mouse-baby prawns you get in plastic coal sacks from the freezer centre.

Slow-baked cheese-and-onion tart = snot in a box. Grilled kipper = smoked postman's odour-eater. The duck pâté was interesting. It was also a Kurdish insurgent duck that had been interrogated to death by Turkish policemen using rubber hoses, then left in a warm, damp cupboard to emulsify. God knows what ghastly, long-buried Freudian memories curried cauliflower, potato and cheese soup would have excavated. *Coq au vin* was thick-skinned chicken knuckles soaked in tepid Brylcreem and aftershave. Chicken-and-mushroom pie came in its own pot. Leaning as far back as possible, I gingerly lifted the sagging, but strangely resilient, lid. It emitted a thin stream of oleaginous vapour. Oh my God, I know what this is. If you live in the country, a man comes with a tanker and a long hose and takes it away. And you don't ask him in for tea.

For pudding (oh yes, we weren't beaten: there was still pudding betwixt us and the exit) we had chocolate pudding and custard, a fine example of the afters that finally put an end to secondary modern schools. Sherry trifle: unspeakable. Black Forest gateau and apple pie: both would have worried gypsy caterers at a Troggs concert in Norwich.

Well, finally we managed it. The girls sat speechless on the summit of all this gastro-porn, nursing warming cups of camomile tea (hot water in a cup; bag on the side). 'You know what this is, dear heart?' quoth Johnny. 'You know what, darling? It's the BBC canteen. In black and white. There's dear old Roland Culver over there. And Valentine Dyall. And Eric Porter. Nyree dear, over here, love.' And he was off.

Out of all the myriad succubus savours and trollish textures, one in particular stayed with me and, indeed, is still with me. I'd quite forgotten the particular insistent insinuation of olde English deep-frying. I haven't smelt it for years. Not exactly rancid, it's as if the oil were slowly cooking the machine it was boiling in. It's as if they deep-fried half a dozen Brillo pads. Quite extraordinary. Brought a lump to my throat. Well, a queue of lumps, like third-class passengers on the *Titanic*.

When you complain about the difficulties and expense of contemporary eating, this is, within living memory, precisely what it used to be like. This was an interactive museum. Catering's Tate.

Starbucks

Have you ever been to a Starbucks? (God, I'm beginning to sound like those judges who say: 'Pray, what is a Rolling Stone? And could you enlighten the court on the exact nature of a T-shirt?') Of course you've been to a Starbucks. Starbucks is your second living-room. The question I should have asked is: why?

I'm not a habitué of these West Coast coffee shops. Not for any snobbish reason – just because I like coffee. An American café sounds like the punch line to one of those jokes in which the Germans end up the lovers, the Italians the soldiers, the French the marriage counsellors and the Greeks the cooks, architects or hairdressers – in fact, anything at all. I can't think of a single thing I'd trust a Greek to do professionally, except make Turkish coffee. (That should get the postman's hernia pulsating.) Asking Americans to make coffee is like asking them to draw a map of the world.

'Okay, so this is your house, that's Disneyland, and what's this squiggle over here? Right, that's everywhere else.' American coffee is only coffee because they say it is. It's actually a pale, scalding infusion of junior-school jam-jar brush water. Americans who drink one a week imagine they're in the grip of a vicious caffeine frenzy that prohibits them from signing legal documents, operating heavy machinery and adopting children, but, oddly, helps if they want to plea bargain a murder – or bomb developing countries. It's not a drink for grown-ups.

Anyway, I did go to a Starbucks recently. And I'm still reeling. I can't remember the last time I was served something as foul as its version of a cappuccino. I say 'version', but that's a bit like saying Dot Cotton's a version of Audrey Hepburn.

To begin with, it took longer to make than a soufflé. I was the only customer, and asked the girl for a cappuccino. There followed an interrogation that would have impressed an SS Scientologist. What size did I want? Did I need anything in it? Was I hungry? By the time she'd finished, I felt like sobbing: 'You've found Tom, and Dick's under the stove in D Hut, but I'll never give away Harry – he's got Dickie Attenborough up him.'

Suspiciously, she passed the order, written in Serbian, to another girl standing all of three inches away, who, in turn, slowly morphed into Marie Curie and did something very dangerous and complicated behind a counter, with a lot of sighing and brow-furrowing.

An hour and a half later, I was presented with a mug. A mug. One of those American mugs where the lip is so thick, you have to be an American or able to disengage your jaw like a python to fit it in your mouth. It contained a semi-permeable white mousse – the sort of stuff they use to drown teenagers in Ibiza, or pump into cavity walls. I dumped in two spoonfuls of sugar. It rejected them. Having beaten the malevolent epidermis with the collection of plastic and wooden things provided, I managed to make it sink. Then, using both hands, I took a sip. Then a gulp. Then chewed.

I had the momentary sense of drowning in snowman's poo, then, after a long moment, a tepid sludge rose from the deep. This was reminiscent of gravy browning and three-year-old Easter eggs.

How can anyone sell this stuff? How can anyone buy this twice? And this was only a small one – a baby. The adult version must be like sucking the outlet of a nuclear power station.

I slumped into a seat. There was a pamphlet about fair trade, and how Starbucks paid some Nicaraguan Sancho a reasonable amount for his coffee so that he now had a mule to go with his thirteen children, leaky roof and fifteen coffee bushes. It made not screwing the little no-hope wetback into penury sound like the most astonishing act of charitable benevolence. And they just had to print a pamphlet about it, so we all know the sort of selfless, munificent, group-hug people we're dealing with.

I've just looked up the origin of cappuccino. I always imagined it was nineteenth-century Italian. Actually, it appears first in 1683, just after the relief of Vienna from the Ottomans. The retreating Turks left behind sacks of coffee, and an enterprising double agent, Franz Georg Kolschitzky, opened the first European coffee shop (disputed with Caffe Florian, in Venice). It was not a success until he added milk, honey and cinnamon. The cappuccino was born. He needed something to go with it, so he got his neighbour, the baker Peter Wendler, to turn his excellent butter buns into Turkish symbols. Ta-ra! The croissant.

All that history, all Sancho's effort, and it ends up as Starbucks. Oh, the pity and the shame. The name, by the way, comes from Capuchin monks, who had white habits. Interestingly, they also donated their name to a monkey, simply by adding a syllable.

The chunky bloke on the door with a telephone wire in his ear doesn't look like he's here to keep out the pressing wannabes so much as drag the lost tourists in. When you get down to it, this crepuscular cellar looks more like a Chinese restaurant in Riga than the centre of international swinging London. It's also studded with girls who look like they know Riga a lot better than they know London. If they aren't, in fact, ladies whose bodies are also their means of production and their men friends have actually filled out full and frank tax returns, then I wholeheartedly apologise. It's just that they'd worked so hard on achieving the steely mercantile come-hither-and-come-fast look that it completely fooled me.

This is interior design that has disappeared up its own fundamental cleverness: a low-slung concrete bunker covered in a caca-coloured collage made of – get this – blown-up stills from a video of the interior when it was a building site. (And to think, once upon a time, Giotto simply painted pretty pictures on the wall. Renaissance? They didn't know they were born.) Oh, and the neon strip lights dim up and down through traffic-light colours, so every three minutes you think you're Bette Davis in Dark Victory *succumbing to a brain tumour.*

At times, the waiters outnumbered the diners, hands came and went, over, under and between my armpits, until I imagined I was being served by an Indian deity doing the macarena.

The service was Teutonically efficient. The waiters were all Argies and seemed to have come from the Gregory Peck school of genetic engineering. They had the restrained, inquisitive politeness of young Gestapo officers. I rather imagined I was going to be asked for my papers and the reason for my journey. The other customers were mostly groups of pinstriped workers and a smattering of office romances taking on protein.

A very nice young man came up with four glasses of beer. 'I know you don't drink, Mr Gill, but would you try our beers?' No, I don't drink. 'We're really very proud of them, will you just taste them?' Sweet of you, but I don't drink. 'No, I know you don't drink, but would you please, please, just have a sip.' No, thank you, I don't drink. 'Just the merest, teeniest one, please.' Have you ever considered a job in heroin? I think you've got a vocation. Look, you really don't want me to taste your beer. Trust me, you've only got the four two-storey silos. 'Really, you're sure, not just an infinitesimal ...' I thought he was going to cry. I tell you what, I'll smell them, okay?

They smelt very nice if you're into snorting beer. Of beer, mostly.

For lunch on a dreary Wednesday it offered the warm welcome and bonhomous hospitality of a Norwegian small-claims court. Sensibly, they'd put in a wood-burning pizza oven (hopefully, they'll get round to incinerating the chairs any day now).

We were led into a room designed by Mr Dan Tay. It was Stygian black – perfect for people with ugly dates, or ugly people with pretty dates. It probably had decoration, but I couldn't see

any. The plates, though, were bright enough to land Harriers on,
with those jolly Portofino patterns that were popular in the 1970s.

It was the hottest day of the month, and a flaming torch,
the sort used to flush out werewolves, sat on the table casting
menacing shadows.

It's a rambling room that appears to have grown organically.
Nobody sane could sit down and design it. The walls are covered
in old junk, most of it weird farming equipment and coffee pots.
The ceiling is a lot of executed mandolins, banjos and ukuleles. The
stools only just function as objects for sitting on. In fact, it looks like
they've been ethnically cleansing folk singers here.

4

HOME

The dining-room used to look like a brothel on the Lusitania. *They've managed to tone it down. Now it looks like a brothel in a boardroom. The restaurant was half-full of men who tuck their napkins into their collars and forget to do up their flies, saying things like 'Suckposset is the best man we've got in the north-west' very loudly. One of them peered into his double armagnac and sighed with a terrible ennui: 'Oh well, another day ruined.'*

I had the stargazey pie, a semi-mythical Cornish dish, with herrings' heads staring out of the pie crust. We owe its rediscovery to the beatified Jane Grigson, as we do the Sussex pond pudding on the dessert menu, an impressive dome of suety pastry for two, containing liquid toffee and a whole stewed lemon, served with cream. It's like finding Elgar snogging Falstaff in a peat bog.

Opening the door, we were met by a wall of braying, a sound I thought I'd never hear again: an old-school donkey sanctuary. Every receding, slightly paunchy Sloane who was ever named after an Arthur Ransome character was here, bellowing at a lady-in-estate-agent-waiting. These people don't go on dates in pairs; they can only manage a tiny percentage of an entire evening's conversation. So they eat in teams. It is a room where everyone knew Tom Fool, so there was a lot of hovering and eye-rolling and muttering and 'just passing'. Indeed, some Tim Nice But Dim came and joined us for no better reason than he thought we'd like it and he was a mate of the owner. They're all mates;

that was the thing with Sloanes – millions of mates and ne'er a mating.

I started with a very good plate of jellied eels, one of those dishes that is generally best left shivering in the memory. The waitress delivered them as if they were a plate of condoms dredged out of a storm drain. The Blonde, whose Keelerish boast is that she'll put anything in her mouth once, quite liked the sensation of slippery cold bottom-feeder in fishy jelly with gum-impaling swastika bones.

The hotel reeks of that English virtue: understatement. It yells, screams, bellows and semaphores understatement until it's puce in the face. Walking into its non-lobby lobby, with its utter absence of charm, welcome or hospitality, you realise why only the English think rigor-mortised understatement is a virtue. And it smells like a boys' prep school: an odour of countless boiled things, which has seeped into the carpet along with any sense of excitement, appetite or exuberance.

The restaurant is hidden up a dark, dank little corridor, as if eating were a distasteful indulgence, and is lit with that peculiar dowdiness that makes everything monochrome. The waiters look like they're made out of the same stuff as the walls, which are brown wood: a brown of a brownness that defies any other colour to ever raise its gaudy little head again; a brown that is biding its time before painting the town drab.

It is a large airy room with Ikea-ish functional furniture and bland little photographs on the walls and, unusually, there are side tables glued to the ceiling. It was full of Hampstead folk, who really are as extraordinary as tables on the ceiling. They all have that intense look of people trying to explain Primo Levi to an eskimo.

The large, glaucoma-dark bar boasts its own DJ and is obviously something of a social club for the serially unattached, shop assistants from Oxford Street and boys from the Middle East here to learn English and crash cars, and the last vestiges of a social subspecies called the Mayfair Mercenaries: glossy girls who wear their sunglasses as Alice bands, have a penchant for miniature suede racing drivers and cutting the crotches out of their boyfriends' suits, and who are the spiritual descendants of Ruth Ellis. If you want to meet one, well, she's here.

Countryside

There are two good things about the country, as in '-side'. One, of course, is the motorway that sprints like a thing possessed to the nearest city. The other is that I never return from the mud museum without something new to hate.

Don't believe what the in-touchy folk with Velcro lives and pitying smiles tell you. Hate is good. Hate is fine. Hate is warm and comforting. Hate lights the darkness and shows the way home. Hate is a doer, a fixer, a trailblazing reformer. Your collection of hates is the most precious thing you own. You will be remembered by the breadth, strength and tempered edge of your hatreds.

Take that smarmy look off your face. I know what you're thinking. You're thinking: 'He's just being a contrarian. He's just doing it to annoy. Don't rise.' But you see, that's what I hate about you – your supine, good-natured, path-of-least-resistance, anything-for-a-quiet-life docility.

Just think about it. It was Wilberforce's hatred that abolished slavery. It was hatred of fascism that won the war. It was hatred that forged the Health Service, marched for civil rights, wrote Magna Carta. It was hating being cold that lit the first fire and hating being wet that built the first house. Hating being picked off, one by one, made the first community. Walk through any great city and feel the hatred and the anger that fuels it. Everything you value most in your life was forged and maintained by hate.

'What about love?' you whine. 'Surely love makes the world go round? What the world needs now is love, sweet love.' Bollocks. It needs better-quality hate. Love is passive, indulgent and myopic. If you're dying in agony, love holds your hand. Hatred and anger go and discover a cure. In 4,000 years, hatred built civilisations. And love? What did love give us? Yoga.

Now, I want you all to concentrate, and think hateful thoughts about animal-lovers. Wildlife-huggers are the measure of everything that's most depressingly, infuriatingly crap about this country: an amorphous, clandestine, fundamentalist grouping that claims its mandate from the speechless and uncomprehending. These are the sort of people who see in nature an anthropomorphic model for their own pathetic lives, who will love an oily guillemot because a sweaty human is just too frightening.

I have a note from my mum saying I'm excused country. The only reason to go to the green stuff is to kill things. I like to make sure there's a little less of it by the time I leave. I do love shooting stuff: small, stupid stuff preferably. I had my first day at the partridge last week. It was heaven; fun, but also a small blow in the international war against terrorism. You've no idea the damage partridges do and the fear they induce. When they get into gangs, they can eat a small house. They lay their eggs in nuclear power stations and are responsible for half of all air disasters.

In between drives (the technical term for avian ethnic cleansing), I came across a man with a dog. That's a nice dog, I said, because he was standing on my foot and staring with mournful awe up my nose (the man, not the dog) and the silence was getting uncomfortable. 'Do you really think so? Really?' he said.

Yes. No. Absolutely. As dogs go, that's a really, really good one. It has everything you could want in a dog.

He beamed (not the dog). 'That's wonderful. Thank you. Thank you. You've made my day. You really have.' Which gives you some indication of the quality of life in the country.

The reason I don't get out and about to restaurants outside

London is because you have to take a quantum drop in standards (can a quantum drop, or do they always leap?). Anyway, it is a giant step down. I suppose I could just make allowances and have double standards, but that's not fair. And actually, when knife meets fork, lunch is lunch wherever you eat it. A view is nice – but you can't chew it. The few places that are worth writing about can already paper their walls with reviews and I don't want to go to Huddersfield to hammer some restaurant that wouldn't last a fortnight in Battersea.

The reason that our cuisine is so capital-based is mostly historical. It is the opposite of France, where you eat better in the country than the city because they have a self-sufficient, peasant-based menu. We, on the other hand, ethnically cleansed all our peasants 200 years ago and our larder has been stocked by trade. London is the biggest port, with the biggest collection of merchants, and so has always kept the best board.

Still, the food renaissance, which is decades old in the city, is taking its time to get to the country. The reason for this is meanness. If you live in the country, it is all your fault. You are just tight-fisted or too poor to pay for dinner. I am sorry, but it's the truth. There is a legion of bright, imaginative chefs who would love to get out of the smoke to where the rents are cheap and the rooms are airy, to grow their own veg and encourage local producers – but the customers aren't up to it. Any rural restaurant that cooks half-decent food has to rely on London trade and tourism. As long as you lot in the tweed trilbys continue to look at a supreme of chicken costing £10 and say, 'I can get a whole one in the cash'n'carry for £3.50', you're not going to get a decent meal out.

Stow-on-the-Wold

Through the miracle of printing, let me whisk you to a gentle fold in the Cotswolds and the soft, lyrically ageless, honey-coloured hell that is Stow-on-the-Wold. Just say it: Stow-on-the-Wold. It's like having a mouthful of the butteriest, sugariest, sucky-glutinous fudge. Stow-on-the-Wold on a Sunday fair takes your breath away, makes you want to hug yourself, wear a cravat, sell your bijou flat in Fulham and move right here, right now. And then set yourself on fire in the market square as a beacon for those who might be foolish enough to follow. Of all the terrible knick-knacky, home-made, detestable places I've seen in this country, Stow takes the biscuit. It will sell you the biscuit first, made from an ancient Gloucestershire granny recipe using only organic pixie nuts.

Where to start? Ah, let's start over there in the organic-food shop with fancy craft den attached. The crafty-wafty shoppy-woppy sells pottery table fountains in runny, pastel iced-cookie colours. I know, I know. How have you ever lived without one? They're £100 each, and together they tinkle like a hymn to incontinence. But the sheer, naked, full-on, peeing nastiness of them isn't the thing that sends you reeling, it's the notices telling you what not to do. Fourteen of them (I counted). Smoking, of course. Eating. Drinking. Babies. Touching. Breaking. Spitting. Loitering. But my favourite is: 'Only serious inquiries, thank you.' Or maybe it was 'sincere'. That boggled beyond Gordian unboggling. How could anyone conceivably be either serious or sincere about portable, moist, plug-in pottery ornaments?

I was brought here by Jeremy Clarkson. It's his neck of the

woods – and it needs to be wrung. He not only chose but paid to live hereabouts. They all know him. 'Hello Jeremy,' they say (even the ones with Alzheimer's). 'You're Jeremy Clarkson, aren't you?' Sitting in the only place you're allowed to drink coffee and smoke simultaneously (hotel garden, residents only, unless you're local hero Clarkson), I pointed out that nothing, but nothing, could make this place worse. It had an unbeatable royal flush of horror. And then the Morris men started.

We escaped to a pub in a nearby village.

Country pubs are buried deep in the collective cerebellum, right at the back in the oldest, black-beamed, rustic bit of our brains. We have a country-pub node that feeds sentimental, Edwardian, Wind-in-the-Willows, cloth-cap-and-tankard, ready-rubbed-shag twaddle into our heads to the sound of Percy Grainger. It's impossible to have been born and bred in this country and be dispassionate about pubs. You know they're foul, but you'd die in a ditch to save them. Even New Labour is trying to pass a bill to stop them renaming the Turk's Head the Slug and Stripper.

Sunday lunch in a country pub is one of those things Englishmen with unspeakable tropical diseases in distant jungles hallucinate about just before they die. And this is the pub they dream of. It's perfect in every particular. Hunting prints. Cross-eyed stuffed Reynards on the yellow-stone walls. Inglenooks a gogo. And things growing all over it. There's a garden with barrows planted with flowers. Everything is so exactly right that it's quite obviously a base for invading Martians.

And the lunch was a perfect pub lunch, just the way you imagine it when you've got a temperature. Roast beef that tastes like it has been cut off the bottom of the Morris men's pantomime horse, Yorkshire pudding like dry rot, kedgeree that's hunt-the-fish and the colour of Chinese cowardice, sticky-toffee pudding, and beers that sound like characters from P.G. Wodehouse. 'Ah, Hook Norton, glad you could make it. Do you know Beamish and Tolly Cobbold? Marston is in the gents.' It all cost nothing, or next to a metropolitan nothing.

We happily watched the weekend locals self-consciously talking greenfly in their stiff Country Casuals cords and Viyella shirts, everyone trying as hard as possible to be a character from a 1950s Shell poster, as if the whole thing were being recorded for posterity; as if they were the ghosts of posterity, and 'contemporary' meant chaps you did National Service with and a joke that happened to art. You see, that's why I could never live in the country. I wouldn't have the stamina to keep up the continual collective pretence, the delusion, that all this was normal.

Yorkshire

You may have noticed that I'm not a great lover of the mud, blood and incest bits of this island – the outside animal toilet we generally refer to as 'the country'. But one of the few pieces of undeveloped suburb that I feel a slight stirring for is the North Yorkshire moors, that thick wedge that languishes to the east of the A1 either side of the precipitous road from Thirsk to Scarborough. I like it despite myself, despite my finer aesthetic best intentions. It's a place where the landscape still holds the upper hand. People live with it, not on it.

It's quite unlike the sentimental cuteness of the Cotswolds, or the hideous good taste and greed that have made Surrey and Cheshire a fitted landscape. Here, property prices and land values haven't wreaked their polished, coy preciousness. The moors are husbanded intensely, not intensively. Livings are scraped, not ploughed. And a walker can still get dangerously lost – though, sadly, not enough of them do.

The moors haven't yet acquired those nick-nack names that infantilise the Dales to the west: Last of the Summer Wine Country, Herriot Country, Hovistry and Nick Berryville. This is a place of violated abbeys and lonely, sodden estates, where squat, gorgon-grey Georgian piles hunch with a gasping, grim depression.

I've been staying at the same hotel there, on and off, for more than a decade and have often toyed with a review, though self-interest and the fact that I'm likely to return have held me back. I do, though, want to dwell on breakfast. I've been meaning to write about hotel breakfasts for ages.

'Breakfast is from 7am to 9.30am,' I'm told firmly. Isn't

9.30am a bit, well, scoutishly enthusiastic? I mean, it is Sunday. 'Well, I'm afraid the dining-room closes at 9.30am. So we can't serve breakfast after that, can we?' This is the sort of brain-shrivelling logic that seems to be the mission belief of every rural service enterprise. So, at five to nine, I blearily drag the Sunday papers and my comfort blanky into the dining-room to be confronted by a scurry of waitresses dressed in the sort of uniforms that even Escoffier would have considered passé. Isn't there a law preventing managements from humiliating their staff with cruel and unnatural hats – in this case, nineteenth-century Parisian prostitutes' garters worn as head tourniquets?

I never cease to be amazed by hotel breakfasts. They're not a meal so much as a pilgrimage. Catholics go to Compostela, Hindus to the Ganges and Muslims to Mecca, but the English go to breakfast. It has nothing to do with hunger or sustenance, or even pleasure. It's a sacrament, a litany of belonging. Hotel breakfast is, corporeally and metaphysically, truly the Full English.

My reverie on the matter of breakfast was deepened by the appearance of Alain de Botton, the cleverest man in the world. Inexplicably, the sight of him always reminds me of that jingle from *Patience*: 'If that young man expresses himself in terms too deep for me, why, what a singularly deep young man that deep young man must be.'

He pulled up a pew and we both chose the unabridged 1666 memorial menu. It was called something like The Wensleydale Chainsaw Hog Massacre (£2 supplement) and was like fighting your way through the gastronomic adaptation of *Lord of the Flies*. That's the other thing about the Full English: it's piggy pelmanism. How many fatty, oinky ingredients can you get on one plate? No other meal slices up a single victim quite so psychotically. What arrives is bacon, sausage, black pudding, kidney (sheep's), egg, potato brick, mushrooms and, by way of decoration, a crumpled, weeping tomato, which looks like nothing so much as an overenthusiastic porcine vasectomy.

Nobody sane would ever consider cooking, let alone eating, all this at home. It only exists in that national chapel of remembrance, the country-hotel dining-room. And it's only consumed among a silent congregation of other Englishmen at prayer, who mutter 'I vow to thee my country' as they slap on the Colman's for added tears of gratitude. The Full English fits with a dribbling, farty, bulldog bellicosity on one side of the breakfast menu, while on the other cowers the weedy Continental: a flaky bun, a smear of jam, some bowel-loosening fruit and Swiss bird seed. Nothing so completely encapsulates the Anglo-Saxon view of abroad – and foreigners in general. There is in the Full English the echo of 'Cry God for Harry' at Agincourt, the volley at Fontenoy and the flutes and drums of Waterloo.

It is as close as most of us will ever get to ancestor-worshipping cannibalism.

As ever, it's the locals that prevent my liking of this place from growing into love. Later, I was buttonholed by a drunk local who looked like a square Toby jug. 'Enjoying it up here, are you?' He waved his little handle expansively as if he'd personally knitted Yorkshire. 'Best place in t'world. Finest place in t'universe. I pity God for having to live in heaven. Where do you live?' London, actually. And you just know what's coming next. That look of ineffable pity, seasoned with moron's contempt, from a bumpkin whose sole interest in the rest of creation is to find confirmation that he is, indeed, the luckiest bugger alive. 'Oh, dear, dear. No, no,' he said with lashings of smug. 'I could never live in London.'

Happily, I was able to reply with just the faintest metropolitan sneer: you know what, you're absolutely right.

Leeds

I have a soft spot for Leeds. Actually – why lie? – I don't have a soft spot for Leeds. But a nice thing happened to me once in Leeds; one of those things that men's magazines call you up about and ask 'When was the first time …?' and magistrate's courts refer to as acts of gross indecency. It happened first in Leeds, and for that I'm grateful. But not grateful enough to want to go back or take her phone number.

I was induced back to Leeds by Jeremy Clarkson – not, I should hasten to make clear, for the same reason. Yorkshire is Clarkson's playpen. It's where he hoves from and, like all Yorkshiremen, he is inexplicably, contrarily, fact-defyingly proud of himself for being himself.

Up here, they speak a sort of personal-column, syllable-saving shorthand – 'Ah bah't t'at? Ah do t' tha'?' – of which Jeremy's particularly proud. 'I can do it,' he chants, 'and you can't. When they hear your big girl's vowels, they're going to beat you up because you're a soft southern poof. They're going to bang your head on the pavement and say Wa' th' f' th' mo' h' th', or something like that.'

It's a thought that gives him vast pleasure all the way up the M1. 'They're going to kick your head in. They're going to crack you one. They're going to give you Chinese burns and flick your ears,' he raps out in a sort of rhythmless macarena. He always does this when we travel north of Notting Hill.

Leeds has two things to attract the inquisitive visitor: the Royal Armoury and Harvey Nichols. Nobody goes to the Armoury. Everybody goes to Harvey Nichols – and they're so proud of it. 'We've got the Harvey Nichols,' they say with that nod that implies it's a wing of the Vatican or the World Bank. It seems impolite to explain that it's just a shop, and that everywhere south of Nottingham has something similar. You see, up here, a shop is a converted front room run by Ronnie Barker and David Jason. And a shop that sells clothes is a double novelty, because clothes aren't bought, they're handed down or left by dead people.

Jeremy insisted that we stay at his favourite hotel. 'It is ...' drops a gear ... 'the best hotel in the world.' Which only goes to prove that travel narrows the mind. It's a perfectly nice little place, made out of an old warehouse on a canal. 'Talk about Venice and their canals. We can give you real canals. Italian ones just have nancy gondolas floating in them. We've got whole fitted kitchens, Honda Civics, condoms and Manchester United fans floating in ours.'

The thing I did like about the hotel was that each room had its own fishing rod. You could just lean out of the window and cast. Which must be nice for visiting forensic pathologists.

We had our dinner (the one in the evening) in the small restaurant, which had a Michelin star. OOooOOoohh! The food was good. A nice tomato jelly 'scented' with basil, embalming lobster, crab and sour cream. A stew of salt cod and clams, with something called 'continental parsley', which I expect is flat leaf. ('We'll have some more of that nice continental parsley, *garçon*.') Then steak *bordelais* and lamb with savoy cabbage and celeriac-infused roasting *jus*. Pudding was handmade lemon ice cream, a chocolate plate or 'Chris's famous crêpes suzette', which beggared the definition of fame.

The customers were – how can I put this without appearing rude? – utterly, fabulously ridiculous. Tossed-up, P&Q-minding, pinky-wagglers. The manager was a miracle of avuncular civility, the sort of master of occasions we just don't get in the south any more. These absurd folk want their money's worth, which means a personal touch akin to molestation. He was a joy to watch as he flambéed crêpes, uttering a stream of mine-host small talk.

When we sat down, Jeremy asked for an ashtray, which we were given. After half an hour, a truly horrendous woman, with a face that should have been attached to the prow of an arctic whaler and hair that looked like a fairground hook-the-bottle prize, came over and, in her best aspirant voice, said: 'Do you mind not smoking while I'm enjoying my meal?' Fine, we said. When she'd finished her 'meal', Jeremy lit up again and she was back, this time with the husband. 'Don't be funny,' she said. 'Don't be funny.' Both Jeremy and I are funny for a living, and I'm perfectly sure we weren't being.

Then the husband, who I swear was three foot tall and ninety-six, went completely, frothingly, berserkly nuclear. No amount of Harvey Nichols and scented *jus* and continental bloody parsley was going to civilise the slum out of him. 'Outside!' he roared. 'Outside! I'll do you. You think you're so big!' (NB: Jeremy is very, very big.) And then this little, white-haired nonagenarian poked Jeremy in the face.

Poked hard. Poked like he wanted to use his nose as a pencil sharpener but didn't have the right glasses.

Anyway, it all ended in tears. Mine mostly. I laughed until I wept. Mine host came over and looked at the ceiling as if he were David Livingstone having a bad missionary day, and said: 'I'm sorry, Mr Gill, but what can you do with these people?' And we chatted. And the words pearls and swine came up more than once. And then he did something I've never ever seen a waiter do before. It was fabulous. A very drunk street-girl person bowled in and rocked round the tables begging a cigarette. As I gave her one, he rushed over on Mach 2 casters, grabbed her, aimed her and ran at the door as if to use her head to open it. There was a bang, a squawk, and he reappeared, all tie-straightening and smiley bonhomie. It was like something out of a Charlie Chaplin movie.

Jeremy, though, was still smoking from his encounter with

the beau monde of Leeds. 'You weren't much help, were you? He poked me and you did nothing. And you smoke twice as much as I do.'

I know, I said. It's just that I was waiting for you to do that accent thing and bond. And you did tell me not to open my smarmy southern mouth.

Isle of Man

We had been on the Isle of Man (or la Isla del Hombre, as we would be calling it if the Argies had been a bit more adventurous) for an hour before I realised what was actually wrong with the place. It's in black and white.

And slightly grainy. And flickering at the edges.

There are a few places in the world that have managed to slip through a crack in the space-time continuum, or fallen off the back of the history lorry to lie amnesiac in the road to progress. And l'Isle d'Homme, as Maurice Chevalier might have jocundly called it, is caught permanently in the pork-pie jelly of 1957.

I was only four, but this island is exactly like my first memories of the forgotten decade: pebble dash and bunion pads, grimy shop windows exhibiting one faded thing on a paper doily (or, occasionally, a pyramid of one thing). It has 1950s weather – dreary, purposeless rain that's just clouds letting themselves go – and it smells of boiled washing, damp wallpaper and fried food. It all came back to me like nasal drip, scraped butter papers and bags of recycled string. I loved it.

'Why are you walking like that?' asked the Blonde. It's my Start-rite shoes and little lamb's-wool reins, I lisped. Quick, get me to something digital, I'm regressing.

Die Menscheninsel, as Dr Goebbels fondly remembered it, is a tax haven, and follows the international law of tax havens, which is that the collective rich will invariably make for a nastier and more miserable colony than the poor. It's God's little joke on the graspingly wealthy that they are forced to live together in places such as Monaco and Bermuda. What is weird about Man is that, even though its main industry is money (laundering, pressing, altering and mending), everyone you actually see is Benny from *Crossroads* or Benny in drag.

While we were there, they announced that the island would be having an alarm drill on Sunday. What's the alarm for, I asked tentatively. 'In case we're invaded.'

How terminally bored would a megalomaniac have to be before he got round to invading the Isle of Man? This was a prison camp in the war, and it is still the last seriously draconian wee country left in western Europe. They're exempt from open borders and EU immigration, their money isn't good anywhere else, and only reluctantly and recently have they been forced to give up public flogging and hunting homosexuals with dogs.

The theatre in Douglas is showing *The Witches of Eastwick*, which is bound to be a hit because they think it's a true story. This is the most pixilated place outside the sixteenth century. There are bits of road where you have to say 'Hello, fairies' out loud. I was told of a visiting American financier who refused, on the grounds that it was silly and humiliating. The taxi driver slammed on the brakes and wouldn't continue. What happened? I asked. 'Well, they sat there for an hour.' Then what? 'The fairies came and beat the crap out of the American.' I reckon the alarm drill isn't about invasion at all, it's in case there's a mass break-out and they all make a run for the mainland.

I saw a Manx cat. I think they must eat the tails, because frankly, there's not much else. The Isle of Man is BED – Before Elizabeth David. The vegetables on sale were extras from *Monty Python and the Holy Grail*. The butchers wear leather aprons, ice-hockey masks and straw boaters. The fish comes out of the sea ready-kippered – Sellafield is just across the way.

When I asked to be taken to the best restaurant on Uomo, as Giorgio Armani inveterately calls it, I was met with a hollow, toothless laugh and told to stick to deep-fried cat tail and grated turnip. Finally, someone named one, but only to say I shouldn't under any circumstances go there. It was an odd-shaped room in a hotel on the seafront in Douglas. Every building with a roof on Man is some sort of hotel for the annual pilgrimage of organ donors who come for the ritual human sacrifice and fairy propitiation that are the TT races.

There was a bar with an ostentatious display of novelty brandy and single-malt bottles, which is the design motif of the provincial money, competitive drinking and wife-swapping that make up rural culture. The menu was short on dishes, but long on ingredients – everything had one thing too many, in order to make the food look sophisticated and to justify the price. How much don't you want to eat smoked goose breast, *foie gras* mousse, grape chutney and the inevitable emetic of truffle oil?

I started with pan-seared scallops, crab risotto cake with garlic and chilli butter (so 2001 that I could barely keep the metropolitan smirk from cutting my head in half). And then I had to swallow it – the smirk, that is. The queenies were beguilingly sweet and fresh, the crab risotto sharp and precise. It was a well considered and impressively made dish.

For main course, I had a tranche of turbot, cooked perfectly plain. Turbot is one of the great four royal fish, and on most Fridays it's my favourite. But I rarely order it, because it's so crucifyingly disappointing if it isn't absolutely in its moment, still wet from the sea. This was the real thing and worth the airfare all on its own.

When I got home, a deeply liberal friend said, 'You didn't go to the Isle of Man?', as if it were like supporting the military junta in Burma. 'You know there aren't any blacks on the Isle of Man? None at all,' she added, with exquisite distaste.

Well, of course there aren't. Why would there be? What black multi-millionaire is going to say: 'Honey, let's go into tax exile on the Isle of Man. The weather's foul, the food's medieval, it's covered in suicidal motorists and honky folk who believe in fairies and whip each other?' For God's sake, they only managed to get the Italians there at gunpoint.

Scotland

There is, in the lowland Scots argot, a place called your calf country, the land of your childhood. Its meaning is more than just geographical. It's the metaphysical, emotional home of your first tastes, smells, sounds, sensations – the place you always return to, if not physically, then in your imagination. It sets the frame within which all experiences are arranged, and the template against which they are measured. The idea of a calf country is a sort of romantic, Presbyterian Freudianism, and the more I learn and understand about food and the way we eat, the more convinced I am that the predilections and prejudices of our palate are laid down before we lose our milk teeth. My calf country is Scotland. I mention this only to make clear that I'm not entirely an impartial eater.

You will eat worse in Scotland than in any other country in the world that isn't suffering a visit from one or more of the Riders of the Apocalypse. As a tourist, finding something decent to pop in your gob is generally colon abuse. It is – and I don't say this lightly – even worse than Wales. Public food is caught either in the parsimony and rolling boil of the 1950s or in the assumed anaesthetic of post-pub. In the big cities and American-patronised country hotels, there is an expensive, raised-pinky cuisine, where the menus read like National Trust brochures and everything comes spiced with a twist of myth and a pinch of tradition. This sort of och-aye-the-nouvelle cuisine is beyond contempt. I may well instigate my own mini clearance of the next kitchen that offers me tomatoes stuffed with haggis, or drappit scones scattered with seasonal fruit and whisky-infused cream, or the latest twist on Atholebrose, flavoured with cardamom. Add to this a raggedy clan of organic salad-bar owners who sell baps with the consistency of the Stone of Scone – or indeed the scones of stone – and zodiac-specific bean salads in the bizarre belief that, because some folk called the Celts once lived here, it must be innately healthy and spiritual.

And yet, I could start that paragraph again by saying: you can eat better in Scotland than anywhere else in northern Europe – you just have to be invited. Porridge made with pinhead oats; cartwheels of fatty black pudding and long bacon; small, loch-caught brown trout; partridge and grouse; real mutton with onion sauce; saddles of venison and rowan jelly; red stag's liver and sweetbreads; wild mushrooms; cullen skink (smoked haddock and potato soup to you); fat raspberries, warm scones and shortbread; thick farls of oatcakes and creamy cheese. Scotland has, bar nowhere, the finest, most varied and naturally unsullied raw ingredients on or in the earth, the air and the sea. Then there are the ones I never got round to: Angus and Highland beef; herring and lobster; scallops and crab; blue hares and neaps; and, of course, haggis.

My favourite ingredient of all is simply the water. There's certainly plenty of it. Soft and crisp and cold and expertly diluted. I never get over being able to drink straight from the earth. And Scots water makes the best tea.

But, as I said, these are the tastes and textures of my calf country. In every mouthful, there are associations of family, heritage and that overwrought sense of belonging that is the leitmotif of the émigré. It wouldn't taste the same to a Serb or a Swazi or a Surreyist.

What's the collective noun for ravens? Too late, I've already googled it. It's a conspiracy or an unkindness. For those of you who guessed a murder or a clamour – close, but no carrion. That's crows and rooks.

Now, a number of things strike me about this (or a crumple,

which is the collective noun for things that strike). First, who says so? Who decides on collective nouns? Is there an international collective-noun collective? And would they be a baptism of collective-noun compilers or a moniker? Did you know, for instance, that it's deemed a stir of teaspoons, but a beatitude of apostle spoons? Or that it's a depilation of ostriches, a frot of poodles, a curmudgeon of rubber bands, a stride of scissors, a tackle of Post-its, a lie of condoms (unused) or a lay (used)? No, you didn't, because I made them all up. They are a merkin: the collective noun for a bogus collection of collective nouns.

I've been stalking in Scotland for the past two weeks, and I saw what I now know to be a conspiracy or unkindness. It's very rare to see more than a pair of ravens, so I wondered if they had a collective noun.

My annual stay in the Highlands is the finest, most invigorating, rewarding, refreshing, hugely fun time I spend all year. Scotland makes up about one third of the mass of mainland Britain. Of the 60-odd million of us, only 5 million live north of the border. Of those, 4.5 million live in the central belt, between Glasgow and Edinburgh. That leaves an expanse of bog, heather, granite and black loch inhabited by just half a million people. Those who live here haven't so much opted out as opted in to being a figure in a landscape.

Take three of the men I went walking with. They looked after the ponies that carried down the stags. None of them was a Scot, but each had escaped to something. Bill, a Yorkshireman, had spent twenty years in a McCain chip factory. Whenever he reached some high point where he could get telephone reception, he'd call his old workmates. 'I'm at the top of a mountain in Scotland with two ponies. What are you doing?'

Mick had left a skilled job as a juvenile-salmon inoculator. 'You turn them on their backs and inject them with a cocktail of antibiotics. You could do thousands in a day. Trouble is, you can only miss and inject yourself twice. Third time, you die of anaphylactic shock. And did you know, it takes three tons of ground-up wild fish to feed two tons of farmed fish?'

And then there was Nick, a quiet Australian, who came to the Highlands to get away from a koala hospital in Queensland. A koala hospital? 'Yup.' Did you get a lot of patients? 'Hundreds.' What do they suffer from mostly? 'Chlamydia.' You're joking? How do they get it? 'From people.' Oh my God. Australians will do anything. 'No, they have a dormant virus that's brought on by stress, which is caused by contact with people.' How do you treat it? 'We put them down.' No? 'You can't give koalas antibiotics. Their digestions are too delicate. I guess there won't be any koalas in Queensland in five years.' Wiped out by a sexually transmitted disease caught by simply looking at Australians. Isn't God weird? 'Yup.'

There's famously nowhere to eat in the Highlands. We were in a small, hunched, granite town with a petrol station, a good butcher and fabulous tweed shop where I make a pilgrimage every year. There is a hotel that sells brown food. Brown is the preferred colour of Scottish hospitality. Brown furniture. Brown food. Brown drink. Brown water. And their conversation is usually pretty broon.

So you could have knocked me down with a well-placed punch to the solar plexus when someone recommended I visit the delicatessen. The Highlands and delicatessens go together like whisky and Coca-Cola. And when I saw it, I must say my hackles rose. I bridled. I had a queeny moment. Here was a neat, modern, brightly lit Fulham deli selling thirty-four types of froggy cheese, a dozen olive oils, exotic mustard and the über-McMissionary of pan-global Mediterraneanism: balsamic bloody vinegar.

We sat down at little wooden tables among the gossiping women and ordered sausage and mash. I started with tomato and lentil soup and we shared a plate of hot-smoked salmon salad, both grudgingly fine. And the sausage and mash was actually very good: a nice local venison banger and tweedy potato. For pudding, we had a clungy, sputoid vanilla slice that was like eating sweet Magimixed maggots, and a cup of tea served in a fiendishly twee little pot arrangement that was the lid of the cup. So you poured the entire contents of one receptacle into the other. Ridiculous.

I know what it was that made me momentarily resent all this. In my annual, touristy, Landseer-eyed way, I didn't think it belonged here. It represented all the things I come to the Highlands to escape. But then, I also make annual jokes about the absence of public food for visitors. This place is a quantum leap, a brave and daring act of faith and taste, which I wouldn't notice in Battersea but which, in all fairness, I should applaud here.

They've painted little bons mots on the walls, which set the tone. Above us was 'A meal without wine is like a day without sunshine', already something of an irony up here, where gay Phoebus can leave you radiantly teetotal from November to March. Could I have a glass of wine, inquired my companion. 'Ooh, I'm afraid not,' apologised the waitress. 'We're not licensed for that sort of thing.'

Ah, the authentic voice of ma haemland. A glum of Scots.

Cornwall

I pulled up in the Ford breeder wagon, the back stuffed with a hundred thou' in potential school fees, private medical insurance, peanut-butter sandwiches, inflatable swans and four hours of 1960s greatest hits on CD, and asked a passing nine-year-old for directions. He paused for a moment, scanning the ineffable, timeless, rolling majesty of Bodmin Moor (his birthright, paid for through my nose), fixed me with a clear, serious eye that belied his tender years and replied: 'Go away.' Ah yes, the voice of the countryman. We're back again. It's the happy, carefree, calloo-calay summer week in Cornwall.

The house, when we finally found it, was a bit of a shock. I would say surprise, but there's nothing in the country that can surprise me any more. Having been gazumped on our usual house, we'd scrambled around the back pages of conservative magazines and found this. No double-glazing salesman could have been more plausible than the lady on the phone: 'A beautiful villa, family home, that comfortably sleeps ten.'

Well, up to a point. It was a villa only in the strictest Edwardian, Pooterish sense: a semi-detached, meanly double-fronted little house. And I suppose the Reichstag bunker could have been described as a family home in its later years.

It slept ten only in the sense that prisons built for 300 can sleep 800. It certainly couldn't feed ten, there being no pot or pan that could hold more than four medium-sized potatoes. The best I can say for the place is that it would have made an entertaining museum of cracks and chips. I have never seen such an elaborate and diverse filigree of decrepitude. Strangers' homes have an aura that seeps into you by osmosis. This one was terminally depressing, from the leatherette-bound one-a-month Hardys and Dickenses in the lounge and the complete paperback set of Georgette Heyer in the bedroom to the wretchedly genteel family portraits. And there was an aspidistra on a plinth in the window of the drawing-room (children not allowed). Actually, the aspidistra was such a monumental cliché that it made the whole place risible. I heard the ghost of George Orwell cackle.

Outside, it was all typically Cornwall. The man next door's hobby was electric motors. He had a dizzying variety and spent happy hours listening to them. Cornwall has all the rural virtues – thousands of bungalows and a miraculous demographic that somehow excludes middle age. The population is either all under fourteen or over sixty. Cornwall is not a place anyone comes from. It's a place they end up in when they are too bad-tempered and sociophobic to live in society.

The Cornish (or those retired ironmongers from Birmingham and junior-school teachers from Leeds who, having bought a cap and smock, pass as Cornish) are irritably trying to mould themselves, like a Blue Peter project, into a real country. What is it with wannabe Celts that makes them such prickly neighbours? The Cornish papers had teach-yourself-Cornish lessons. What can you say about a place that wants to grow up into an imitation Wales? Wanting to be like Wales is like being a limbo dancer of low expectations.

Gastronomically, of course, it already is Wales. For my own information I wanted to settle the question of the Cornish pasty once and for all. Is it or isn't it a food? Now, I know that some people say that friends of friends or distant relatives have actually enjoyed one, but I think these stories are apocryphal. I actually ate nine in a day. Well, when I say 'ate', I bit them in the way a dachshund might bite a line-up of particularly smelly postmen. And I can tell you that they're definitely, categorically not supposed to be eaten. My guess is that they were some ancient Cornish craft, the purpose of which has been lost in the mists of time.

My great pleasure in this week is cooking. I never get to cook any more, and here I can cook for lots of people. Not dinner parties – I'll never cook a dinner party again – but proper food, eaten at dinner time. I know from experience that you have to bring your own victuals to Cornwall. And you can forget fish. If you want Cornish fish, go to Barcelona.

The Cornish – no, let's be accurate: the people who have lived in Cornwall long enough for their neighbours to forget that they're actually retired schoolteachers from Warrington – call us summer visitors emmets. It's derogatory, naturally, and means ants. I'm thinking of having T-shirts made next year, saying: 'Emmets on tour – shag your women and drink your beer.'

Truth to tell, they're the ants. We're greenfly – we sit in long queues and get milked.

Tourism is Cornwall's more profitable fishing industry. Who in their right mind would go out in a little boat and get cold and wet for dabs, when they can hang around in a nice dry smock and sell seashell kirby grips for cash? Now you would have thought that, having murdered their first fishing industry, the born-again Corns would be a little careful with their second. But get a load of this. There's a big fishmonger's in Padstow on the quay. Should be good. The front of the shop is a depressing mortuary slab of peppered mackerel fillets and the sort of prawns you'd have to take a day trip to the Pacific to get fresh. But in the back there are tanks of live lobsters and crabs. Wonderful, I'll go and choose a couple of cocks.

A surly boy stopped me. 'That'll be 20p.'

Any crab for 20p? 'No mate, it's 20p if you want to go and look at the crabs.' Hang on, let me get this straight. You're trying to fleece me of money to look at your stock? 'No, I'm charging you 20p to view the crabs.' Well, I just held my sides and howled. He looked stony. Pray, what other shop in Britain would charge you to browse? Sonny, has it ever occurred to you why you're sitting in a smelly fish shop next to a plastic tub of crabs instead of on the prow of a fishing boat like your dad and grandfather? Does 'exploitation of natural resources' ring any bells? He looked even stonier. Do you not think that if you cynically exploit the fish-buying public they may well go the same way as the fish? He didn't. Ah, born and bred in Cornwall, were you? Yes, I thought so.

Despite it all, this is still my favourite week of the year. The joy of feeding the kids whitebait for the first time – 'All of it? Eyes and everything?' – and watching Ali, four, shamble across the vast sands of Daymer Bay, head down.

'What's the matter, darling?'

'I've got lazy legs, dada, they can't do anything. They can't swim or climb or hop. All the girls run faster. They're just lazy. Give me a piggy-back?' Bless.

Elizabeth David

Two appalling things happened to British food in the twentieth century. One was the Second World War, the other was Elizabeth David. Of the two, Elizabeth David was probably the worse. She might have been avoided if it had not been for Hitler.

Rationing had a devastating effect on British food. It went on until 1954. Rationing destroyed the heritage of our national cuisine quite as efficiently as the Luftwaffe flattened Coventry. In the same vein, where we built horrible ersatz boxes to replace smashed medieval cities, so we also served up horrible ersatz food. A generation of women grew up judging the quality of their board against their ability to make do. The relay of mothers teaching their daughters was swept aside, and in its place we got the beginning of the ghastly, uniquely British parsimony, the 'instead of' recipe: use margarine instead of butter; use a chicken instead of a duck, if you cannot afford sole, any white fish will do.

For the first time in our history we had civil servants stocking our larders and organising our kitchens. A whole industry of stretch and compromise spewed out of the Ministry of Food. Wartime women had to forget six hundred years of cooking and learn to cater. There is a world of difference between cooking and catering. Wartime brides pretended to cut iced cardboard cakes. Factory workers came home to a nourishing plateful of Woolton pie, a dish named after the food minister that so exemplified the drabness of rationing that it became a grim national joke. (Woolton pie: a stew of root vegetables covered in a white sauce, with or without cheese, smothered in mashed potato.) This is a recipe invented by committee.

Britain lived for twenty years under committee catering and never recovered. The values of food changed for ever. British housewives expected things that were not rationed, like indigenous vegetables, to be cheap, and bought quantity rather than quality. But ingredients that were rationed or only available on the black market gained a mythic value out of all proportion to their gastronomic worth, so sugar was used in medicinal quantities, and old butter papers were kept in the fridge, like white fivers in a bank vault, to be carefully laid on dishes of peas or boiled potatoes.

I remember it, it was surreal. Like saying you cannot have real butter on your sprouts, so here is the word butter laid on top. When I first started to cook, I would always run my finger around the inside of a cracked eggshell to get out the last dribble of albumen. I did it because my grandmother did it. She did it because eggs had been so precious that the possibility of even the smallest waste was truly sinful. I would still rather drop a plate than an egg. The twisted values of rationing have travelled three generations.

As we were fighting a war, guns were necessarily more important than butter. Rationing and the 'make-do' ethos were a necessity. Elizabeth David was not. The position Elizabeth David holds in the kitchens of the nation is disproportionate to her value as a food writer. Her Mediterranean books are used like dictionaries or encyclopedias. If you want the definitive word on *coq au vin* or what to do with a red mullet, then the beatified David will give you a definitive answer. The absurdity of this genuflecting reverence was shown by the price paid at auction for her kitchen equipment: £80 for a wooden spoon.

Elizabeth David came at a tired grey nation out of the sun. Her books caught a great yearning for colour and warmth and exotic flavours. She spoke of a style of life that seemed a million miles from the drab, empty shops of provincial Britain, where a treat was a tin of watery ham or a banana. On a deeper level, she spoke to a country that was desperate for a new start, to do away with the old order of things. We had elected the first Labour government and wanted to put behind us the old net curtain, Victorian sideboard, waistcoat-and-chain Britain. Being an island worked both ways: it kept the bloody foreigners out, but it also made European food seem sophisticated and modern, the taste of the future.

In the introduction to *Mediterranean Food*, her first book, published in 1950, David quotes Marcel Boulestin: 'Peace and happiness begin geographically where garlic is used in cooking' (actually garlic grows wild in Scotland). She goes on to write lists of countries and ingredients as exciting and foreign to the average British cook as the Kama Sutra '... pimentoes, aubergines, tomatoes, olives, melons, figs and limes. The great heaps of shiny fish, silver, vermilion or tiger-striped ...' It goes on like this for paragraphs. This is the first purple beginnings of food pornography, now a vast, glossy industry. It is writing for people to salivate over, to have fantasies about. It is the sensation of gluttony without the peeling.

But surely the bare bones of her books, the recipes, are benchmarks? Unfortunately not. The first recipe in her first book is for pistou soup from Genoa. You boil French beans, potatoes and tomatoes, with salt and pepper, in three pints of water, adding a handful of vermicelli and a mush of garlic, tomato and basil, and there you are. I'm sorry, but if you were served that at a dinner party today, you would send it back. This is food as a metaphor, recipes as escapism, cookery books to be read in bed with a packet of chocolate wholemeal biscuits. Metaphor and simile are something food lends itself to. Elizabeth David's life was itself desperate when she wrote her Mediterranean books. Her husband had left her after a short, unhappy marriage, and she had started to drink heavily. She ran to the Mediterranean and wrote. Her writing can be read as self-help, as a passionate therapy. It struck a chord in an unhappy and damaged country.

Her books were not the best, but they were the first. Today there are five cookery books published a week, about half of them devoted to Mediterranean food. Under a dozen a year will deal with indigenous food. If Elizabeth David's *Italian Food* landed on an editor's desk tomorrow, it would barely raise an eyebrow. Certainly, the recipes would seem immensely pedestrian. But even after all these years, to say anything even mildly critical about her in public is to court howls of protest. It is like saying Mother Teresa was a bad Catholic. The truth is, David was not a very good food writer by today's standards. Her vision of oily, garlicky and languid lunches on the terrace under a fig tree has led us directly to the horrible Euro-chameleon food we eat today.

David was a good travel writer of the Peter Mayle type, and an excellent journalist, but what we got from her was a handful of olive-stones compared with what we lost. I understand that this is a little like blaming Christopher Columbus for the state America is in today, but I do think it is time we stopped treating her books as if they were the best thing since garlic bread. That said, she did write one very useful book, and I bet it is the one most of you have not got: *Spices, Salt and Aromatics in the English Kitchen*. There are only five references to garlic in the index. It was published in 1970, and by then the damage was already done.

So what actually is the problem? What is wrong with the cooks in this country preferring pasta to potatoes? Why shouldn't we eat lasagne instead of cottage pie, drench everything in olive oil, eat anchovies instead of herring, know the names of fifteen sorts of foreign lettuce and sixteen ways to prepare a mango? After all, we can now get ingredients from the far corners of the globe within hours. The world is our oyster, clam, scallop and spiny lobster. Surely this is a good thing, and anyway wasn't British food always disgusting and unhealthy? Wasn't it all boiled to death and swimming in fat? The answer to the last question is a resounding no. British food was as unique and diverse as any in Europe. But our memories of it are collective and only stretch back to the time when food was poor and in short supply.

It is difficult to say succinctly what it is that makes one country's food different from another. Of course, you can taste it in an instant. Ingredients may easily travel across borders, and cooks are naturally inquisitive and experimental, but dishes remain fiercely national. Our kitchens are like our language, words are absorbed from all over the place. Some dishes, like some words, become fashionable and then fall into obscurity. But underneath there is a style, a character, that is identifiably our own. Two factors stand out as being nationally important: our position as a maritime trading and colonial nation, and our weather. Trade meant that from the Roman invasion the British have made foreign ingredients indigenous from chickens to rabbits, from apples to tea. The climate has meant that we have incomparably good grazing for livestock. Because we are so far north, there is a very long period between harvest and new season crops. This dictates that an awful lot of typically British food is preserved: ham, bacon, salt beef and mutton, smoked fish, pickles, jam, dried fruit, fruit cakes and potted meat and fish. The dishes we used to eat did not come down to us from the court or up to us from the peasantry, as they did in France or Italy, but from the country house and manor farm. British food is essentially middle-class, squire and parsons' food, deceptively simple, filling and almost always unpretentious. Carefully tended kitchen gardens and the British obsession for breeding and husbandry produce the finest varieties of meat, fruit and vegetables in the world. Every country has an indigenous fat that is the key to its cooking. Fat is the base taste. In Britain our fats were always animal: lard, dripping, goose fat, suet and butter. More than anything else, their loss in favour of oil for spurious reasons of health and snobbery has changed the taste of what we eat.

There is no heritage in this country of British food in

restaurants. Our cuisine is generally slow-cooked and made in family-sized dishes, not individual servings. An individual steamed pudding is a sad thing, an individual Yorkshire pudding is an abomination. Do you know what the difference is between a pork pie and pâté *en croute*? It's about £6.50 and a Conran catalogue of pretension.

The history of British food was made by women cooks. From Hannah Glasse through Elinor Fettiplace and Meg Dodds, from Eliza Acton and Mrs Beeton to Jane Grigson, British recipes have been cooked by women feeding their families for love. We have turned our backs on them to listen to a lot of French and Italian men who cook for profit.

If selling our gastronomic birthright for a mess of potage du jour was a good idea, then we are the only country in the civilised world that has seen fit to do it. There are not thousands of Sicilian women scouring the delicatessens of Palermo in search of suet to make their jam roly-poly. There are, however, women in Portsmouth filling their baskets with unripe peppers, parmesan and prosciutto.

The real problem is not just that we cook Italian food day in, day out, it is that we cook it so jolly badly. Part of the catering mentality that is left over from rationing in this country is the primary concern for economy. We as a nation expect a lot for our money. We spend less per capita on food than any of our European neighbours. Housewives try to cook dishes that may be cheap to put together in Milan or Rheims, but cost a lot in Bolton or Penzance. Take those two staples of Italian cooking, the tomato and sweet basil. The plum tomatoes that grow in the heat of Italy taste totally different from the forced-under-polythene ones that we get here. Most cooks who want something actually to taste of a tomato are reduced to using tins. Basil in Italy is a few pence a handful, it grows like a weed. Here we have to buy it by the sad little leaf. Consequently, robust peasant food tastes insipid and second-rate when it is prepared by urban foreigners.

The habit of cooking from recipe books that was learned during the war has continued. Housewives now cook recipes rather than ingredients. Again, we are unique in Europe for our addiction to self-help cookery books. Visit any Italian, French or Spanish kitchen and you'll be amazed at the absence of foodie porn. There is no Italian or French equivalent to Elizabeth David because cooks on the continent do their menu-planning in the market, not while reading women's magazines. We have a slavish reverence for pictures with instructions because we have never seen most of the things we eat made by anyone else. I bet 90 per cent of the food being prepared in kitchens up and down the country this week will have been here for less than a generation.

Because we have lost confidence and facility in the kitchen, raw ingredients have become frightening, disgusting and too complicated. We are terrified of getting our hands bloody or poisoning the boss. How much easier and safer to buy a packet of something that does not bear any resemblance to its origins; if it should make you throw up, you can always sue someone, it is not your responsibility. A whole generation of women are now defiantly proud of their complete inability to cook. We consume tons of committee-designed heat-and-eat meals, the contents and mechanics of which are as obscure and mysterious as the inside of a computer or a chicken. There is a generation of thrusting young families who can read a menu in three languages, but cannot write a recipe in their own.

British cooks graze round the world, trying a bit of this and a bit of that, never really becoming proficient at anything. Our kitchens are junkyards of unused pasta rollers, woks, tagines, dim sum baskets, raclette grills and sushi mats. We are tourists at our own dining-tables and, like tourists, we are being ripped off. As any chef will tell you, you get good by cooking one thing twenty times, not twenty things once.

Glynn Christian, the food writer (*The New Delicatessen Food Handbook*) and broadcaster, says: 'Of course, the British have always imported food from abroad. We are a maritime trading nation. Actually, the base tastes of our national cuisine date back to the Crusades. One of the biggest changes since the war has been the use of herbs as opposed to spices. The English used to spice things; if you think about old English food, you inevitably think of allspice and cinnamon and nutmeg, not basil and tarragon. The use of green clippings in everything is quite inappropriate. Most of the herbs we buy in supermarkets don't taste of much and they're used indiscriminately.

'Think of game: you don't want to muck around with hydroponic Mediterranean herbs, you want juniper and mace. British food ought to be about strong tastes: rosewater, all those wonderful dried fruits – raisins, sultanas and currants – that were used uniquely here. Because of our trading heritage, British cuisine was quite different from the insular peasant dishes you get across the Channel. Today, the dining tables in Calais and Dover are probably set much the same. I'd just much rather eat in Calais, where the food's original, rather than here, where it's a copy.'

To see how depressing food has become in this country, all one needs to do is visit a good butcher. I could not count the number of times I have written 'a good butcher' in articles about food, and each time I know that the majority of readers will interpret it as 'a good supermarket'. Good butchers are as rare as well-made chitterlings. Curnick's on the Fulham Road in London is a good butcher. Kevin, the head butcher, explains how his trade has not only shrunk, but the cuts of meat that people now cook have dwindled to a handful. 'I can't remember the last time I sold a Jacob's Ladder or a Flat Iron or an H-bone or, come to think of it, an oven buster. They're all wonderful cuts, they just need slower cooking. Of course, we sell yards of fillet; very good it is, too, but expensive. And loads of veal escalopes and chops. But all the stuff that we used to make when my dad was a butcher, there's no call for it now.

'I'd love to stock mutton, but I only get asked for it twice a year. I'd love to make faggots, but who's going to buy faggots in Fulham? Sometimes I wonder if people actually know what a cow looks like, they never ask for any of the fore-end cuts. Maybe they think it's a long, thin animal, like a dachshund, with a big bottom and no head. People always ask for lean meat; you can tell them the taste's in the fat until you're blue in the face. You know what I think is a shame, the fact that we have bred the best livestock in the world for more than two hundred years and now there's nobody who will eat it. All that work, all that care. If all that weren't bad enough, we've got the bloody EC to contend with.'

The EC and the regulators in our own ministries are busy finishing off what is left of British cuisine. Occasionally a piece of particularly amusing nannying legislation comes to the public's attention through the tabloid press, such as when is a *Wurst* a sausage, but most food law slips past without a by-your-leave. For instance, you cannot now buy a pork chop with a kidney; you cannot buy an ox heart to stuff, because all hearts have to be slashed; you cannot get fresh suet, the basis of so many savoury and sweet puddings, because it is illegal to move the carcass with fat inside. Chickens can only be sold eviscerated, which halves their shelf life – a gutted chicken goes off much faster than a whole one. You cannot even buy the giblets separately to make gravy, because the packaging would cost more than the bits.

Europe is passing health laws that specifically eradicate our food, while the French and the Italians fight ferociously to set up *appellations contrôlées* to protect their own specialist ingredients. In Britain, we have only one name that is protected by law, and that is Stilton. But, as far as I know, the last creamery using unpasteurised milk to make it gave up in exasperation at our own ministry's red tape. The final, shaming ignominy is the unmarked passing of the Baron of Beef, a joint from just below the waist to just above the knee that is the symbol of all that was very best in British husbandry, butchery and cooking. Now all carcasses have to be split down the middle. The Baron is the joint Hogarth painted to taunt the poor, underfed French with in his picture *O the Roast Beef of Old England*.

British food never flourished or belonged in restaurants. Restaurants are what foreigners have, we have homes. British food belongs in the domestic kitchen, where lunch is not portion-controlled, and where the chef does not have to make your main course as you sit down to your starter. Our national cuisine has become a quaint oddity to be offered as an unusual alternative to standard Eurofare. There is another side to this supposed British foodie revival: numerous small-craftsmen food producers are offering handmade cheeses, carefully smoked meats and organic bits and bobs. With a few notable exceptions, these are pale foreign imitations. We are being tempted by Cornish brie, Welsh parma ham and Gloucestershire Bavarian smoked boar. Real British hard cheese and proper bacon that does not melt in the pan are still just a memory.

For the first time in our history, we have enough food to feed everyone. In this country nobody starves to death. Yet, what most of us eat is junk, rubbish and fake. You may feel that food is not that important, that we should just sit down to eat so that we can then get up to live, and who cares because there will always be some crank making salmagundi or neat's tongue. I think our food is as much part of our culture, our birthright, as our landscape or our poetry or our music. And now it is gone, probably for ever.

Cuisine needs to be eaten and cooked as a matter of course, or it becomes a self-conscious exercise, like speaking a dead language. Now, to cook British food is as bizarre as being conversational in Anglo-Saxon. We can go for treats to visit our food in restaurants. But it is like National Trust houses: when the family moves out it is just dead history, interesting but irrelevant. There is one small ray of good news: there is still food that is cooked in the Great British tradition of strong flavours, slow cooking, using tasty, cheaper cuts of meat and the old spices. Unselfconscious and flourishing and cooked by British people in Indian restaurants. What could be more British than a curry?

The room doesn't encourage you to gawp. It looks like the set for an opulent production of Blithe Spirit. *It's gloomily panelled with what might have been left over from Elgar's coffin. The other diners were a serious fugue of people from a Somerset Maugham novel and a surprising number of women dining à deux in polished brogues, who may or may not have been on Radclyffe Hall adventure weekends.*

We made our way into a bar, which is one of those rooms decorated not with taste or enthusiasm, but with the mortal fear of being passé. You want to know how to give every creative in Notting Hill a nervous breakdown? Just tell them that irony is totally naff. This place has enough juvenile irony to get it an import ban in the United States. The bar's half-dozen denizens, whose veins ran with Botox, regarded us with that sixth-form common-room look, the heavy lidded sneer that says: 'I'm not looking at you, you're looking at me.'

Excuse me, where's the restaurant? I inquired. 'Duh! Upstairs,' I was told with heavy incredulity. (In these parts, not knowing is the most embarrassing affliction. They'd rather pee in their own soup than ask the way to the loo.)

Out of some ancient reflex, my hand reached for the brown sauce and the first mouthful made everything go wavy. My head spun. I think I passed out. When I came round, everything was in black-and-white. All the men looked like Edgar Lustgarten, the city

smelt of coal smoke, someone was playing a harmonica.

Brown sauce is the most extraordinary concoction. Only a nation that thought of food as an extension of engineering could have invented brown sauce. You can clean silver with it. It doesn't go with anything. It's a culinary assassin, an olfactory blackout. And it's got tamarinds in it: ''Ere, guv, we've got these weird little fruit from out east. What shall we do with 'em?' 'Chuck 'em in the brown sauce.'

Brown sauce was invented by a man like Barnes Wallis or Frank Whittle. 'Well chaps, I think I've cracked it. Let's give it a spin. Chips away. If this does what I think it'll do, it'll shorten the war by 3ft 6in and we'll be home in time for tea, which is really breakfast all over again.' It's a cacophonous, sledgehammer taste, more reminiscent of the foundry, the garage and the printer's shop than the kitchen. Unless you've been inoculated with it at an early and impressionable age, you'll never eat it twice.

By every gastronomic criterion, it's utterly indefensible. And yet – and yet – despite all that, despite the years of sophistication and fine dining, it was the most powerfully delicious thing I've tasted for ages. You can train your tastebuds until they jump through hoops of fire and balance on a sturgeon's egg, but underneath they're still wild and free.

5

AWAY

Tom yum kung, a chilli prawn soup that was sharp and sour and utterly brilliant, like putting a battery on your tongue, but without the concomitant implication of being interviewed by the Burmese police.

I'm naturally wary of cannelloni – once bitten … This one arrived inescapably imitating a nuked sanitary towel. It was fine in the sense that the overriding sensation was relief and that it tasted better than it looked. The lemon chicken stew was lumps of bedridden, soft chicken in a sauce with constituent parts that were mostly lemon rind and cornflour. The panna cotta was the colour of tramps' teeth and appeared to have espresso dregs tipped over it. At £12.95, you couldn't fault the price, but then neither could you imagine it was £13 well spent.

Chicken consomme with duck and noodles was called mi ga, a truly frightful, insipid infusion, which, with the simple addition of an exclamation mark, might have been the noise you made when tasting it. Though it was bland to a whisper, I devoutly wished that it had tasted of less rather than more.

Lime-cured seafood ceviche was a huddle of ingredients hiding a fish that, sadly, hadn't been improved by its cure – you wouldn't have fed it to a starving penguin. The wok-fried collection of oriental mushrooms looked very similar, but was repellent in a different way. It might have been used as a tie-break for a Japanese endurance show; the layers of odoriferous, dark, slimy slither were a plate of Hitchcockian suspense. Nem ran was, we were told, traditional Vietnamese spring rolls, and proof that traditions are best left well and truly alone.

Foie gras sushi. Like eating a vet's biopsy tray.

The dining room is stuffed with those lunching people you only see in New York: women who are going to leave their heads to the Natural History Museum, Formula One folk who can't get out of the house unless they have been tweaked by a team of maquillage mechanics, and men who look like they've breakfasted on small children and iron filings. I'm very rarely made to feel nervous by dining-rooms, but I checked my flies twice before walking into this one.

The food is Thai, the fashion for which has always escaped me. Siamese dinner is fusion food. It's China meets Portugal, and it ends in a draw. I can bring myself to almost like the starters – chewed leather on sticks in peanut butter and fishy biscuits with runny jam – but after the imperative of hunger has been satayed and it's just about pleasure, my capacity wanes.

I'd forgotten how shiversomely ghastly an insipid, underpowered bavarois can be. It was a quivering, pink, vaguely fishy gelatinous mush, the sort of thing that collects in dark corners and incubates unspeakable pustular contagions. A forkful was like being beak-fed by a penguin with emphysema. I should say that it was perfectly well made. That's how it's supposed to be. There's a market in provincial France for penguin snot.

Working around the sushi bowl, I like the tuna, I love the eel, I can swallow the salmon – it's better smoked – but the cuttlefish, I don't know, one moment it's sort of unusual, nearly pleasant, and the next it's the closest you'll get to chewing a suicide's armpit.

America

Tex-Mex

I think it's time you knew. I think you deserve to be told. I'm going to let you in on one of the great secrets of transcontinental catering. You see, there's been a conspiracy to keep you in the dark. They'll probably throw me out of the confederation of witty gastronauts, tear up my magic circle napkin and embossed cloakroom ticket. They might even spit in my amuse-bouche. But you really ought to know. So, fearlessly, I break the cartel of silence: There Is No Such Thing As Nice Tex-Mex Food. There, I feel better already. They can do their worst. Feed my pug poisoned tortillas, post guacamole through my letterbox, stuff mescal maggots up my nose. I don't care.

When I first went to America, some time during the Depression, almost the very first thing that was said to me – by an immigration officer on Ellis Island who was dusting me down with pesticide and marking my back with a chalk question mark – was: 'There is out there in the great expanse the perfect Tex-Mex restaurant. And it is every American's dream to find it. Now it is your dream. Have a nice burrito.'

It's carved in stone on the Statue of Liberty: bring me your tired and your hungry yearning to be fajitas and we will feed them huddled messes. Tex-Mex food is the great crusade of the new world. We in the old crusty world had our pilgrimages, our searches for the Holy Grail, but here in the bright dawn of modernism they had the Holy Enchilada. The struggle for the West was not against Indians and an indomitable unforgiving terrain, it was to swallow chillies so fearsome they could Dynorod drains.

The first dinner I ate in the land of the brave was Tex-Mex.

My host said: 'I'm going to take you out for a nachos with best baby backribs that will make you dribble.' And I thought, hello, that's nice, but can't we eat first. The expectation was high. The Americans talk of border food with an old-time Baptist fervour. Their eyes roll. They ululate and become nachos evangelists.

To say it was disappointing is really not to do justice to the boundless possibilities of disappointment. It was a little like being promised a dark date with Kate Moss in a tight sleeping bag and waking up underneath Stirling Moss. The things that weren't simply odorously disgusting hurt like scrubbing your uvula with a rusty wire brush. I decided then and there that that was it with me and the border. But every American I have met since has said: 'You can't not like Tex-Mex food. It's just because you've never had it good.'

And so it's gone on for years. I've been forced by the iron dictate of guestdom to recreate the storming of the Alamo every morning after. Not liking Tex-Mex in America is a heresy akin to printing the Stars and Stripes on a tampon applicator. Americans all dreamily look west and imagine the perfect cantina. The American dream. It doesn't exist. It's a fantasy and a pretty lowbrow one at that. It's born out of the greatest, oldest, hoariest fantasy in America: the cowboy film. Tex-Mex food is your own private plastic-bibbed *Shane* and *High Noon* made for fat, sedentary people who hyperventilate if they're not standing on concrete, who don't like horses or loud noises but feel a little Gregory Peckish.

From an outsider's perspective it's perfectly obvious that cowboy food will be hideous. Cowboys are hideous. Only a country as remedially sentimental as America could have made its core fantasy out of transient farmworkers. Cowboys were ignorant, poor, venal, uncultured, tasteless, violent dimwits. What on earth made anyone imagine that when they happened upon the ignorant, poor, venal, uncultured, tasteless, violent dimwits in basketwork donkey hats on the other side of the Rio Grande, it was going to result in a great cuisine? The legacy of cowboys is some of the most hysterically kitsch, maudlin songs ever sung, a uniquely appalling canon of penny-dreadful novellas, and hours and hours of B movies with plots and dialogue that would embarrass a trepanned mule.

How could their food be anything other than the equivalent of sucking John Wayne's lariat's pommel? Ah, but as they say in Abilene, there's no sucker like a well-informed sucker with a wealth of previous experience. And so it was that I found myself herding fourteen children into a Mexican restaurant in the middle of London. No poke on the Chisholm Trail had a more testing task. Don't make any loud noises; they'll stampede and we'll be picking up stragglers in the badlands of the Strand. As usual, it was made up to look like all the Diamante Lils' saloons you've ever seen. How come this food can't exist outside a cheesy film set? You have never seen a Tex-Mex restaurant with carpet or tablecloths or waiters that were over nineteen. It can only be eaten bolstered by the clichéd tat of horns and free-form plasterwork, sticky pine and bogus wanted posters. It's as if we had a national obsession to endlessly recreate the Blitz with faux bomb-damaged caffs serving snoek and powdered egg.

The menu was as predictable and fulsome as Dolly Parton's lungs. It's not that I've anything against poor food, you understand, or repetitive food. In fact, most of the best dinners in the world are of peasant origin and use limited ingredients. But I really don't want food that was originally prepared for people who didn't care what they ate and, in fact, thought that noticing what you ate at all was justifiable grounds for a hot-lead enema.

There are two abiding themes in Tex-Mex food. One is that it is not designed to be consumed by mouth. It's designed to be absorbed by osmosis. For every filthy mouthful you manage to secure, your trousers, shirt and the table glean two. It slithers and squirts, meanders and sidles over everything. A tortilla is a primitive vegetable Slinky. The other thing is that it's constructed for people who have tertiary gingivitis.

Everything has been systematically and thoroughly chewed already. I've often toyed with the idea of asking the waitress to bring me the Mexican who ate my food before I got it, but have resisted because of the faint possibility that she just might.

We ordered almost everything on the card. It came plate after plate: dung-coloured, squidgy, slug cud. From the kitchen's point of view, the joy of Tex-Mex food is that it needs no presentation. However you arrange it, it looks like radical colonic surgery on a large ruminant. We ate very little, the children moodily staying on the safe ground of tepid flabby chips dipped in shootout ketchup. I managed to draw the line at something called 'flautas', which is just too like the medical term for socially compromising wind.

The high point was something called a Texas Rose, which was a vastly deformed onion bisected from stem to stern repeatedly then dipped in muddy batter and deep fried. It came on dramatically looking like a cancerous thistle and made you wonder why anyone ever imagined doing it in the first place. Perhaps Jim Bowie had an inventive afternoon whittling with his knife. Although hyperbolically vaunted, all the plates had a torpidly repetitive taupe-coloured flavour, occasionally spiked with something unpleasantly hot or worryingly crunchy.

Hours later, the Blonde mentioned that, like a trusty Winchester, that doggone lunch kept repeating on her. I know. It was a second helping of flautas. And I hadn't even eaten it the first time.

Colorado

One of the oblique ways of telling what a new place is like is to see what sort of books are in the junk shop. Cortez is a town in Colorado, between the desert canyons of the

Navajo reservation and the pine mountains and aspen-fringed meadows of the high San Juans. On the thrifty shelves, along with the knackered cowboy boots, herniated belt buckles and saccharine china tchochke, there was a small selection of callously thumbed books. Most were cookbooks and maps of other places – which sums up Cortez, a push-me-pull-you of wanderlust and homeliness.

I bagged *Chuck-Wagon Cooking*: 'An authentic collection of round-up law, cowboy humour and more than 100 old-time recipes.' The cover is a fetching photo of stew, biscuits and a .45. No well-fitted kitchen should be without one. Then there was a collection of recipes from the pinto-bean cooking contest, with classics such as pinto-bean mock chicken legs and pinto-bean fudge. And there was a book with one of those titles that makes you kick yourself for not having thought of it first: *Best Recipes from the Backs of Boxes, Bottles, Cans and Jars.* Isn't that brilliant?

America has a particularly intimate relationship with proprietary processed food, and these recipes were as bizarre, touching, occasionally delicious but mostly palate-scrapingly disgusting as the States itself. How about oven-fried chicken and bananas, from the Coco Casa cream-of-coconut label? The ingredients are chicken bits, cream of coconut, lemon juice, bananas, three-quarters of a cup of melted margarine and two and a half cups of cornflakes. I'm not going to give you the method for Jell-o Artichoke Salad. You'll just have to imagine. The Jell-o flavour is lime, naturally.

One of the best things about coming back to this bit of Colorado is that it's home to one of the best natural cooks I've ever met. She's a doctor who delivers babies for the Indians. It's a sexist truth that chefs tend to be men, while cooks are usually women. Men make food with arrogance, vanity and enthusiasm; women with love. I know that's a syrupy stereotype, and there are humble chefs and women who couldn't cook a marshmallow with a blowtorch, yet the most moving and memorable things you eat will be given to you by a woman. And they'll be free. Occasionally, they'll prepare food that is greater than the sum of its ingredients and becomes an edible parable, a secular transubstantiation, a communion of hospitality and sustenance – not the flavour of heaven, but, far more elegiac, the taste of humanity.

Emily gave me a tomato sandwich on sliced white and an egg stuffed with coriander. She grew the tomatoes and raised the hen. It sounds so prosaically absurd, so lumpy with banal bathos, but I could barely say thank you for fear that I might sob. We taste and experience food in the part of the brain that came before language. Sometimes it is beyond words.

Later, my boy, Ali, said: 'That tomato sandwich, it's the best I've ever eaten. What was in it?' Tomato. 'Just tomato?' Yes, and no. He gave me the 'whatever' look.

Breakfast

I think I've put on half a stone. I'm not actually sure, because I don't own a pair of scales. If I ever do weigh myself – in a hotel, a rural German railway station or at the butchers – they're always different calibrations. I'm 200 somethings and then, next time, I'm 15,000, or three minutes past 12. My waistband is my true Plimsoll line, and I assume that half an inch is about 10 bob, or a baker's dozen, or 13 degrees.

Anyway, I've just reached the outer limits of my tailor's tolerance and the Blonde is giggling that she can pinch a cubit. All by spending a week in America. America just clings to you. It used to be said that you could eat very well in England, just as long as you ate breakfast three times a day. It's not true here any more, but it is in America. Breakfast is a majestic thing, so complex that most Americans have to go out to eat it rather than attempt it in their own kitchens. It's best in cheap diners.

In Blighty, the Full English means only one thing – or one

collection of things. But in America, breakfast has more options than a Nevada brothel. The children and I went to the Candy Kitchen every morning, and they'd stare with shock and awe at the cornucopia of waffles, omelettes, pancakes, french toast, hot sandwiches, bagels, muffins, pastries, coffee cakes (not made with coffee, but for coffee), oatmeal, smoked fish, potatoes, porky bits, ironed bacon and eggorama. Not to mention the juices and variations on a theme of coffee.

There is something properly egalitarian about American breakfast. Everyone from the Mexican delivery boy to the industrial Gorgon and his fifth wife sits in the same plastic booths and eats with the same concentrated appetite. It's a big, generous, can-do start to the day, sweet and unctuously bounteous, taking on fuel for the honest travail of building a righteous society. It says every dawn is a new beginning and the day will be what you choose to make of it. And you've got to love a country that allows you to have ice cream first thing.

If you're going to America this summer, you might like to try a game we played that was, I think, invented by Jeremy Clarkson's producer, Andy Wilman: you have to order an entire breakfast without ever prompting a question. It's surprisingly hard. Every choice spawns options, like edible malaria. Toast is wholewheat or white, buttered or dry, real butter or low fat, jelly or honey. My kids got very good at it.

Of course, the truth about American breakfast is that its sense of democratic, free-market choice is illusory. The bewildering alternatives of coffee are all still just bad, weak coffee, and the rest is mostly delicious variations of flour, fat and sugar. Not that that's a bad thing: flour, fat and sugar are the three refined graces of gastronomy – big lasses with generous asses.

Arizona

A couple of weekends ago, I went to Arizona. With a thudding symbolism, Phoenix rises out of volcanic ash. It's a rather wonderful place that's full of get-up, but with nowhere to go except the desert. One of the fastest-growing towns on the planet, a heady, if incongruous, mix of new-age digital nerds and the nearly dead from the Bakelite age, who've come to rummage and desiccate and shuffle in white Velcro trainers that are practising for nothing but a final sprinkle of more ash into the hot desert wind.

The big problem with Phoenix is the water. So naturally, septically, subtly, the place has three hundred golf courses and enough fountains to colonically irrigate the entire bulgingly prostrated population. The water comes from the mighty Colorado river, which greenly snickers its way through the Grand Canyon. But by the time it has reached Mexico, it's an undrinkable, brackish trickle. The Gatt treaty and the global free market obviously don't include sharing water with your neighbours. They're only wetbacks if they splash about a bit.

In the Biltmore, a hotel allegedly influenced by the designs of Frank Lloyd Wright (not in his wildest dreams), where the elastic-waist shop is unavoidably called The Wright Stuff, I had a pudding called s'mores. Assuming that you were never an American Girl Guide, let me tell you that this is possibly the most childishly moronic dessert ever offered to a grown-up and, therefore, well worth the journey.

A flaming pot comes to the table with satay sticks skewering marshmallows. You roast the marshmallows, then smear them on Graham crackers (a nasty, indigenous cheese biscuit) before adding a slab of Hershey's chocolate – only Hershey's will do, only Hershey's is ersatz enough – and another Graham cracker. It's an eating experience that's about as subtle and sophisticated as having the Easter bunny sit on your face. Repulsively moreish.

Fat

It's official: 45 per cent of Americans are fat. Obese. And that's on the Yankee fatometer, which I expect isn't quite the same as the Balinese or Botswanan one. American fat seems to be of a different species to everyone else's. I've noticed that they can store it in ingenious places. They get fat ears (I've seen Americans carrying the equivalent of a Big Mac and fries in their lobes). And they get extra knees (American women can support up to five knees on each leg). And fat armpits: how do they do that?

Of course, most of their conspicuous consumption is carried in the big breadbasket of the Mid-West: the buttock area. I say area, because Americans can grow buttocks that circumnavigate their bodies and hang in interesting garlands: the hanging buttocks of Kansas. They are what I think is technically known in farming circles as 'double muscled': that is, they have essentially two bums, one on top of the other.

I once met a doctor from Illinois who told me that 30 per cent of Americans have grown too corpulent to mount each other and now have to be mated by a third party, like turkeys. It was, he said, rewarding work, though you had to be fit. His specialist tools included a miner's helmet, one of those dampometers that surveyors use, and, of course, a ball of string to find his way back.

Pregnancy is a problem for Americans. My doctor friend said that 20 per cent of the women don't even know they are pregnant until they hear an insistent crying from inside the easy-fit spandex ski pants, putting the contractions down to the ever-present trapped wind. In some of the more reactionary states, where sex education is a capital offence, 10 per cent of overweight women actually think they are pregnant, sometimes for years on end. One septuagenarian was convinced that she had been gravid with sextuplets for thirty years, the father being a hot-dog salesman who had winked while selling her a snack of twelve jumbo chilli-dogs at a Neil Diamond concert.

This is no laughing matter. Obesity is a killer – 48 per cent of Americans will die prematurely, taking half a hundredweight of Cheesy Wotsits with them. But there is a downside, too. Fat has now taken over from illegal immigration as the main cause of overcrowding. The federal government reckons that, at the present rate of consumption, America will be completely full of Americans in a hundred years. Just one vast, elasticated, smelly, undulating prairie of flesh, which will cause a severe downturn in the pizza-delivery industry.

In a truly, uniquely American way, they've decided that the answer is to sue the food manufacturers and tax them for selling fat. Only in America does this make sense. After all, it's what they do with drugs: blame Colombian peasants for Los Angeles crack addicts. It's not going to work, is it? Fat chance. We know where this ends: you get finger-food dealers hanging round schools, the price of Doritos rockets, and old people are going to be mugged by Gargantua, desperate for a Twinkie fix.

I have a much better solution. I know a slim something about addiction, radical life changes and food. What fat people need is tough love and caring confrontation. The worst thing is if we collude that it's all right to be mega.

It isn't. It's killing them.

Whenever you meet a fat person, at work or socially, you must point, laugh and shriek, in a high-pitched voice: 'My, but you're hideous! Do you find a lot of loose change and old socks down those folds?' Or 'Hey, being two-faced is one thing, but are you supposed to wear them both at once?' And shout at fat kids in the street as well: they should have their whole lives in front of them, not an inverted belly button and man-breasts. On no account use euphemisms: none of this chubby, rotund, big-boned, Junoesque stuff. And let's get one thing perfectly clear: none of it has got anything to do with glands.

I know this all sounds cruel, but the true cruelty is pretending that fat isn't an affront to human aesthetics. And just remember the last time you had to sit next to a fat person on an aeroplane.

California

Californian eating is extraordinary. Not the food – the eating. There's a Darwinian thing going on here: the ability to use cutlery is atrophying. I sat for hours, spellbound, just watching Californians try to get to grips with a knife and fork. They can't do it. I think it's the fact that they've got two, differently shaped objects to manipulate at the same time that stumps them. Grown-up Californians stare at the ironmongery as if it were some sort of Mensa co-ordination and intelligence test. 'Wow, you expect me to pick the pointy thing and the sharp thing up simultaneously? That's tough. It's a kind of patting your head and rubbing your tummy deal. Okay, here we go.' Nearly. 'But it's not supposed to end up in my ear, is it?' They use the fork perpendicularly as a stick to stop the food running away. They place a thumb over the top for maximum pressure. They then grip the knife in the fist and hack in a Jean-Claude Van Damme frenzy until the plate looks like dogfood. Then they lose the knife, transfer the fork to the other hand, plaiting it through their fingers, and then – and this is the good bit – pretend it's a spoon.

I don't think I've ever seen it mentioned before, but the *raison d'être* behind the much copied, much lauded, cool Californian fusion food isn't health, or happy ingredients, or sophisticated palates. It's the inability of the customers to eat with two hands. If it can't be shovelled or picked up in the fingers, they really don't like it. It took three hundred years for Europe to learn how to use the Italian invention of a fork plus a knife. Californians have managed to forget it in less than a generation.

Hamburgers

Hamburgers are synonymous with American cultural sleep-over, of course, but they have an interesting history. They're exactly contemporary with the Model T Ford. The first burger diner was built on one of the first Californian motorways, and its popularity has grown alongside roads by way of the car.

They asked me how I'd like mine. I said medium rare. I could have said anything. Skin on. Rotten. Radioactive. It was obviously one of those inquiries, such as 'How are you?', where no meaningful answer is expected. What came was an overdone, thin burger in a bun that had the consistency of candyfloss, with a scab of cheese and hard bacon. The whole thing oozed a wholesome puddle of watery fat. And it tasted just like a burger.

If heaven is eating *foie gras* to the sound of trumpets, then purgatory is a hamburger consumed to the sound of the same shrill, flat note being blown on a harmonica over and over. No dish ever invented starts off so engagingly and becomes so boring so fast. It's yum to yuk in four inches. This hamburger was precisely what you'll find everywhere and anywhere in America. Indeed, hamburgers, the original hybrid meal – not a snack, not a lunch, but a solitary low-aspiration indulgence – are fundamentally symbolic of America. They are the eternal triumph of hope over experience.

Corn

I think it was Thomas Jefferson, but it might have been one of those other smart, ugly terrorists in wigs, who complained that the bald eagle was a dumb bird to have as a national symbol: opportunism and scavenging are not the sort of ideals with which a new state-of-the-art nation ought to associate itself. The man with wire glasses and a barn full of black slaves said that it would be far better to adopt the turkey, a fowl of some use and merit. The turkey that had sustained the pilgrim fathers was a model parent and made a halfway decent duvet, but the bank notes had already been printed – so an eagle it was.

Ever since its inception, America has been obsessed with a national, provincial and parochial animism: the ancient desire to totemise bits of the natural world. Every state has its figure-head bird and flower. Sports teams take on the ferocity and strength of animals. There are national days allocated to bits and pieces of nature, like Gopher Day. As far as the gophers are concerned, every day since the flood has been National Gopher Day – just one long breakfast.

In Britain, our towns marry with other European towns: Hull is twinned with St Tropez (I wonder what St Tropez gets out of the deal). To drive across America is to pass hundreds of places that are twinned with vegetables, or rather towns that have offered homes to things that have lived outdoors all their lives – Blow-out Flats, home of the Lima Bean. Everything in America must have a home. All those bits of flora and fauna that existed quite contentedly where the wind dropped them now have zip codes and statues. No denizen of the Darwinian order of things is too insignificant to have a place on the map, a day, a stamp and its picture on the town hall wall of Dole Queue, Louisiana, Home of those Tiny Black Bug Things you only see Dead Behind the Glass of Old Engravings.

Now, having said all that, I'm not sure that America lays claim to a national plant. You can imagine the fuss they'd make over choosing one: the lobbying, the arguments. Cotton would be good but the blacks would veto it; oranges would be fine, but the Hispanics have to pick them; whites would hate watermelon, and don't even *mention* tobacco. Idaho would put in a bid for potatoes, but who wants to belong to the land of the free, the home of the brave and chip?

I know what it should be. I know the plant that epitomises everything that's best about the States. Corn. You see, even the name is a truism about Yanks. Corn, or maize, is the biggest of the edible seed grasses. It is fantastically versatile, producing everything from syrup to oil, popcorn to custard powder, cattlecake and laundry starch. The old cobs, I'm told, also make efficient if abrasive loo paper.

Years ago I lived for a short while in Kentucky. We grew corn and sugar cane. There was this joke: you'd stand in the field of corn and a guy in a pick-up would pull over, take off his redneck cap and say 'Yep, fine corn. How many gallons do you get to the acre?' Then you'd both laugh. That was it. They'd been doing that joke two, maybe three times a week for four generations and it still got a laugh. Corn is the raw material of moonshine and there were hundreds of small shine distilleries in the hills and hollows.

North of Kentucky is Ohio, where you can drive for two days and not see a gradient that would make a billiard ball roll: in fact you won't see anything except corn, miles and bloody miles of it. In 1910, America grew three billion bushels of it, which would be more impressive if I knew what a bushel was. Corn is Midwestern manna: the locals are eternally grateful for it. They dry the stuff for decoration, invent things to hold it, have patented napkins to stop it dribbling on their Terylene ties and most of all they talk about it. In Ohio you can put corn on the cob on the table three times a day and they will break in to perfect kernel-stripping grins and say 'Mmmm. Corn, I love it.' I must say, it does taste better there. The second biggest industry in Ohio is, of course, dental floss.

Miami

Miami. It's a hoot. A hot, oily hoot. I'm lying here in a thong, by the pool of the Delano Hotel on South Beach, a seal colony with breasts. This is Silicon Valley without brains. Think St Tropez crossed with Cheshire. Miami is a place that has lived its life in reverse. Ten years ago it was a heart-bypass nature reserve, with 10,000 New York deli-owners left out on the sidewalk to roast to death like hot eskimos. Now it's the Versace memorial drive-by pick-up. In a generation it will probably have regressed to being a crèche without any discernible decline in mental agility.

This is a middle-aged, mini-skirted vice Olympics, the last place where you can find truly brave men. Brave enough to wear ponytails in broad daylight and sunglasses in the dark, and only ever do up three shirt buttons. This is a place where the watches are the size of strippers' nipples and the nipples tell the time like sundials. Miami vice is vice with valet parking; it's pasteurised naughtiness, dressing-up-box Berlin. The urges are kept in check by the huge Jell-o egos. Miami is just too self-obsessed to get down and dirty and ladder its tights. But it likes to think about it.

It's a long time since I've been to the States outside New York. New York gives you a false sense of what America's really like. It's a proper, grown-up place, a European city that got lost. But Miami could only be American. It wouldn't survive anywhere else: someone would spank its silly bottom.

There is this extraordinary place in Miami called Joe's Stone Crab Restaurant. It's an event restaurant, something of a venerable institution. In American terms it's older than God: it opened in 1913. The point of Joe's Stone Crab Restaurant, you'll be unsurprised to learn, is stone crabs; in particular, the left arms of stone crabs. A stone crab is a pretty bog-standard crab, not as sweet as your Norfolk or as interesting as your soft-shell, or as convivial as your genital (and not as much fun to catch). The restaurant has grown to about a thousand covers over the years, and you can't smoke at a single one of them. They do serve other things, but crabs' left arms are their speciality. A basket of about a trillion arrives in front of you, boiled and expertly cracked, with melted butter on the side.

'Enjoy!' as almost everyone, including the tattooists, says in Florida.

Being of an inquisitive nature, I wondered in an en passant

kind of way what happened to the rest of the crab. Well, would you coco?

They throw them back and, nature being miraculous and stone crabs being stupid and Candide-ishly hopeful, the dismembered appurtenances grow back again ready to be reamputated. The arms are of uniform size and perfectly un-blemished and they taste of virtually nothing, least of all crab, which is the way Americans like their food.

As I chewed, I did a little light maths: 1,000 covers twice a day, 10 sinister crab arms per person and overnight mail order anywhere in the country: that's ... that's ... well, that's how many? That's a truly disturbing number of one-armed crabs living out there in the bay.

And then you think of the men sitting in the kitchen, shak-ing hands with thousands and thousands of crabs and not let-ting go, and the whole business becomes very creepy. I know this is a genuine example of ecologically renewable resources, but it makes my skin crawl. It's really unpleasant. In fact, almost everything about renewable resources is unpleasant. I don't want to eat the same optimistic crab for ever, or a pig, or a carrot, or a cornflake. I always knew that ecology would end up ripping the arms off things.

Las Vegas

I was back in America last week – Las Vegas, which is a very odd place to eat in.

Time loses the pegs and guy ropes that keep it secured to a normal human day. Daylight means nothing, sleep means little and meals are a distracting bodily function. The death of meals is a fact for many Americans. They don't eat regularly, they eat constantly. They walk around the fruit machines eat-ing everything but fruit. They clutch slices of goo, fat-stuck lumps, buckets of dead crustacea dunked in vinegar-sweet pink slime, and cartons of carbonated corn syrup that taste of fruit gums and tar. They eat without appetite or enthusiasm, almost without noticing. It's sub-consumption. I love Americans, but boy, does Las Vegas put a strain on the relationship.

However, I did discover two fast-food outlets that were pretty fabulous, and available all over the States if you're going there this year. First, Krispy Kreme Doughnuts, which makes just the best doughnuts ever; the minute you bite one, you know it's the first of a chain that will last longer than your teeth. Americans don't buy them in ones or twos, they buy them in dozens in huge cardboard boxes and then eat them in solitary darkness. The other chain is In-n-Out Burger, which is everything McDonald's should be, but isn't. Decent cheeseburgers and proper chips. Of course, only Americans can name a shop In-n-Out Burger without collapsing into a heap of dirty sniggers. You know the difference between them and us? To us, a double entendre means only one thing: to them, it means absolutely nothing.

Argentina

My first mistake with Argentina was imagining, foolishly, that it was somewhere in South America. Getting off the plane in what the captain had confidently declared to be Buenos Aires, I imbibed a deep breath, looked out over the river Plate and said, with a conquistador's confidence: 'Ah, South America.' At which the small, aerobic woman who was carrying my steamer trunk on her head displayed an expression of timeless pain and sadness. 'Oh no. No, no, no. This is not South America. You have been misinformed. This is Europe.'

Now, hold it right there, I replied a little testily. I have just spent three generations of fruit-fly lives on a plane and eaten the meat option twice, not to mention been felt up and X-rayed, on the strict understanding that I would be deposited in South America. If I wanted to go to Europe, I could have put my head out of my bedroom window and sighed, 'Ah, Europe,' saving myself a considerable amount of bother.

'It is a common misconception,' she said, conciliatorily.

Look, I'm not going to let this go. I'm supposed to be in South America. I've paid to be in South America. I'm being paid to be in South America. If this isn't South America, I want to complain. I want someone to bring me South America, right here, right now. And anyway, I've seen maps. Argentina is definitely in South America, tangoed next to Chile beneath Brazil.

'Oh dear,' she whispered. 'Mere cartography. Maps mean nothing. Columbus, he thought he'd discovered India. You think you've come to South America. This is not what it appears. It's Europe. See Buenos Aires and you'll understand.'

And indeed, I did. There is nothing here that would lead you to believe that you're not actually in Latin Europe – except for the fashions, which are all a year or two out of date, giving the odd impression that the new world is older than the old. As European cities go, Buenos Aires is quite lovely, with wide, shady boulevards and pretty, neat women. The men are a bit of a worry, though. How can so many chaps be so obviously, glutinously handsome? It's like an open casting for a Jilly Cooper novel.

Gastronomically, the Argentine means one thing: beef. Now, everywhere with enough room for a cow boasts it has the best beef in the world, and, as beef is one of my all-time top ten pop-in-the-gob things, it's easiest and politest to agree: 'Yes, of course your Texan/Scottish/Irish/Florentine/Japanese beef is the best.' (Actually, Japanese Kobe beef is rather disturbing: it's not so much like eating a manly steer, as secretly partaking in some sort of chubby fetish.) But I can now say, with absolute conviction, that Argentine beef is head and shoulders, buttock and prairie oyster above the rest. If you think this is a little unpatriotic of me and that I ought to be championing the cattle of the Borders or the West Country, let me say in mitigation that their breeds are all British – mostly Hereford, with a smattering of Black Angus – and as Argentina is really in Europe, it might as well be just off the M4.

The reason the meat is so good is that nobody makes the European mistake of trying to improve on God. The cattle only eat what they can find, and what they can find grows where they find it. They have sex and give birth when they want, where they want, and there is no word for 'vet' or 'Rolf Harris'. They only come into intimate contact with man when they're having graffiti burnt into their bums, or their testicles removed, or being turned into lunch and a handbag. This is as close to wild beef as you can get. After the war, when rationing was at its most enervating, Attlee's government sold the Argentine railways (which we'd built) for corned beef. Having seen the Argentine railways, I can say it was the best deal a Labour government ever made.

Now, there's no question that Patagonia really is in South America. The landscape is staggering, the Imax version of Scotland. Here, I ate beef with the gauchos, cowherds attired with a louche, chic vanity that makes Peter York look like Kenneth Clarke. After a hard morning abusing bovines, they set up some meat on a barbecue. 'This will make you feel at home,' they said. 'It is an English joint.' Not to my butcher, it wasn't – it was the better half of a spine with the ribs neatly cut off. But the meat around the discs was historic.

You cut off a slab, sprinkled it with salt, grabbed it with your teeth and, slicing a cheekful with your trusty gaucho knife, being careful not to remove portions of your own nose, chewed while listening to the nervous lowing of tomorrow's lunch. The gauchos watched the Blonde and me with a sullen disgust, which is not something she's used to. They don't like it rare. They only like their beef very, very well done. Perhaps that was what they meant about reminding me of home.

Germany

One of my most precious possessions is a book called, teasingly, *A Culinary Voyage through Germany*. Now a voyage is, of course, a journey made by sea, and the image of Germany covered in twenty fathoms of water is a pleasantly heartwarming one. If only it were possible to set out from Harwich and view Teutonia from a glass-bottomed pleasure-steamer. Entrepreneurial salvagers could try to raise it for fun and profit, and the rest of us could sign petitions opposing it on the grounds that, like the imperial fleet at Scapa Flow, Germany was best left underwater as a memorial to the Dambusters raid.

In this fragmented continent, studded though it is with winsome good intentions and well-meaning handshakes, the only thing that really and truly unites us all is a deep and obsessive desire to see Germany sink under the North Sea. Ah, but children, it is only a happy reverie, a pleasant dream. And yet, perhaps one day, if global warming keeps up, who knows?

A Culinary Voyage through Germany is compiled by Hannelore Kohl. (Why aren't more children, or indeed herring, called Hannelore these days?) Mrs Kohl is credited as general editor, which I imagine is some sort of Teutonic military title. She is accompanied on her gastronomic journey by her husband, Helmut, who you will remember was chancellor of Germany. A culinary progress round the old electorate is the sort of thing ageing politicians cleave to. I imagine that at this very moment the Majors are compiling *A Cosy Weekend Bed and Breakfast Directory*; the Blairs will do their home constituency in *Juice Bars of Central Tuscany*; and dare we hope for Mandy Mandelson's *Rough Guide to Room Service*?

You can understand why politicians are drawn to eulogise the food of their countries. Food is an easy metaphor for who you are. If, in Germany, wrapping yourself in the flag and singing 'Tomorrow Belongs to Me' has uncomfortable historic resonances, then you can just wrap yourself round a steaming sausage without being accused of wanting Poland for afters.

It's a pathetic nationalist truth that citizens of all countries consider their cuisine second to none. Even Egyptians, Nigerians and the Swiss are convinced their national cuisine is the best, despite voluminous, indeed, vomitous, evidence to the contrary. For Germany, the idea of an über-national cuisine – ridiculous, risible and oxymoronic as that may sound to the rest of us – is vital to the body politic. Germany hasn't been a country for very long and a sense of belonging is best homogenised in the kitchen. Italians could have much the same problem, but they never talk about Italian food; they have Ligurian, Neapolitan or Piedmontese food and are, in fact, only united by a national belief in avoiding taxes and traffic lights.

But back to Chancellor Kohl. Herr Kohl is to food writing what German food is to European cuisine. This is Herr Kohl on cabbage, a subject close to German hearts and not far from their heads: 'The salty ground of the Dith marshes forms the largest cabbage-growing area in the whole of Germany. Every year a girl is crowned Cabbage Queen in a big folk festival. A popular and true local saying is "cabbage may cause wind but it also nourishes man". I like this saying and it's very true!' Isn't that just heaven? It sings off the page, a true insight into the German soul. It has everything: dull statistics, folklore, bowels, wooden delivery and – my favourite bit – an oompah-pah exclamation mark.

Somewhere out there is a girl who, even as we speak, is a Cabbage Queen and doesn't care who knows it. And what about the joke? German wit at its finest. Ho, ho, Helmut, you wag. Slap my lederhosen.

I need hardly point out that Hannelore's recipes are of a vileness unsurpassed in the civilised world. When we eat foreign food, we don't just consume meat and veg prepared in a different way, we feel that somehow we are taking on a taste of the *joie de vivre* of the host country. So, rightly, there are millions of Italian restaurants, and loads of Frenchish ones, hundreds of Americans, and even the occasional Mexican is awarded a culinary embassy. But where are the German restaurants? Where, indeed. There used to be one in London called Schmidt's, but it got gotterdammerunged ages ago.

Last week, however, I passed a small Teutonic establishment.

'We've got to try that,' I said. 'Do we really, really have to?' whined the Blonde.

'Ja, ja, my little blonde knackwurst, wind your hair into earphones and I will sing Weill for you.'

Oddly, everyone we asked to join us found that they had another appointment that night, which turned out to be a blessing because it was a very small restaurant and only seemed to take couples. At the other half-dozen tables were half-a-dozen men with very low self-esteem dining half-a-dozen girls whose collective body language screamed 'not a hope in hell, schweinehund'. I mean, would you melt for a chap whose idea of a romantic first date was dinner from Dortmund? The room was simple and unassuming, with a window at one end and a bar at the other. And it wasn't altogether authentically German; it wasn't quite Sixtiesly hideous enough, and they didn't have any Iron Maiden posters or laminated instructions on how to perform the Heimlich manoeuvre on Belgium.

I went for the Wiener schnitzel.

The best thing about Wiener schnitzel is saying it. It sounds like a man with a handlebar moustache sneezing minestrone out of his nose. The most a Wiener schnitzel can aim for is utter indifference. It is about as forgettably minimal as food can be and still be food. Bland is too emphatic a word for Wiener schnitzel. If it doesn't come with a lemon, it doesn't really exist at all. I can't remember a thing about this one, so it must have been jolly good, a credit to the dull grey civil servant's soul of schnitzeldom. The Blonde had chicken paprika 'braised on the bone with a sour cream sauce'. Aha, at last: this was more like it, this is what I expected. I've been told it is actually illegal to be a German and not eat at least a pint of sour cream a day. If they think you're getting subversive with yoghurt, they come round with a Friesian and make you juggle her udders for an hour.

The chicken paprika was utterly German, in that the muscle let go of the bone like an exhausted suicide losing grip of a window ledge. The sauce was a glutinous pink congealing thing that resembled – and possibly tasted of – anti-rust paint. We also had spatzel, a sort of cancerous macaroni that tastes strongly of water with an exotic touch of flour.

For pudding, there was, of course, a strudel, with cream or ice cream. Might I have cream and ice cream? 'That is permissible.' Thank God for that, then. Again the pleasure of strudel is in saying it: 'strudel' makes a good alternative all-purpose verb, adjective and rude-bit noun.

There were a million types of that fruit-flavoured spirit that's the German equivalent of tequila, but without the concomitant singing, dancing and sex. As I was paying the bill I asked which bit of Germany the cook came from. There was some shuffling: 'Actually, he's a Croat.' Oh well, that explains everything, he's not German at all. I got a slow, hooded, beady look that seemed to say: 'Not yet my friend, not yet.'

Outside, the Blonde waited for me underneath a street lamp looking very Ute Lemper. My mind strayed to strudel.

Peshawar

I've lost count of the number of querulous people who have tugged at my sleeve and quoted the old cliché:

'As ever, the first casualty of war is restaurant criticism.' How true. Where are the reviews of Normandy in 1944? Where is the critic to pass judgment on the invention of a new fricassee at Marengo? Where is the star rating for the doners of Omdurman?

Well, I'm not just a good-time restaurant critic. I'm staunch when it gets tough; when the bivalves come like bullets and the soup's a colonic landmine. And so it was that, last week, I donned the trusty flak napkin and yomped to the Northwest Frontier to review the restaurant at the end of the world.

Now there are some of you who will say that sending a restaurant critic to a dirty little war zone is, frankly, in bad taste. To go and raise a nicely-nicely pinky in a region with 4 million starving refugees is to stretch the knicker elastic of satire to breaking point. Well, I hear you. But surely starvation is no reason to let standards slip.

Peshawar, ancient city of Alexander and Akbar, backdrop for Kipling's *Kim*, is a sprawling stew on the grand trunk road, a hot stuffed naan on the old Silk Route, a place of intrigue and anger, conspiracy and prophecy, of ragged dignity and gossamer elegance, a place of feuds and feudalism, of fearsome beauty and unimaginable filth, a city of a million prayers and countless curses, down whose brindled wynds a chap's shadow is rarely his own, a labyrinth of dead ends (and ends where you might as well be dead), a burgh where strange men tell stranger tales, where boys are men and girls are lamp shades.

In short, I have never been to a more exciting and intoxicating place. Peshawar simmers with rumours of holy war, while its markets are swagged with smugglers' booty. The streets lurch in a confusion of stoic donkeys, bony horses, gaudy lorries, motorbike taxis and sinewy men who have walked a thousand miles from the high places on empty stomachs. You can get anything on the streets of Peshawar – except the antibiotics to cure whatever it was you got. There are huddled stalls selling diamonds and gold from India, spinels and rubies from Burma, and the Madonna-blue, gold-flecked lapis of Afghanistan. You can buy a home-made Kalashnikov or an Uzbek bride's dowry, woollen shawls that are softer than a third wife's moan, fairy embroidery from Waziristan, rose-pink silks from Swat and self-cleaning microwaves from Taiwan.

But it's the food we've come for; it's plain tales of the meals you yearn to hear. The food of the North-West Frontier is the finest in central Asia. It is here that the disgusting plov of the central Asian steppe is finessed into the aromatic and delicate pilau. On this frontier, the mountain-bred mutton is spiced with a magician's hand.

Peshawar has given its name to stuffed bread, and Afghanistan was once famous for the gravid fruit trees that shaded the streets of Kabul. And still the barrows in the market are piled high in season with fabulous produce smuggled from beyond the Khyber. Now is the pomegranate season, and every morning I drank foaming, choleric glasses of deep red juice. Now is also the time for the tiny yellow grapes, so sweet they make your eyes water, and a yellow fruit that looks like a misshapen pear, whose perfume is so powerful that it wafts away all the odours of corruption. Its softly juicy flavour reminded me of something. Finally, I discovered its English name – it was a guava, but far, far removed from the insipid cousins further east.

In the poultry market, I watched a man delicately eviscerate a chicken, with its friend watching intently under his arm, hoping for titbits. In another stall, a group sat plucking tiny bundles of feathers, laying out the naked corpses in neat rows. They were sparrows, a Pathan aphrodisiac – which doesn't make you feel that Afghan women have much to look forward to when they get their burkas off.

The greatest dish hereabouts is Kabuli pilau, basmati rice poached in lamb stock, finished with grated carrot and those little grapes. Up here, you eat with your hands. To lose a hand to war or villainy is to lose either the cutlery or the bog roll.

One of the two best restaurants is in the Khan Klub, a fabulously Graham Greeneish hotel, where I stayed in a room of dark wood and brass with a shuttered ladies' balcony and a bed set into the wall up winding library stairs. The muezzin woke me at five every morning, presumably to stop me having misguided, unhealthy, heathen dreams. In the blood-red restaurant, you sit on cushions, and a waiter comes with a ewer and bowl to wash your hands (if you have them), and you eat the most aromatic *karahis*, stuffed naan, pilau and the only kulfi I've ever felt fond of.

The other place is on the roof of the Frontier Hotel, where you can look out over the great dun fortress, at the kites circling, the sprawling, steaming, cacophonous city, and eat salads of onion and white radish, bowls of setting mutton, kebabs in the central Asian style, alternating lumps of meat and fat, and shredded chicken, okra and chickpeas.

But above and beyond the food, you should really come here for the truly humbling, dignified hospitality of the Afghans, which in itself is a truth worth a ream of speculative foreign-policy briefings.

Pakistan is, of course, a dry country – which suits me fine. At a particularly stuffy dinner in Islamabad, I was pleased to see a waiter circumnavigating the table offering red or white: i.e., Coke or Seven Up. And that, too, is worth a quire of columnists' musings.

Go with God.

Japan

Market

Tokyo's Tsukiji fish market is one of the great wonders of the world. Or great disasters, depending on how you organise your breathing. For a man called Gill, it's a family reunion. This is the biggest fish market in the world. The size of a small ocean, it gets through 2,500 tons of fish, worth £16 million, every day – from things the size of an eyelash to whales. That's 670,000 tons of fish and more than £4 billion a year. It's a lot. How can there be that many fish in the sea? How can there be that many fishermen? And the variety: there are things here with fins that defy natural selection and digestion. If it swims, it dies.

A lot of it dies quite slowly. Boxes wriggle and squirm. Mouths gape and gulp on slabs. Exoskeletons clatter and clack. Antennae search for a familiar ecology. And round your ankles, eels slither, making a break for it. It's God's great blessing that fish can't scream.

The market is a frenetic Nintendo game where you have to make your way through a labyrinth of alleys past monsters of the deep while dodging kamikaze delivery vans. The high point of the morning is the tuna auction. Picture a hangar the size of a couple of football pitches. The tuna lie in neat lines stretching as far as the eye can see. They've been iced on the ships and gently smoke. The floor is shrouded in mist. They look like unexploded bombs.

The bidding is frantic and high-pitched. Each fish is beautifully calligraphied with red paint to denote its owner. Dealers stand in tense huddles wearing ninja headbands, kneading fingers of flesh like bonsai Hannibal Lecters.

In one of the hundreds of wholesalers' stalls I watched as the

Kabuki-mongers neatly butchered the morning's catch with razor knives the size and shape of samurai swords. Their blue fin tuna the size of an obese nine-year-old had cost £4,000. By this evening, it will have made £17,000.

There are 125 million Japanese. (I know, there seem to be at least that number on Sloane Street.) And they all eat fish every day. If you're of a hand-wringing temperament and mind this vast pillaging of the seas, where everything from infants and eggs measured in trillions to lumps of nameless, boneless, faceless jelly are consumed with a slurping verve, then stick to tofu. The Japanese manage both.

Personally, I have no problem with this daily massacre. When I see the miserable, wizened and parsimonious thing our fishing industry has become, I can't find it in myself to blame the Japanese (or indeed the Spanish). All I feel is envy. These people don't just enjoy fish in all its comprehensive schools of variety. In preparing and perfecting it, they rise to the pinnacle of civilisation. If all we can do is eat fish shapes and dumb fillets battered in concrete overcoats, then frankly all we deserve is a smear of fish paste. The good things from the bottom of the world's barrel belong to those who know how to enjoy them, not merely endure them.

It's virtually impossible to eat a bad meal in Japan (although I see that the Zagat guide has just crowned Starbucks as one of the top ten places to go in Tokyo, which has convinced me never to open any of their ridiculous books ever again) and you can sit down to some of the most vauntingly sublime things ever offered to pleasure. At its finest, Japanese food has a pitch of aesthetic excellence that is rarely conceived of elsewhere.

In Hiroshima, as I sat at a sushi bar, the cook showed me a fish – what they call a lionfish: a beautiful pied and speckled thing, a foot long, with spinnaker fins and sinister spines. Not a fishmonger in Britain would sell it as food, not even for cats. On the plate, it transmuted into five sorts of sushi: slices of muscle, liver slivers, shoulder and head flakes, and the fine, silky jelly that lurks just below the skin. And it was presented with the intact skeleton set like a flower arrangement or a Philip Treacy hat. At the end of dinner, which included a cold fish head no bigger than a goldfish that you dissected with chopsticks for minute morsels of intense achievement, we finished with a soup made from the lionfish bones. It was beggaring.

When we got back, we went to a Japanese restaurant in London's West End. As it happens, this place made the first Japanese food both the Blonde and I ever ate – though before we met. It's one of those little bonding coincidences that turn couples into cooing doves and turn their friends to sticking their fingers down their throats. I can still remember the surprise and joy at my first mouthful of maguro and the shock of my first daikon. And then there was the giddy, junky excitement of not being able to stop. Not for anything. Not ever. I had to have more. Had to have everything. That first lunch was the most expensive thing I've ever bought. It cost me all the money I had in the world and I didn't regret a penny. The Blonde's the same – though I bet hers didn't cost cash (it still doesn't).

This time, I took Blind Pugh, the Afghan and an American friend of hers, called Jonah, who I dearly hoped was eating raw fish as a piecemeal revenge for his name. It wasn't good, the food. It was okay, but not great. Maybe it was their bad luck that I had just got back from Tokyo, but the sushi and sashimi seemed tired and sweaty and thick-fingered. And my udon noodles with tempura was a mess, which is the one thing Japanese food should never be. The noodles were dun spaghetti in thin miso; the tempura sloughed slime into the mix, leaving wobbly prawns like skinned ET fingers.

As I left, I asked for a copy of the menu, which I always do and am invariably given.

'No, you can't have a menu. We haven't got one.' Now don't tease – I've seen it. 'Well, we can't find one.' Didn't have any trouble finding Pearl Harbor, did you?

It's nice to be able to use the old jokes, and there's no reason why a new infatuation should dull the old puerile sense of humour.

Manners

In a restaurant in Kyoto that served only fish seventy ways, and all of it mackerel, I asked my charming and sophisticated guide, a man who bore an uncanny resemblance to the bonsai teacher in *The Karate Kid*, and who had spent a professional life fixing for Western journalists, if he would teach me about Japanese table manners.

'Oh, no, I couldn't,' he said, staring modestly at the table.

No, please, I won't be insulted, tell me when I get it wrong and tell me why. 'No, no, I couldn't.'

Look, I write about food, I need to know, so please teach me. I won't be offended. 'No, no, I couldn't.'

Look here, I'm paying you. He had an agonised mien. 'No, I mean I couldn't, because it isn't possible. You wouldn't understand. You are not sensitive to Japanese thinking. We,' he waved a chopstick at the room, 'have all agreed that foreigners are excused table manners. When you make infantile mess and clumsy, embarrassing mistake with fingers and gross rudeness with your mouth, when you eat with insulting selfishness, when you are ungrateful and Western, we don't see it. We are blind to your lack of finesse and sensitivity.'

Oh, righty-ho, then. Well, just tell me one thing. 'Don't leave chopsticks in rice. It is sign of death.'

Right. And, I suppose, don't make rude noises eating soup. 'No, Benny Hill noises very good and pleasant.'

Right. Well, you know we laugh at you because you can't pronounce your rs? 'Weally?'

Japan is the only country I've ever been to that wants tourists not to understand what they are looking at. It thinks people who aren't born Japanese are psychologically, intellectually, spiritually and aesthetically incapable of understanding their culture. Each time you are confronted by seven rocks in gravel, two lilies in a pot, a dwarf Christmas tree, a bedroom without a bed or a limerick without a joke, a polite little local will say: 'Sorry, very Japanese, difficult to explain,' which translates as: 'You are too cretinously oafish and hairy to comprehend the finer feelings that are needed to admire this teapot in all its sublime simplicity.'

To respond, smile with as much patronage as you can muster and say: 'Yes, it's a pity you'll never know what your decorative plagiarised trinket civilisation looks like through sophisticated Western eyes.' Or: 'How droll of you to have so many Elvis impersonators, and to make one of them prime minister.'

The one area where we really do have to doff our bowlers to the children of the rising sun is in the kitchen. No community goes to the same neurotic and aesthetic lengths for lunch as the Japanese. The skills involved in preparing, growing and serving food are way beyond those considered decent, necessary or appropriate in other cultures. What is particularly memorable (and here, my admiration is irony-free) is that the exhaustingly complex dexterity and care of preparation produces the purest form of simplicity. That is some trick.

Vietnam

Dog is the dish at the wild frontier of gastronomy. It's a roast dog that guards the custom post between epicurean inquisitiveness and uncivilised barbarism. Most of us think of ourselves as being sophisticated and adventurous, but we draw the line at puppy.

It's irrational, of course. Why make distinctions between species? As a rule of paw, we tend not to eat other carnivores, but it's only a recommendation, not an injunction. Piggywiggies are omnivores like us, cleverer than mutts and much more human in their biology – and we eat every single scrap of them, including their scratchings. But in the West, we've decided that dog is the line in the sand; a species too far. It's a sort of proxy cannibalism: you just don't eat your best friends.

You know where all this is leading ...

It was, without a smear of doubt, the filthiest room I've ever sat down in. Not just eaten in, but been in. It was in Vietnam. Hue, on the Perfumed River. The temperature was in the high 80s, humidity in the 90s.

The distempered blue walls were patinated with a thick flock of suppurating mould with occasional H-block flourishes. The concrete floor was ankle-deep in detritus, the main constituent of which was screwed-up sodden loo paper. The tables were sticky white plastic, a Braille health exclamation of cigarette burns and nameless viscous pools. The seats were minute infant-school stools. The neon light attached to a pole beside my seat was insulated with the bodies and defunct pupal sleeping bags of a trillion winged things.

The menu, scribbled on a wall, offered five ways with dog, one of them being boiled brain. The waitress, a lady of uncertain age, with a face that was a sanctuary for abused make-up and a mouth big enough to swallow a fox terrier whole, smiled until her gob looked like a row of marble beach huts. What did we fancy? We demanded the finest dog known to man.

The Vietnamese eat a lot of dog – but only in the winter, and only at the end of the month (the first fifteen days are thought to be unpropitious, though it's quite the reverse if you're a dog). Pooch, they say, is warming, and should traditionally be eaten when old friends meet.

What arrived was three dishes: cold sliced boiled dog, dog stew, and dog heart and liver sausage. The Blonde took a long hard look and passed. Gastronomically, we've grazed the world together, matched dish for dish; we've been horses for courses. But she wasn't swallowing this. She said she wasn't that old, and didn't like me enough to wolf a dog.

Now I've always said, as a professional conceit, that I'd eat anything that anyone else in the world ate, as long as it didn't involve a bet. But even I paused before slipping cold Fido onto the tongue. I could feel civilisation tugging at my sleeve.

But only briefly. It tasted slightly gamey; a soft, dense meat – a bit musty. Actually, what it tasted like was cold dog's breath. The stew was better, though it had apparently been butchered with a hammer and was as chilli-hot as a Dobermann's bite on the buttocks. Frankly, the meat could have been anything. But the sausage – my dears, the sausage – was by far and away the best. Turdy little black puddings, rich and unctuous, they had the dark savour of a really good illegal pâté.

It is perfectly possible to eat dog back here in Blighty. You'll just have to prepare it yourself. You can eat any dog, but unless you're having a lot of mates round, I suggest you stick to the smaller breeds.

If you don't have one handy, any of the animal charities or dogs' homes will sell you one for very little. Pound for pound,

mongrel puppy is cheaper than chicken. Dog is low in fat and
high in protein and natural minerals. It is, as far as I am aware,
the only mammalian carnivore that's bred for food, the general
kitchen rule being, don't eat anything that might eat you or
has more offensive droppings than yours.

Of course, if you want to splash out, make an occasion of
it, you can spend a lot more on pedigree. There are, surprisingly, sixteen types of dog that have been bred exclusively for
meat, ranging from the family-sized chow-chow with its black
tongue and easy-to-kill unfriendly nature, to the unorderable
izcuintlipotzotli and xoloitzcuintli, both from Mexico. Table
dogs, as opposed to lapdogs, are indigenous all over the Far
East and the Americas. I recommend one of the miniature hair-
less varieties, such as the Peruvian Inca orchid or the Bolivian
khala. They come oven-ready – and you get crackling.

There's a general misconception that it's illegal to kill your
own domestic animals here. Good news. It isn't. It's only illegal
if you enjoy it (so the traditional tenderising slow beating-to-
death is probably out). What you're not allowed to do is sell
privately butchered meat. For your own consumption, it's perfectly kosher. In fact, you can eat the whole pet shop: hamster,
parrot, shire horse – though not the girl behind the till.

When we'd finished – when I'd finished – I asked politely
if I could see the kitchen. The moment it was translated, the
restaurant fell utterly silent. You could have heard a chopstick
drop. The waitress's smile came down like a wet weekend in
Worthing, and I suddenly felt like a Bateman cartoon: The
Man Who Asked to See the Kitchen in a Vietnamese Dog
Restaurant. Life's a bitch and then you diarrhoea.

The Vietnamese do another delicacy – unborn duck, boiled
in the shell – and when someone kindly gave me one, it seemed
churlish not to eat it. I don't want to be lying on my deathbed
and be asked if I have any regrets, and gasp: 'Yes, I didn't play
hunt the thimble in a sleeping bag with Elle Macpherson, and
I didn't eat the pre-natal duck.'

You consume the unborn in much the same way you do your breakfast egg – though without the soldiers. The foetus is twelve days old, so there's not much in the way of break and bone, and there's still a lot of yolk. Rather worryingly, there's also a seepage of ducky liquid in the bottom of the shell, which the Vietnamese are insistent you don't waste. It's supposed to be particularly propitious for something or other. Probably the other.

What's it like? Well, it's edible. In fact, it's quite decent. It's just not actually an improvement on a nice boiled barren egg, and certainly no competition for a roast duck. Medical benefits aside, my feeling is: get in quicker or wait a bit longer. I don't know that I'm in favour of an age of consent for ingredients, but twelve days does seem a bit premature for a duck.

There's also the turtle. For all of you preparing to frogmarch (or toadwalk) me to the World Wildlife Fund, let me say that this was actually a large terrapin. Tortoises and their kin have a symbolic gravitas in the East. They represent great age, and age is synonymous with respect and wisdom. I really like the metaphysical and metaphoric aspect of eating here. Everything has a meaning and power beyond the peristaltic, which, frankly, is bad luck for the terrapin, because you probably wouldn't eat one simply because you were hungry, even though it does come as a ready-made serving suggestion.

It isn't bad either, although perhaps interesting would be a better word. I've never been more fascinated to see what was under the cloche. I half expected clockwork. But it's actually a gelatinous, bony goo, that texture the Chinese so prize. The skin is like savoury green rubber, and gingerly working your way through a foot with its metatarsals, tarsals and claws is barely worth the bother. Still, a boiled terrapin on the table is a talking point, and some of you may like to consider it for Christmas this year as an adventurous alternative to turkey.

The restaurant that did the hot-gravy turtle also advertised a number of other off-piste gastronomic items. Rat, for instance, and something called scent weasels, which I was shown, stacked in a corner. They were sad little things, with black eyes that glowed from inside bamboo corset cages. They looked a bit like possums, only less friendly, and their given name went ahead of them. I'd be interested if anyone can tell me what these little delicacies actually are.

I was truly bowled over by the food in Vietnam. More than anything, I was entranced by the sheer range, invention and skill at balancing sparkling, vivid flavours. Even the lowliest trishaw driver would approach his morning pho with an epicurean concentration. It was a humbling lesson in how to eat – and proof that sophistication comes with appetite, skill and taste, not with china and downlighters.

After the sharp clear flavours of Vietnam, our grub seems muddy and out of focus, as if it has been airbrushed with fat, or is eaten through a veil.

Oh God, I nearly forgot: the last bit of the turtle. When we'd finished, the waitress brought out its liver, heart and pancreas, raw on a plate, with a cupful of its blood. She then took out a medical syringe and carefully extracted the bile from the gall bladder. 'Hang about,' I thought. 'Sod the spirit of adventure. I'm not jacking that up.' And she squirted it into a cupful of rice alcohol that smelt like surgical spirit. This little elixir, I was breathlessly told, would turn a man into a buffalo with a pylon between its legs. It would supply an erection of such unsurpassed quality and fecundity that I would resemble the Eiffel Tower on Millennium night. I gave it to my driver, who was as wide as he was tall and as ugly as he was short.

Next morning, grinning through the obvious wreckage of his deflated body, he said he'd shared it with his old dad and they'd hit the town and become not just sexual pile drivers, but irresistible to boot. (This might have been a mistake in translation – it might have been 'as a boot'.) If you're going the turtle route this Christmas, you could bear this in mind instead of the sherry for the loyal toast.

Chinese

Chinese restaurant

I vividly remember my first Chinese restaurant. It was just the same as your first Chinese restaurant – unless you actually come from China, in which case it will have been utterly different from any Chinese restaurant you ever saw. Light porcelain bowls with chrysanthemums in the bottom, brush drawings of cranes, dragons and mountains that floated in mist, the fretwork pagoda over the bar and all those little red tassels on everything. And I can remember being taught how to use chopsticks by my mother.

What Subbuteo is to real football, chopsticks are to catching a greased piglet in a fair on stilts. Picking up the last slimy mushroom is an exciting game for all the family. Thrills, spills and a combination of nerve and skill. No dice, no batteries, all the luck of the fortune cookie.

I learnt fluent chopstick at a very young age. I was inordinately proud of my dexterity. It's one of those little signs that separate us middle-class boys from hoi polloi, like having a thirty-year-old haircut and stuffed olives instead of bubble gum. Other oiks might be able to fake broken backs to get penalties, they might be able to french-kiss Tizer bottles, but the Chinese restaurant separated those of us who had dinner in the evening from those of us who had it at midday.

'Ah, I see you use your chopstick as a pilum,' I used to say to northern chums at college. 'How droll. A pilum? Oh, it was the Roman short stabbing spear. Shall we ask the waiter for a spoon?'

Chinese restaurants produced the first exotic food to get into this brown-palate post-war country, and they were given a traditional hearty British welcome – that is, loads of jokes about Alsatians in the fridge, 'This duck is rubbery', 'Grad you enjoyed it' and lots of lager puke on the pavement, leading to the commonly held belief that the food was actually fried poison, botulism in a bowl, and that the only antidote was a huge inoculation of alcohol and stout Britishness.

Native resistance and suspicion have remained undimmed, undented and undaunted for forty years. Most of us eat in Chinese restaurants because they're cheap, you don't have to book and they take orders after the pub's closed. Most of us have eaten the same four dishes off the longest menus in the country all our lives. But still the wily orientals persist, and Chinese restaurants have opened in every town and village in the country that boasts a pub.

Why they bothered is an opaque oriental mystery. The hideously, hysterically depressing existence of life as a Chinese waiter in a suburb in the Midlands is beyond imagination. Mao's long march was a stroll in the park, compared with Chinese restaurants' yomp for respectability. Constrained by the absurdly low prices their customers reckon Chinese food is worth, these Peking Stars, Jade Dragons and Oriental Gardens have persevered and accommodated. The accommodation has produced a style of food that has only a passing acquaintance with its roots. A stunted pidgin cuisine dictated by the most tasteless, parsimonious, uncouth clientele in the world: the British lower classes. So terrified of novelty and menus that they have to order dishes by number or, most embarrassingly, a whole dinner with a single letter: 'We'll have set menu A and four pints of Carlsberg, chop chop, tee-hee.'

Chinese food transformed itself into soup-kitchen dinner that was cheaper than you could eat at home. It imitated the familiar brassy flavours favoured by the gastronomically illiterate: sweet and vinegary, the muddled fruit and spice of brown sauce and ketchup. How it must have galled the chefs to come from one of the oldest and most sophisticated tables in the world to produce gallons of the nastiest dish ever consumed by choice, Chinglish sweet and sour prawns: sauce the colour of a stripper's knickers and the consistency of a politician's promise, the swimming chunks of tinned African pineapple and frozen, watery farmed prawns with a splash of white malt vinegar and a spoonful of cornstarch.

On top of all that – the unpleasantness, the low wages, the ignorance, the drunkenness, the weather, the years of being patronised and ignored by the foodie establishment. (I am as guilty as any.) Then, just when the fashion turns to the East, when all the tastes that have been kept in the cupboard for a generation have become flavour of the month, just when it looks at last as if Chinese food is set to break through, along come the Thais and take all the laurels, or bean sprouts. Thai food – that crass, limited imitation. It's just not fair, like having a wardrobe full of Balenciaga and wearing C&A.

Chinese food in this country has become a prisoner of its reputation. The one or two attempts to drag it out of the takeaway to make it classy have foundered on celebrity gimmicks such as the dreadful Mr Chow's, with its Italian waiters and tables reserved for Terry Venables. And talking of waiters, the rudeness of the Chinese is another piece of collective received wisdom. Nobody ever comments on the unbelievably foul behaviour of the customers, the surliness, the dismissiveness, the barely contained racism. The Chinese have got every reason, every reason from one to 110 and set reasons from A to D, to be not just rude, but ruddy murderous.

Shark's fin soup

The problem with judging Chinese food is that we long-nosed milk-eaters have to use our round-gullet Western mouths. We may all share the same taste buds the world over, but we actually taste food with a complicated set of culturally nurtured preferences and prejudices. We don't taste the same thing. I

may like a dish, but I may be liking it for completely different reasons from the waiter. For instance, the Chinese value
texture much more than we do, particularly things that can
only be described as snottish.

We started off with the usual stuff: sweet and vinegary
nuggets, bits of shredded lettuce, crabs' claws that looked like
they'd been slammed in a drawer. All very good. Better than
that really: excellent. But you see, that's the thing with your
chinky, the first mouthful is always the best; it's all invariably
downhill after the first course. Except here. I saw that they had
shark's fin soup for £44.

Now what does £44 soup taste like? Well, you've got to
know, haven't you? You can't go through life having passed up
the most expensive soup in the world. It came in two varieties:
with crab or with cabbage. I had cabbage. A very small bowl
appeared, according to the menu direct from Hong Kong. I
dipped my spoon, faint with expectation. Sip, savour. Yes, yes?
Sip again to get the full benefit. Yes, yes? I was regarded by six
round eyes. Yes, yes? Well, um, nice. Thin, but nice. Thin but
nice chicken stock with a shy pair of underage bok choi and
three lumps of overboiled chook breast. Anastasia had the one
with crab. It was better, gloopily tasting of crab.

I must say in favour of my soup that I have never concentrated quite so hard on anaemic chicken stock before. Forty-
four pounds' worth of clearish water does arrest the attention,
as does the palpable absence of shark. That was unnerving. I'd
have settled for a sluggish dogfish. You knew it was there, somewhere, you just couldn't see it. Just when you thought it was
safe to go back into the soup ... Dumdumdumdumdumdum
... I imagined the gently rippling surface would be suddenly
broken by the jaws of a great white and I'd be sucked off the
table like Robert Shaw. I hummed 'Ladies of Spain' to keep
up my spirits.

Was it worth £44? Well, that depends. Was it soup or was it
art? I was put in mind of Damien Hirst's shark in a tank and,

I thought, this is probably what the water tastes like. Cup for cup, it probably costs about the same. In fact, they should call it 'The Impossibility of Something Living to Imagine – a £44 Bowl of Soup'.

Along with soup we had a £49 abalone.

Now, they said it was a whole abalone, but frankly it could have been half an abalone or indeed any fraction of abalone. I'm not altogether au fait with abalone and they have no discernible features. Although I can put a ballpark figure on a bowl of soup, when it comes to abalone the sky's the limit.

The Blonde asked me what an abalone was, and because we were with company, and I didn't wish to look a fool, I said with some authority that it was a member of the abalone family and lived in an abalone's house. 'What does an abalone's house look like?' she quizzed, spitefully. I'm glad you asked: a cross between a cockleshell and a thatched cottage, but different.

It was a brown thing, about this big, and sort of this shape. The waiter cut it into four bite-size bits and suggested we eat it with mustard. I knew that. Abalone doesn't want to be eaten. It does its utmost to avoid the combined utensils of two continents, slithering and skittering around the plate in its oyster sauce. Finally, owing to their carnivore's nails, the ladies managed to secure a lump and pop it into their mouths.

Their faces were a picture. A picture probably painted by Edvard Munch. The collective expression was of horror, abject, regurgitant horror. James and I snagged our morsels and gingerly pouched them. For those of you with a sensitive disposition, or who haven't been to church yet, I strongly suggest you skip the rest of this paragraph. I have searched hither and yon for a polite description of the essence of abalone and I am afraid there is only one possible simile.

It's private – positively, undeniably, deeply, femininely private. 'Yum,' said James. 'Yum, I could eat another one.' 'You're mad,' said the girls. 'It's utterly disgusting.' 'Don't worry your little heads about it,' I interjected. 'It's a boy thing.'

The rest of the meal was a bit of an anticlimax after that. Well, it would be.

Sichuan

The capsicum family hails from America. The peppers – bell, sweet, hot, quite hot, bearably hot, uncomfortably hot, seriously hot, drunk-dare hot and hobbit flaming-ring hot – didn't get to the rest of the world's kitchens until the sixteenth century. There are two good-golly-gosh things that strike you about this. First, what did Indians do for curry before stout Cortes? And second, why on earth did anyone put one in their mouth twice?

Imagine Walter Raleigh returning to James I's court. 'Majesty, unfortunately we didn't manage to find El Dorado and the uncountable riches of the New World. However, I think it's fair to say the trip wasn't a complete failure. We have brought back some fascinating new comestibles. Try a bit of this.' 'Och aye, and what do you call this, Sir Walter? Chilli, is it? Give us a wee one, then. Aaarrgh! Jings! Off with the regicidal murthering ned's heed!'

The desire to have severe pain inflicted on the most intimate, delicate and sensitive bits of your body defies explanation. No amount of boffinry explaining that chillis remind us of orgasms really seems to make sense. I've had an orgasm and it's not remotely reminiscent of inadvertently chewing a little red jobbie. But still, chillies have made their way into virtually every national larder. I think only the French are sparing with the heat.

The people who are most addicted to chillies are not Mexicans, Sri Lankans or Hungarians, but Serbs. Their consumption of insanely psycho pickled chilli has nothing to do with food, it's simply part of their rudimentary, sadomasochistic bonding that involves drink, stomach ulcers and recreational pogroms. But as part of a nutritious, balanced and varied diet, nobody gets as hot under the epiglottis as the Sichuan Chinese. Sichuan food makes Mexican taste like sorbet.

There was a new Sichuan restaurant which had been given some of the best reviews I've ever seen. Paul Levy, the Alf Ramsey of food, sent me a postcard ordering me to go. When I actually found it, there was nothing to indicate that this might be foodie nirvana, one of the greatest restaurants at the heart of the most food-obsessed city in the world – and that is one of the reasons critics will have loved it.

We are all different, we critics. We have individual peccadilloes and prejudices and gastro G-spots. But there are also certain things that draw us together. The moment I walked in, I realised it ticked every box. For a start, it plainly hadn't had £1 million spent on its interior. In fact, it came from the school of Jordan anti-design: every penny spent had made it uglier.

Then there was the food, which is an authentic cuisine rooted in geography and history, not a Jabberwocky fusion or personal interpretation. It was not a chain or a copycat – and there was no black cod or chocolate fondant. Chinese food has been declining in London, and the cheap restaurants across the road in Chinatown are now just rude tourist clip joints; instead, we have the high-camp chinoiserie of Hakkasan and China Tang. But this was a rare Sichuan restaurant, not the usual Hong Kong Cantonese. And food doesn't exist in a cultural vacuum. China is the nation of the moment. It has power and energy and the Zeitgeist.

The final chummy attraction for critics was the menu: it had tons of offal on it. Nothing attracts us like the soft internal bits. If you eat a lot, you end up eating colon, udder and testicles, sucking weird glands and licking lungs. We live for the vibrant vitals without bone or muscle. I know you think it's disgusting, but actually, it makes us all very, very good in bed. Except Giles Coren, of course.

I'm unsure about exactly what we ate because almost everything looked like disembodied shards of gloop submerged in an oily miasma with a grated topping of chilli. The first mouthful thudded me back in my chair and I emitted a small strangulated, 'Wow!' It was almost the last coherent thing I said. After that, a painful numbness spread through my mouth and each new dish was experienced as a mugger's stab behind the eyes. It seemed as if an unseen hand was roughly injecting Algipan up my nose. My cheeks began to melt and my lips quivered with an involuntary palsy. Sticky sweat ran down my back into pools in my soggy underpants. With a strangulated falsetto, I managed to ask the waiter to bring the specially mixed offal stewed in medieval dragon spit. 'Very hot,' said the waiter. 'You sure?' Bring it on, China boy, I sighed.

What arrived was another cauldron – an inferno of blood-curdled oil, Bruegelishly bobbing with tripe and lurking flesh, scabbed with chilli. I prodded with my chopsticks and came out with a corner of pig's liver that collapsed like hot jelly. The whole thing looked like nothing so much as the bucket under a field-hospital operating table. I put a piece of nameless gut in my mouth and it was as if everything that had come before had merely been toying with me. I heard a distant choir, a white light exploded in my head, and I went to a place beyond physical agony, beyond understanding, a place of pure pain outside worldly vanity. I looked down and could see myself, my face glazed with my own juices, my hair standing in sticky fronds, puce eyeballs protruding and revolving like dashboard compasses, my mouth codding with mumbles as I shook and hiccupped with involuntary spasms. All the major junctions of my body oozed with a noisome effluvium.

If this isn't a good look on you, I don't recommend a Sichuan restaurant as a first-date destination. But for critics, this dish was nirvana – like being granted a taste of the godhead – and the restaurant an unctuous chapel in the pantheon of epicureanism.

Sichuan is extreme eating. Try it if you dare. Whether or not it will end up being a success, I can't say. As Mao said, when he was asked what he thought of the French Revolution, it's still too early to tell. I can, though, offer you a fortune cookie of advice. Confucius, he say: 'Put the wet wipes in the fridge before you go to bed.'

Indian

Butter

'If you really want to know Indian food, then you need to understand our relationship with butter,' I was told by Camellia Panjabi, a lady of formidable knowledge and even more formidable appetite. One of the nice things about playing with your food, which is essentially what I do for a living, is that you automatically become a member of a fascinating and gluttonous dining club. Gourmands and epicureans aren't always nice, and they're not always entirely sane, but they are always interesting – and the best of them enlightening, in a way that transcends recipes and digestion.

The brotherhood of greed amounts to an introduction, so I wasn't surprised to find a note from a person I'd never met attached to a cookery book in my Bombay hotel room last week. And Camellia wasn't remotely surprised when I called and suggested we should eat as much as possible, as soon as possible. So she started with the butter. Indians think of butter as a semi-mystical substance. Cows are sacred and all their by-products are blessed. Ghee, the clarified butter for cooking, and the golden stuff itself 'is the soul of our food. It's luxurious, extravagant, generous and the epitome of goodness.'

But it just isn't, I pointed out, pointlessly. Camellia took us to a street stall, with a large wok in which a slab of about a pound of best butter spluttered and sank into itself like a yellow *Titanic*. In the street, a chap was cutting bread rolls in half, the sort of cheap, square white rolls that they sell in packs of six and fill with grated cheese in canteens. Before the English tipped up here, white bread had been brought to the Maharashtran coast by the Portuguese, and ever since, the people of Bombay have taken it to their hearts – quite literally. The split rolls were liberally dunked and turned in the foaming butter, then set aside, while a melange of finely chopped, masala'd vegetables was slopped into the well of unctuousness. More fresh butter was added in 8oz slabs. The vegetables were mollycoddled into the slick. 'It's important that the customers see how much butter is being used in the cooking. They have to witness the extravagance, the expense.'

We sat at a little Formica table and plates of vegetable mush – which I conservatively guessed were, by this time, 40 per cent butter – were plopped in front of us, with slabs of yet more fresh butter sitting like a soft sunhat on top. The glistening rolls were dipped in and … bon appétit. As a taste sensation, you couldn't fault it. It was right up there with deep-fried Mars bars: silky, delicious and repellent in equal measure. Coming from a culture that lies awake at night listening to its arteries silt up, and for whom cholesterol has replaced Beelzebub as the quintessence of evil, it wasn't naughty but nice – naughty but nice is a profiterole. It was a catastrophic medical pile-up.

'Ah,' explained Camellia, as another plate appeared. 'I just wanted you to try this.' A thick layer of grated cheese covered more buttery vegetable curry. Oh, and what's this here, in the middle, hiding like an elephant behind a palm tree? Another vast pat of butter. This was all, by the way, as an addendum, a savoury, to lunch. 'Snacks,' said Camellia. 'Bombayans love their snacks.' Out of the corner of my head, I remembered the end of *Little Black Sambo*, where the tiger runs round and round the tree until he turns into ghee. Fear magically becomes pleasure, rather like the dead lion surrounded by bees on the Golden Syrup tin – 'Out of the strong came forth sweetness.'

Curry

Lots of plates came. What they contained, I can't really say, because like all Indian food the dishes are so stewed and have such a similar consistency, are so baroquely, intricately wired with smells and flavours that they're impossible to deconstruct. That's not a criticism: I enjoy the breadable, soupy, sloppy nature of it all, encouraging mutual finger-licking and action painting. Altogether, it was an interesting diversion, like going through a selection of edible wallpaper swatches, but I don't think it's quite dinner. You're left with that overall subcontinental dark brown taste. There was something still missing – the M word. If I were absolutely forced on the limbs and lives of my children to live the rest of my life on a vegetarian diet, I guess I'd choose southern Indian. But I'd probably let them lose a couple of fingers before I gave in.

South Africa

Game park

I imagine that 90 per cent of restaurateurs would, if asked, say that location was the single most important element when starting a restaurant. But, in my random and exhaustive questioning of punters, location comes fairly low down the list of things people look for. The customers' top answer is atmosphere. Customers don't, in my experience, generally say: 'Let's go to Polenta-U-Like because it's got a really smart postal address.' They don't say: 'You really must try Gob-Stuffers because they have a dear little car park just round the corner.'

Restaurateurs, on the other hand, seem to think that atmosphere is something the customers ought to bring with them. A head waiter once told me that the punters in his restaurant were a big disappointment: 'Their standard of conversation is very poor, they don't seem to know how to enjoy themselves.' I pointed out that maybe it was because the room had all the welcome of a headmaster's study, his staff had the charm of Serbian gravediggers and the intrusive and hideous pianist apparently could only play 'It's a Quarter to Three, There's No One in the Place Except You and Me'. He shrugged my suggestions aside as mere amateur speculation. 'No, no. We're situated on a corner of the most expensive street in Mayfair.' The actual food on both lists comes somewhere after value for money – whatever that is – cleanliness and service, which punters interpret as speed and restaurateurs as dexterity.

I've recently had an amazing dinner in a place that had more atmosphere than Disney World on Snow White's birthday. As a location it's one of the most unlikely on the planet. To get there you have to be taken by a guide carrying a rifle. It's set in hundreds of miles of wilderness and the nearest fast-food takeaway is patronised exclusively by vultures. Londolozi is a game park in the Eastern Transvaal. Well, it was in the Transvaal when we arrived, but it was Mpumalanga when we left. South Africa is in the process of renaming things. As a gesture of good will, we might consider giving them back all those Mandela crescents, avenues and community centres that spent the apartheid years seeking political asylum here.

Garry with the rifle and Patterson, our tracker with the sixth sense and the torch, led the Blonde and me to a rough boma (stockaded camp) on the veld. Inside the fence a large fire crackles and trestle tables are lit by paraffin lamps. Above us, that remarkable African sky you've heard so much about, a scythe moon and the Southern Cross glaring down at the dancing sparks from the logs. The smell of bush mixes with wood smoke and grilling meat. Outside, things snort, shuffle and growl. To anyone who has read a page of *King Solomon's Mines*, it's all utterly, hugely, hypnotically romantic.

'This is a traditional Shangaan camp site; the Shangaan are the indigenous tribe here,' says Garry helpfully, and there beside the fire is the traditional Shangaan drinks table with five sorts of gin. The traditional Shangaan welcome was offered by Katherine, our hostess, who used to be food and beverage manager at the equally traditional but somewhat less romantic Lygon Arms in Broadway, Gloucestershire.

There were a dozen of us dining. It was an odd collection of people. No, a bizarre collection, like those Wells Fargo stop-offs in cowboy films where everyone on the stagecoach has been thrown together by circumstance. You spend the first ten minutes guessing who's not going to make it to the second reel. The American couple with the Diet Cokes are definitely about to buy the farm. She's so mellowed out on her why-worry-who-needs-orgasm pills she's still trying to work out why this restaurant doesn't have a roof. Her husband has a beard and a cap that says 'Gleneagles'; he's ripe for an arrow between the shoulder blades.

The chef walks into the circle of firelight and, in traditional style, intones the oral menu. She's so large that if she stood still for too long they'd rename her and hold elections. We start with green mealie soup and marog pesto. To you and me that's cream of sweetcorn, warming and thick and a bit like savoury porridge. The marog is a type of wild spinach, and interestingly reminiscent of buffalo cud. Next, there is warthog with fig sauce. The north London couple opposite have a whispered argument about whether or not warthog is kosher. Purely gastronomically, to confuse warthog with pork is an insult to pigs. It's a dense grey meat with no fat and a thin gamey taste. I'm glad I've tried it and I'm glad we don't have them here. Warthogs are sociable creatures; they trot about in single files of decreasing size like muddy Russian dolls. Lions are very partial to them, but then, if you've ever watched a lion eat, you'll know they're not one of nature's epicureans.

An awful lot of being on a game park is watching things eat. Everyone's chewing someone else and it does make you realise that being at the top of the food chain has the priceless advantage of not having continually to look over your shoulder worrying that you're about to be the object of a snack attack. The American woman's annual consumption of Prozac and Valium wouldn't begin to take the edge off the anxiety of being an impala for a night.

Pudding is a traditional whisky and almond gateau with apricot ice cream and chocolate sauce, sweet and stodgy, perfectly made and perfectly incongruous. The man next to me is a bright red expat, whose wife has got on the outside of a quart of the Shangaans' traditional Beefeater gin. He is complaining bitterly about the old country and the new country: 'I used to get the *Spectator* sent out, but it's too bloody left-wing now.' He's off like a warthog harrumphing about the unions, the National Health Service, the EC.

All around us nature lurks and stalks either diner or dinner, and I think how spectacularly lucky I feel to be well fed and safe and sitting in front of the fire in this remarkable place. I also think, as the blimp drones on, that even if nothing out there wants to eat you, you can still end up consumed by bitterness, envy, anger and spleen. A camp fire tends to make me a touch philosophical. Wherever you go, the weirdest animals you ever see come from the Home Counties.

Garry the guide has found a scorpion; he palms it lovingly. Is it dangerous? 'No, not really. Your leg might balloon up to three times its natural size, the pain would be bearable after a couple of days and you'd walk again in a week.' You wouldn't like to just slip it into this bloke's pocket, would you? Garry's shocked: it might hurt the scorpion. As we left, the eyes of a pack of hyenas shone in the headlights. It was just like being Richard Gere leaving Daphne's.

Ostrich

When I was Mr Chips and taught cooking, I used to say that if you could cook a chicken, you ought to be able to cook an ostrich. The general principles and the engineering were the same. I said it with the casual insouciant authority of a man who has never actually tried to stuff a trussed ostrich into the Baby Belling.

I am not really sure what I think about ostrich as dinner. It's becoming quite commonplace. Five years ago it was novelty meat, along with alligator, kangaroo and fruit bat. But now that provincial hotels serve ostrich with Yorkshire pudding and all the trimmings for Sunday lunch, it's rather ho hum. As the novelty wears off, so the cooking has calmed down. A new ingredient always inspires chefs to invent recipes that sound like a list of newlyweds' Christmas decorations. There was a short vogue for smoked ostrich, which happily seems to have passed. Smoked ostrich was like chewing Tony Benn's used pipe cleaners.

My problem with ostrich is that I don't know what it's supposed to taste like. 'A large flightless bird, obviously,' I hear you yell helpfully. Well, yes and no. It's not as simple as that. At the heart of all food there is a memory, a recall of all the other times you've eaten this ingredient. A Proustian Rolodex. Pop a Brussels sprout in your mouth and you unconsciously compare it with all the other sprouts that have passed this way and you decide whether it's up to Belgian standards.

The keener and clearer your memory, the better your palate. I became really aware of this problem when I taught. Flushed and dubious young chaps would thrust spoons of grey glob at me and inquire: 'Is this what it's supposed to taste like?' The answer was usually: 'If you're getting your recipes from the Book of Revelation, then probably.'

With a new ingredient, you are more than likely to have eaten one of its close relatives, so you have some idea of what to expect. If you've eaten quail, then thrush comes as no surprise. But ostrich doesn't taste the way I imagined. It should be like a big turkey crossed with Stewart Granger's hat, but it isn't.

I've just had an ostrich steak, quite a good one. It was a bit like lamb, a bit like underhung beef, a bit like roe deer. It's got a texture that's very unavian. I have a horrible premonition that ostrich will be the post-modern all-purpose uniflesh. Every recipe from Lancashire hotpot to chicken biryani will have 'or use ostrich' written into them. My particular fillet came with monkey gland sauce. You see, here we are again. I'm shockingly unfamiliar with monkey gland. I couldn't even tell you what species of monkey it was or what vital function the gland had once performed. However, I was mildly surprised that any ape should have an organ that so exactly tasted of worcester sauce.

As for ostriches, I'm still not happy about eating anything that eats keys and watches.

Johannesburg

Johannesburg is 120. In urban years, that's newborn – barely out of tents. They used to say that all great cities were built on bays, rivers or crossroads. Jo'burg has none of them. It was dumped in dusty Transvaal, on the way from nothing to nowhere. It grew out of earth, born from a golden reef that was the largest deposit of ore in the world. And it is a worldly truth that, while poverty forms the rural landscape, it's money that makes a city.

Jo'burg is not architecturally memorable, though it has more trees per hectare than any similar-sized burgh, and when the jacarandas are out, it's a purple haze. It is a strange and dysfunctional place, a bitter gruel of pain, guilt, misery, raging unfairness, intransigent greed and sullen self-interest. Other cities – Rome, Istanbul, Venice, Pontypridd – have been built on grander inhumanity, but none was so perversely, stubbornly out of kilter with the morality of the times as Jo'burg.

When I was last here, about six years ago, it felt like a city on parole, a criminal place that had come back to live next door to its victim. It lurked behind a Passchendaele of barbed wire. Every deadlocked door greeted you with the promise of lethal response and psycho ridgeback bitches. The white city kept its fingers in its ears and stared at its knees as a terrible random violence ran through the streets and crept in through the windows. I wasn't looking forward to going back.

But, blow me down with a wind of change, it's like a new city. It's 'Tonight, Nelson, I'm going to be somewhere else completely.' The centre of town, which was doughnutted of hotels, business and residents by robbery and murder, has been repopulated. Areas you would never have walked in now have bijou galleries and roadside cappuccinos. You can drive with your window open. This is not to say it has come over all Zurich with Zulus – razor wire and spikes are still a growth business – but you sense it is a place that has turned a corner, that has made a decision. Soweto is now a tourist destination. There is a shedload of investment. The rand is on steroids. And that delicate hybrid of black and middle class is now marginally less rare than the white rhino.

Ten years ago, I prophesied that South African food would be the next big thing. I have repeated that prediction with conviction ever since. South Africa has a wealth of ingredients (fruit, vegetables, fish, cattle, sheep, game) and a great mix of indigenous cuisines (Dutch, Malay, Indian, Huguenot, Jewish, Portuguese and African). But it hasn't happened. And this time, dinner at the fine dining-room of a Jo'burg hotel finally showed me why.

It was a menu of unfounded self-importance, frenchified in snobbery, though not in taste, decorated with amuse-bouches, palate-clearers and sweetmeats, and made with gastric juxtapositions that were pointlessly daring. The service was overheated and cloying. I watched a family with two small children work their way through dinner in silent, good-mannered misery, digestive foreigners in their own country. It's a long time since I've wanted to go into a kitchen and drag out the chef, shouting: 'Here he is, I've got him.'

This was dinner pretending to be somewhere else. I saw a truth that I should have known all along: it's not cooks or ingredients that make great food, it's hungry people. National cuisines must be egalitarian. I don't mean that everyone eats together, or that they can afford the same, but that the national recipe book is held by all in common, that everyone will have experienced the same cooking. And that's not yet true of South Africa. There is still plate apartheid.

Ethiopia

Right, see if you can guess what Ethiopia and Argentina have in common. You couldn't imagine two more different and disparate places. In every single respect these countries are polar opposites – except for this one thing. You're not going to get it. It's Italians.

I know, strange but true. During the depression, more Italians emigrated to the Argentine than to New York, and they just managed to rescue the food before it fell into the soiled-nappy hell of southern Mexican. Also in the 1930s, the Italians briefly invaded Abyssinia, leaving behind a few intrepid colonists – very intrepid considering what the Ethiopians traditionally do to invaders ('For you, Luigi, fatherhood is over') – who did what Italians invariably do when they come second in a war: cook.

Let me whisk you in the comfort of your fleecy tartan slippers to the searing heat, gaudy sights and enigmatic smells of the oldest country in Africa. (Actually, there's nothing remotely enigmatic about the smell of Addis Ababa; if anything deserves the appellation 'in your face', it does.)

Ethiopian food sounds like the beginning of a joke in very poor taste (ooh, bit of a pun there): 'I say, I say. What does Ethiopian food taste like? Bob Geldof's B-side'; 'What's an Ethiopian three-course meal? A two-course meal where you get to eat the vultures'; 'What do they call throwing up in Ethiopia? Showing off.' Oh, I've got a million of them.

But forget all that. Ethiopian cuisine is far from a joke. And it's far more than an Oxfam high-protein snack or imported pasta. If you think about all the plants in the world (actually, don't try to think about all the plants in the world – you'll become very boring, with a head full of compost), it's a lot. But of that lot, we eat very little. Or few. A very fewish little. Considering that, as a species, we crave variety, and given that so many of them are edible (in the sense that they won't actively poison us), we regularly only consume fifteen types of plant in any volume. I know that you can count more than fifteen vegetables in your supermarket, but they tend to be family members.

When it comes to staple carbohydrates, we eat even less – or fewer. We eat rice and wheat, with a few added potatoes, maize and sorghum. But Ethiopia has a unique staple carbohydrate that nobody else in the world eats, or even bothers to grow. It's called teff, and it's a grass with very fine seeds that are difficult to mill. It's of great antiquity. Ten thousand years ago, we all ate lots of different grasses before settling on wheat, barley, oats and maize as the most efficient and versatile. But for some reason, known only to themselves, the Ethiopians went with teff.

They make a bread from it called *injeera*, preparing a sort of pancake batter with yeast that's left to ferment then poured into flat, shallow pans, covered with a conical lid and cooked. What comes out is a damp grey sheet that resembles nothing so much as old foam rubber crossed with tripe. This is used as a plate and on it are poured various hot stews made from lamb or beef or chicken and vegetables, all of them sinus-searingly potent. You tear a bit of plate, scoop up stew and, with particularly noisome bits, you compress balls the size of plums and pop them into the mouth of the person next to you. Extra *injeera* comes in cold, soggy rolls like the towels offered in Japanese restaurants.

Now if I'm making this sound repellent, I apologise. I quite liked it. If you're a food critic, then finding a completely new carbohydrate is pathetically and nerdishly exciting. The Blonde, on the other hand, was utterly disgusted – and I must say, you do need a broad gullet to get the benefit. The texture is cold and flabbily slimy. The stew is secretive, viscous and snottish, with little detonations of motherless 'aahs', 'eehs' and 'yeuchs'. But even she couldn't deny that it was both a rustically sophisticated and ancient cuisine. Using bread as a plate is one of the oldest forms of eating. In England we called them trenchers – hence trencherman – and it's the most absurd myth that sandwiches were invented by a gambling earl. The sandwich is as old as sliced bread, and that's very old indeed.

Morocco

(1)

I was just talking about those league tables that executive magazines – the type you find in hotel lobbies with prostitutes' numbers scrawled on their man-of-the-moment covers – publish every year. You know, the ones where they make incredibly complex equations comparing things like education, crime, prevailing wind, velocity of sewerage, width of smile and sandwich, and come up with a top ten of the very, very best places in the world to live.

The answer is always Canada – and, more specifically, somewhere called something like Domestos, Ontario: 'Happy to greet careful drivers.' Which just goes to show that the sort of people who compile business-class analysis don't live in any known real world.

Come to think of it, they probably live in Canada, or one of the many small satellite Canadas that sprout within commuting distance of everywhere else. You look at all the new, private-gated, fecundity-friendly, sensor-lit, barbecue-smoked developments and you think: this was designed by a committee whose idea of a honeymoon is Vancouver. Indeed, whose idea of a perfect wife is Meg Ryan, the Canada of actresses.

There is a whole other world of Canada out there. Saturday-evening rural murder mysteries with John Nettles are Canada. Louis Vuitton sponge bags and cordless electric razors are Canada. Having flu shots and drinking schooners of bio-alien yoghurt are Canada. Owning a weekend hat, choosing shoes primarily for comfort and silence, transferring pulses and shaped pasta into co-ordinated airtight storage jars, and learning a language after you're thirty because you like the music are all very Canada. So is the ozone layer and having a favourite tree. The list is sadly, tundra-ishly endless.

Canada-isation is being slyly, politely foisted upon us. It is the last great imperial invasion, colonising the world not with gun and Bible, but with picnic-area nature walks and plug-in, refillable, guilt-fresh room deodorisers.

I was discussing all this in the souk in Marrakesh – which must be so far down the list of perfect places to live that they probably haven't even bothered to print it – with a man who lives in Tuscany, another place that would have the suits shaking their heads and putting crosses in boxes. We looked round at the teeming market and attempted to see it in Canadian terms. It's a Gomorrah with extra Sodom, the sort of place that wakes health-and-safety workers sweating and screaming, and has them reaching with trembling hands for the double-strength wet wipes. It is a chaos and confusion beyond the can of Canada. In fact, Marrakesh is anti-Canada, and one of the most wonderful places ever not invented. As Stephen Fry once said: 'You can divide the world into people who split things in half and those who don't.' It is a continuing dark struggle between the forces of Canada and the forces of Morocco, between those who want to keep the windows shut for the benefit of the air-conditioning and those who want to throw them open and let in the heat.

All this was of particular importance to me because, it being half-term, I'd taken my children. Marrakesh is by far the most exotic place they have ever been, and it's a worry at the back of every parent's mind that they might have spawned Canadians. You never can tell. One day, your son comes home and says: 'Mum, dad, sit down. I've got something to tell you. I'm a Canadian. I've tried to fight it, but it's who I really am. I want to introduce you to my Subaru.'

Well, within a day, I'd lost them both to the souk. Alasdair was ordering boiled snails from stalls and collecting reptiles – I had to check his pockets for chameleons (not as easy as you may think). And I found Flora in the back of an apothecary's with a pair of hysterically cackling, veiled Berber women, who were rubbing camel dung into her hair, which, two hours later, turned out to be henna and now she has a Disney sunset on her head.

I needn't have worried. They're far more Maghreb than Montreal, though, given the way of things, they'll probably go off and marry Mounties.

(2)

The open square, the Djemaa el Fna, is one of the greatest restaurants in the world, a collective of temporary kitchens put up every evening, each serving a speciality. Dark, heavily spiced sausages; snails cooked in a broth of ginger, thyme, garlic and chilli; great tumblers of fresh orange juice; coconut macaroons; intense little marzipan cakes. All around you, in the smoke and steam, are thousands of people: tourists and Moroccans out for the evening, snake-charmers, monkey-handlers, herbalists, roving dentists, henna artists, Berber drummers, water-carriers, storytellers, soothsayers, dancers, beggars and seven blind men sitting in a row, singing for their supper in close harmony.

Eating with children is a way of vicariously retasting the spectacular strangeness and mystery of food. Flora wanted to eat a sheep's head – my favourite stall. We sat on a bench, crammed in with taxi-drivers and slipper-sellers. In front of us, a chef in a pinny the colour of the last sultan's soul hooked heads out of a bubbling vat and dumped them on a greasy chopping board, then, with hot, dextrous fingers, pulled them to bits, cheek by jowl. Crenellated jaws were disengaged.

Strong, dark tongues were peeled and sliced. A handful of chopped, glutinous baa-baa bits was piled on paper napkins in front of us. Flat bread was dipped into thin soup. We sprinkled a mixture of salt and cumin, and drank tooth-meltingly sweet mint tea. Flora tastes new things with a homeopathic wariness. I watched her face, the creeping, uncertain surprise of pleasure and the smugness at having overcome the squeams.

There was a yellow lump that got added to the head meat. I didn't immediately recognise it. It had the texture of tofu and the bland, fugitive flavour of unworked muscle, with a sour, acid hint of July milk bottles. It was udder. What do you think of that, I asked Flora. She pursed her lips: 'Tits up.'

There was one flavour that was completely new to me: *amelou*, a peanutty, oily spread, sweetened with hot Moroccan honey. I'm told Berbers have it on their breakfast croissant. It doesn't appear in Alan Davidson's exhaustive *Oxford Companion to Food*, but it is deliciously addictive, a sort of sophisticated Nutella. I was as pleased to meet it as I was when I first tasted *dulce de leche* in Argentina.

Amelou is a by-product of an oil made from the seeds of the argan tree, which grows only in south-western Morocco. The oil is reddish, with a nutty, musky flavour. Imagine olive oil that has been used to marinate a flatulent squirrel. The Blonde wasn't sure about it. She thought it smelt like Berber morning breath. They say it's full of good trace-y things and fights bad, cloggy, cancery stuff. But they say that about everything. It is already being made into cosmetics.

The argan tree is gnarly and uncultivated, like Bill Wyman with bark. Goats climb its branches to feed on the green fruit. The kernels are hard, so pass through the goats and are collected by strolling Berbers who press them between stones for their oil. I do like the idea of Knightsbridge women buying expensive face cream made from goat shit.

As argan oil becomes more fashionable, the supermarkets will go in search of mass bottlings and ways of selling it cheaper. They will make sentimental advertisements with wrinkly-faced, smiling Maghrebis pinching each other's bottoms to show that they are vital well into their nineties. The oil will become 'argan style': pale, slick, anaemic, without a breath of Berber.

And, you can bet, unpassed through the rectum of Billy.

Greece

There's this condition, very rare, called Stendhal's syndrome. It can strike anyone, though it tends to be found in Mid-Western Americans on trips to Florence, where the guards at the Uffizi are said to be trained to treat it. It is the effect of being suddenly, cataclysmically overcome by beauty and it usually strikes those who unknowingly live in surroundings of banal aesthetic indifference (hence the Mid-West). But it can affect particularly sensitive souls – Lord Clarke used to suffer from it.

It's a thunderbolt, a psychic stigmata, a ripping away of veils. The symptoms include fainting, shaking, transfixation and uncontrolled weeping. It happened to me once. I'm not proud, I don't mind admitting it. I was eighteen, it was hot and I was in a museum in Athens traipsing through rooms of sharded pots, verdigris and lines of blankly monolithic *kouroi*. I walked into a room and burst into tears.

It was the damnedest thing, I felt light and cold and numb. For the first and only time I saw the bronze statue of Zeus or perhaps Poseidon. There he was, lifesize, arms outstretched to fling his lost trident or thunderous javelin. I can't for the life of me explain why I wept and I can't re-create the feeling. As I remember it there were just the two of us in the room, though I doubt that was the case. All I do remember is the shock, and his grave bronze balance poised just on the balls of his feet and his blind eyes, the empty sockets staring out over his pointing arm to an unseeable future.

The Greek renaissance must have been the most remarkable, vital and profound moment in human history. Its achievements dwarf every movement and school since. In the space of a few generations the Greeks invented from scratch a way through the dark into the light that we still see by.

Even with the added halogen of hindsight it's impossible to do anything but marvel at the concentrated, pristine, breathtaking collected effort of imagination and will that set Western civilisation on the rails. Everything since has been merely decoration and polishing.

Try and imagine our world without the Greeks: architecture, sculpture, theatre, poetry, philosophy, medicine, mathematics, politics – all unrecognisable, inconceivable without that first thunderbolt of energy flung blindly into the future. Sadly, miserably, deeply to be regretted, having created the classical world they didn't find the time to stop for lunch.

Like so many creatives, the Ancient Greeks must have been sublimely unconcerned about what they put in their mouths. Even the Epicureans, who insouciantly handed us the word for grubaphilia, actually preached a sort of aesthetic stinginess. Supper was for symposia not greed. You'd have felt a bit of a derr-brain if you'd said: 'Look, sorry to interrupt Plato, but this doner is filth. Why don't we get a takeaway Babylonian?' Unfortunately, the other blot on the Greeks' book is that they also invented competitive sport and were consequently a nation who watched their waistlines.

It seems a little churlish to carp about Greek food when they gave us so much else; on the other hand they have had 2,500 years since to make good in the kitchen. The Italians managed an empire, the architectural arch, a renaissance and the River Café Cook Book, but the Greeks, you see, suffer from being the children of famous parents. It is in every sense a classic condition: dad was a genius, the kids are never going to live up to him, so they give up and become a bad-mannered, misogynist, lazy, self-important fat bunch who sneer: 'When you were still running round in woad my dad was building in marble and the *Iliad* was book at bedtime.' Yes, we reply, but what have you produced in the last two millennia? Nana

Mouskouri, Mikis Theodorakis and Kojak? Even the Isle of Man's done better than that.

Greek food is unremittingly ghastly. The Greeks, having invented tragedy, went on to serve it in paper bags to students. Outside of Greece I think we are the only country in the world to offer a home to Greek restaurants. So who said we're not a country that takes in unwanted refugees? If you went to Rome, for instance, and said I'm going to open a Greek restaurant here, they would hyperventilate with mirth and give you your own primetime sitcom.

Greek food is best eaten drunk, but even that they don't make easy. In Greece, the disinfectant has a health warning that says: 'Do not serve at mealtimes.' Millions have. Greek restaurants are primarily famous for plate-smashing. Why? you may ask, but then if you do you've probably never tasted the stuff or you brush your teeth with creosote. Greek plates are the only known example of inanimate objects committing spontaneous suicide through guilt. You don't have to chuck them, they leap off the table.

I haven't been for a decade, but I dimly remembered that Greece was the answer to a question. After a day there, I remembered what it was. The Green movement asserts that the only way to put off the end of life as we know it is to halt technological innovation and go back to the old ways. The question is: what happens if you put progress into reverse? And the answer is: Greece.

I landed on Mykonos in the Cyclades and, viewing the little white buildings, thought: how did the people who built the Acropolis end up living in these crooked, whitewashed garden sheds? They have actually gone and reinvented the box. You look at the lean, elegant, svelte figures on antique vases, then gander in awe at your contemporary Greek and wonder: can these be the same people?

Well, I have a theory. They're not. The folk who are squatting in Greece at the moment are, in fact, a criminal consortium of Bulgarians, Turks and Albanians. They are holding the real Greeks hostage on an airfield in Cephalonia – hence the weirdness about plane-spotters. Any day now, Brussels will get a ransom note demanding one million sheep, five tons of disposable razors and the Elgin marbles. Or it will be Thermopylae all over again.

Clarkson and I (for it was he I sojourned with) had a competition to discover the very worst cup of coffee on the island. This is the last place in the civilised world where they advertise Nescafé as a chic alternative to freshly brewed. Jeremy won by simply ordering a double.

Their local fish is Meccano and thorns covered in wet lavatory paper. If you find a bit that tastes of something, you should run, not walk, to the nearest stomach pump. Calamari is the rehearsal for an appearance in German porn movies. Dolmades are designed to be consumed in the manner of Italian headache pills. Moussaka is shepherd's pie with pus. For taramasalata, they invented the funky name first, then looked in the bottom of a plastic bucket for something to attach it to.

I know why Greek men (and women) have long, straggly moustaches: it's to strain the lumps out of their wine. 'Don't drink the water,' we were told. Drink it? You wouldn't wash your socks in it.

A weekend on Mykonos is just about long enough. After that, you start chewing strangers' fingernails and get rickets. But I couldn't leave without trying an authentic doner kebab. It came with chips stuffed into the pitta bread. To save my life, I couldn't have told you what the meat was: chicken, pork, lamb, mythological. The thing turning on the spit looked like it had been discovered on an archaeological dig through an abattoir's midden. There were teeth sticking out of it.

I have a piece of advice: if you really must eat Greek, then go to a Lebanese restaurant – they do it all much, much better. All the food prepared in the hinge of Europe is much the same and the Lebanese – not having famous parents, and being utterly unafflicted by artistic or philosophical brilliance of any sort – have spent the past 2,000 years in the kitchen, chopping parsley.

So there you are. Think Athens, eat Beirut.

Lebanese

This will make you laugh. The first proper restaurant in France was opened in Paris in 1782 and it was called La Grande Taverne de Londres. 'Alors, Danton, why don't we check out that chic new restaurant place, the Big London Pub?'

The word 'restaurant' was just seventeen years old. Before that, taverns and inns specialised in poor travellers' lodgings and working-class drinking, while cooking in public was the monopoly of the guild of caterers, the antecedents of the modern hot-dog stand. These greasy, odoriferous trailers are the direct descendants of medieval catering and when you eat from one, you see why their life expectancy was so short. The restaurant was the invention of a tavern-keeper called Boulanger, who served a dish of cow's heels in white sauce and was taken to court by the guild for his troubles. The caterers lost and a man called Baker was allowed to serve food in his all-night café. He called his dish of bovine extremities a divine restorative – *divin restorant* – and that, best beloved, is where the name came from. The rest was histrionics.

The person who really made the restaurant possible and popular wasn't a restaurateur or even a chef, he was a prince. The Russian Prince Aleksandr Kurakin. He brought Russian service to Paris in 1830. *Service à la russe* was the revolutionary idea of serving courses, as opposed to the old *à la française*, which was having all the food laid out at once on a banqueting table, like a buffet. *Service russe* changed public eating and, as they say in Hollywood, life as we know it. Kurakin is the great unsung architect of Western society. He broke more jelly moulds than Marx, Freud and Keynes fricasseed together.

And, of course, he was the great-grandfather of Ilya, Napoleon Solo's partner in *The Man from UNCLE*. As far as I know, there is no statue to the prince. His abiding memorial is that most exciting statement of adult life: 'Your table is ready now, sir.'

Russian service changed everything. Purely practically, it meant you could eat hot food. It meant you could have separate tables. It meant a menu and choice. It led to a boom in the number of waiters and cooks. It made splitting the bill easier, if not easy. Socially, it changed the way we talked, flirted and generally got on. At the old long tables, guests sat much closer together, conversation was semi-public. With Russian service, waiters must be able to get between each diner. The long homogeneous benches, which had been symbolic of the social order for a thousand years, where placement denoted status and where everyone ate from the same dishes, were split and fragmented into small islands, seated by sex, with our backs to the other people in the room. We had personal, private food. It was a sign of a social revolution: social, sexual, political, spiritual, an end to the old huggermugger hierarchical, inclusive order.

It has been said that the course structure of dinner can be seen to represent the march of evolution. We start with nothing, then the word, then the primeval soup from which emerged fish and invertebrates, then fowl and mammals with forest and savanna, and finally man arrives, represented by the artifice, architecture and sweet cunning of pudding. I should hasten to say that it was not me who said it, it was Anthony Burgess. He could keep a straight face and say things like that. I might, if expansively joshed, if flattered and pushed, be tempted to posit that Russian service is symbolic of the age of inquiry and reason, representing individual responsibility, choice and personal morality in a predestined, ordered, ethical format. You might say that the old-style banquets were Catholic, and the new-fangled courses Protestant. You might think buffets Whig, and menus free-market Tory. You might think any damn thing that came into your head, but I want to get on to a Lebanese restaurant.

Lebanese food is one of the few dinners left to us that are eaten in the old medieval way, with the meze piled high. It doesn't have the reputation it might in this country, probably for two reasons. First, a lot of the dishes are similar to Greek food. The second reason is that grown-up aesthetics stop at Istanbul. You can have any colour you like as long as it's gold. Arabs, Persians, Hashemites, Berbers and Bashibazouks, all have the style of acquisitive five-year-olds. I have yet to see a Middle Eastern restaurant that doesn't look like an interior designer's practical joke.

To get the benefit of this sort of food you've got to forget a hundred years of ordering for yourself and order for the table. There is nothing so depressing as hearing someone in a party say, 'Oh dear, our eyes were bigger than our stomachs,' because they haven't managed to eat every scrap of garnish. For God's sake, leave as much as you eat; it's not a waste, it's hospitality, conviviality, luxury and generosity. We must be the only country in the world where you can call something generous as a term of disapproval. The point here is variety and opulence rather than greed.

Well, perhaps just a side order of greed. We ordered twenty-five dishes, to give the kitchen a fair crack. I wanted to eat as many pieces of sheep as possible. We managed muscles, sweetbreads, tongue, liver, brains and balls. The brains were everything you always imagined sheep's brains would be: soft and stupid and nice enough to feed cows. The tongues took some bleating, but sadly my balls were overcooked and had become granular, like old school rubbers.

I have a particular passion for the Lebanese raw lamb, *kibbey nayeh*, a fillet pounded to a fine paste with bulgur wheat and onion, moulded into bite-size shapes. Sort of steak baa baa. You can have it grilled in sausages if you're squeamish.

I should also mention *batrakh*, smoked fish roe with slices of garlic; and the *moutabal*, baked aubergine with sesame seed and lemon juice; *arayess*, minced meat and parsley grilled on Lebanese bread – a cross between pizza and bruschetta.

Altogether, the overall effect is a huge raucous harmony of tastes and textures. We drank raki, the hideous pastis of the Levant, and Lebanese wine that the Blonde said was so-so. We passed on the grilled meat main courses and finished with small sweet cakes and thick sweet coffee, and a drink they call white coffee, which isn't coffee at all, but seasoned and sugared hot orange flower water.

Lebanese meze is best eaten in large friendly groups or even large unfriendly groups. The business of sharing dishes makes not just the food, but the conversation, communal and co-operative. It's declamatory dining, a bit like the Middle East: everyone shouting at once and grabbing the Golan Heights.

Russian service may have given us intimacy, haute cuisine, soufflés and meat and two veg, and it probably was progress, but once in a while it's good to get away from the neat ranks of cutlery, get your fingers dirty, and grab someone's testicles.

Jewish food

Jerusalem

Jerusalem last week. I've always wanted to be able to write that. 'Join the back of the queue, goy-boy. The whole diaspora has wanted to write that for 1,500 years.'

One of the many things I was looking forward to in Jerusalem was Jewish food. The bottom line is, what you want from dinner is something that doesn't come in the recipe. It's a taste of place or history, of heritage and hospitality and hope, the intimation that there's more on your plate than the sum of a few heated vegetables and a dead animal's bum. Before soul food got to mean anything burnt to cinders and served with bananas, Jewish food was the original soul food. If you have a mind to, you can taste it even in a bagel. Given that transubstantiation is a Christian concept, the closest thing to the metaphor of food becoming body and soul is the meal of Passover, the most moving and sad and memorable dinner on earth (albeit virtually inedible).

So I was looking forward to eating in Jerusalem. But do you know what? There wasn't any Jewish food. Not as I know it. Not obviously available. There might have been an underground Haganah dealing in secret gefilte fish or passing small baggies of chopped liver, but I never found it. I felt like going out in the street and shouting, to quote Bernard Levin: 'Doesn't anyone here have a Jewish mother?'

It was my own fault, of course: I hadn't read the menu. There wasn't any Jewish food, because there was Israeli food instead – and they're not the same thing. Israel is a Middle Eastern country (I did know, but I'd sort of forgotten) and its food is that stuff that you get all the way from the Carpathians to the Atlas: basically, lumps on sticks and saucers of salad.

It's nice, but it's not what I was looking for. What I mean by Jewish is really Yiddish, mittel-European, and just as they've made a new country for themselves, so they've taken on the stony earth's indigenous cuisine: eminently sensible, but also disappointing. There was, as everywhere, the pandemic curse of international food, which gets progressively more noisome the hotter the climate. At my hotel in Tel Aviv (a hostelry I would highly recommend if you ever needed reminding that, all things considered, life could be a whole lot worse), I found the most unappetising menu of the year. It was short and to the point, like a punch to the gut, and included pasta 'Old Tel Aviv: curry, cream, mushrooms and tomato' and just plain pasta, which came winningly in 'tomato sauce and custard'. Enjoy.

The first – and still, with the sweet pickle of memory, the best – Jewish food I ate was when I worked in a sex shop in Soho twenty-five years ago. Just down the road in Great Windmill Street was the Nosh Bar, a kosher café that was warmly uninviting, run by very old men with severely pomaded thin hair, who wore white coats and looks of the utmost world-weary malevolence. There were a lot of pictures of fierce, forgotten boxers, a reminder of an East End tradition of pugilistic immigrants taking to the ring to escape tailoring.

The thing here was the pastrami. Long, slippery escarpments of warm, bright red meat seeping onto a wooden board, sliced with the precision and delicacy of a gay mohel, always combining the right proportions of fat and lean, and slapped onto dense, aromatic rye bread – no butter, of course, but a deft smear of sinus-searing mustard, accompanied with a crunchy salt pickle and sweet tea with lemon.

It was one of the great meals, deceptively simple, but actually as mysterious and complex a combination of tastes, textures and temperatures as you would find in any sophisticated three-plate meal. It had simile and philosophy as deep as you chose to look: the bitter salt-tears taste of the pickle; the clear, clean asceticism of the tea; the earthiness of the bread; the hot anger of mustard; and the warm, soft, hospitable, generous heart of the meat. Pastrami on rye is my desert island sarnie and, of all the remarkable things that Judaism has donated to a cruel world – from nuclear physics to David Kossoff – this is the finest.

Kosher

The Blonde decided we'd eat Jewish. Sadly, kosher food is disappearing from central London. Bloom's is no longer in Whitechapel, and the two salt beef bars in Windmill Street are no more. The few restaurants that are left are to be found in the northern suburbs, in the land of the waving palms (a visual pun, that: trees – hands). There are still old German bakeries and kosher delis, but the warm, irritated, funny communal eating thing that immigrants brought to London in the nineteenth and early twentieth century has all but vanished. The community has assimilated and gone on to be successful at other stuff.

I love Jewish food. I love it despite the way it tastes – because, frankly, a lot of it is not all that nice. But it is, first and foremost, a symbol of belonging. When the Jews had no homeland, their cooking was their country. Jewish food is communion. It's also some of the nastiest stuff people have ever forced children to eat.

We started with boiled gefilte fish, a large ball of damply sticky, pale mushed fish, like a large cat's fur ball. To you: horrible. The chopped liver was better, but too much like pâté for my goy taste. I like it a bit soggier. Calves' foot jelly is a dish that strangely links the pre-war Habsburg empire with the back-to-backs of Lancashire. It's repellent in both: an uncompromising block of cloudy glue with slices of hard-boiled egg suspended in it, like something from *Jurassic Park*. The texture is part industrial, part mollusc; the flavour, insipid garlic powder. The famous chicken soup, of which there were four varieties, I thought rather underpowered, though my kids loved it.

Beef viennas are electric pink sausages that Americans, imitating the old Jewish habit of pronouncing Vs as Ws, call wieners. They're pretty horrible, but in a moreish, oh-God-did-I-finish-the-plate sort of way. The Blonde had fried chicken livers with onion and mashed potato, which was excellent, having a strong and unctuous liver taste without being too renally bitter. It came piled on a plate that screamed: 'You're nothing but skin and bone; you need to put on a few curves if you ever want to catch a nice Jewish boy.'

In any other country's larder, this stuff really wouldn't amount to much. But here, in this restaurant, there was a proper sense of wellbeing, and it's the pudding-proof of something else I keep banging on about: that all food is much, much more than the sum of its ingredients and preparation. Jewish food is history and insecurity and jokes and brilliance and comfort and sympathy and being useless at ball games. It's a pleasure and a bit of a privilege to be able to dip into it.

The rest of the customers were a testament to the observational accuracy of Jewish jokes. All blissful stereotypes. Two old chaps sitting next to us ate companionably, the way very old friends do. When the waitress asked how they wanted their bill, affronted and in unison they replied, 'Separately,' having plainly said it every Sunday for thirty years. And, over in a corner, a very old man, who I think must have been a tailor – his tweed suit was exquisitely cut, though he'd shrunk inside it – ate pastrami with a slow gusto, never addressing a word to his companion, a West Indian woman a quarter his age, who looked out of place, ate little and watched him. I guessed she was his social services helper, who'd taken him out for a mouthful of his heritage, to sit for an hour with his culture and lemon tea and be not just an old man, but an old Jewish man.

Part of something. It was a tableau of pity beyond violins and, in that uniquely Jewish way, spiked with sentiment, kindness, humour and hope. What am I? Chopped liver.

France

Paris

Even the beggars have that certain *je ne sais quoi*, that inimitable Parisian touch of *misère de vivre*. Along the rue du Faubourg St Honoré, in the doorways of the *corsetières* and the little cake shops, the beggars are going for it in a big way. As any French mistress will tell you, the secret of style is all in the accessories, and this year the beggars accessorise with the effortless chic of a little cripple's stick and no shoes. So daring, so déclassé – bare feet. Each mendicant is a witty homage to Courbet or Géricault. They crouch in attitudes of histrionic torment. You find yourself stopping and saying: 'No, don't tell me, let me guess – The Raft of the Medusa?' It's worth a couple of francs simply to save on the queue for the Louvre. You see, that's the difference between them and us. Here, the beggars draw the National Gallery with chalk on the pavement. There, they do Marcel Marceau impressions of it.

So stylish.

We're in Paris because it's *prêt-à-porter* fashion week and the Blonde's doing the shows. Actually, she's taking her Philip Treacy leopardskin trilby for a dirty weekend and I'm tagging along to watch. Paris is not having a good time. She always was a bad-tempered old tart, but now she's a down-at-heel, unemployed, bad-tempered old tart. The first thing I noticed was the women. They don't look like Parisians. They've lost that slightly petulant polish, the style that implied they slept in display cabinets. Now they could be from anywhere, on the way to the supermarket in Düsseldorf or Leeds. Paris is not a movable feast any more. It's an itinerant soup kitchen.

Gastronomically, it's been going downhill for a generation.

It's not simply economics and bloody-minded socialist politics, it's a more fundamental malaise that is neatly encapsulated at Dehillerin, the kitchen-equipment shop on rue Coquillière. This is probably the greatest, most civilised hardware store in the world.

There is nothing remotely comparable in this country. It doesn't sell lifestyle accessories for fitted country-style kitchens or polished-steel bibelots for Manhattan food-fetish chapels. This is utensil Valhalla, a starched Dexion warehouse of the greatest kitchen equipment ever devised. It's as beautiful and awe-inspiring as the stock room of the Louvre or the Vatican sideboard. It's the beauty of function, designed by trial and error, heat, sweat and oaths in a million kitchens over a thousand years. And it's still state-of-the-art.

The trouble is, the art stopped two generations ago. You look at this amazing kit and you wonder who still cooks with four sizes of paring knife, who uses a turbot kettle, or a hundred delicate miniature dariole moulds. Or, for that matter, an adjustable marzipan cutter, three grades of conical passing sieve and that must-have, the five-bladed gherkin fanner.

This is the workshop of the greatest cuisine ever invented, the most sophisticated and culturally ravishing stuff that ever passed a lip, and it's as obsolete as the steam-engine room in the Science Museum. Here, Japanese ladies in a fit of francophilia buy matching sets of copper pans. They'll use them once, then discover that their delicately silvered tummies have to be cleaned with rock salt and elbow grease, and they'll be stuck facing the wall next to the amusing Philippe Starck Alphabetti-Spaghetti Scrabble board. I watched an American man pick up an escargot dish and ask: 'Waddya use this for?' His corpulent wife took one look and said: 'Dips,' with the absolute certainty of someone for whom using a knife and fork simultaneously made her a member of the Magic Circle.

This place, and these people, are the real reason Parisian cuisine is dying. It's weighed down by a heritage that is both unimprovable and archaic. Cooking isn't timeless, it's as much a product of fashion as the Blonde's hats. French food is caught on its own duck press. All attempts at modernising it diminish it. Cuisine minceur, nouvelle cuisine, the arbitrary addition of eastern spices and twiddly garnishes all make it absurd. It's food caught in aspic, and you either eat history or you move on, like the rest of Europe, to easier, dumber food.

We did have one simply ravishing dinner, though, in a very unexpected place: our hotel. Frankly, you go to Paris and the last place you think of eating is in a hotel. But the nice manager said his wife was from Yorkshire and read everything I wrote, and would I possibly see my way to gracing the restaurant one evening. So with the vaunting self-importance of a Halifax alderman, I strode into a spectacular French dining-room, a splendid wood-panelled oval with chandeliers that would have been sniggeringly *de trop* anywhere else in the world.

The food was pretty close to historically perfect, but I'm going to glide over it to eulogise one course: my roast chicken. A roast chicken that was the template, the benchmark for all roast chicken.

Shared between two, the hen was brought to the table like the condemned man's last meal, its little black feet pointing at the ceiling in supplication or surrender. Too late, mate. Just the choicest pieces of breast were carved. The skin was a starched, ochre linen; the flesh was white and chewy and had a flavour that could only be described as like eating Beatrix Potter. Caught betwixt the crispy Wonderbra and pert bosom was a discreet padding of shaved truffle. It came with its own delicate juice and *pommes purées*. Now *pommes purées* are to mashed potatoes what Carrera marble is to crazy paving. This *purée* had a warm, orange moran egg yolk nestling in the middle and was covered in an embarrassment of Périgord truffle. Unbelievable.

I was caught on the eternal dilemma of gluttony: which comes first, the chicken or the egg? It was like eating an entire family, a dynasty on a plate. The dish was everything that is contradictory and incomparable about France and French food: simple yet sophisticated, straightforward yet duplicitous, and utterly, arrogantly self-confident. There was no fiddly garnish, no nervous fanning or arrangement. It was philosophy, and it was also just roast chicken. How can you hate a country that produces that?

Well, you just have to keep trying, I suppose.

Nice

Nice. Let me sing you a restaurant. Elton John and David Furnish took the Blonde and me to a restaurant in the middle of town. The room was big and unremarkable, in that it had not been decorated by anyone whose only job is decorating. It had the light, organic, functional feel of a proper French dining-room that has grown through constant use.

We started with a tapenade, an act of gross indecency involving olives and garlic. Then caviar with boiled potatoes. Then crisp toasted squares of buttered baguette stuffed with thick seams of shaved black truffle that was so utterly sublime, made such perfect gastronomic sense that, embarrassingly, I was unmanned with joy. Then perfect prawns. Then fried calamari with aioli. Then – get this – scrambled buttery egg yolks with more black truffle. Then nude spaghetti, this time with testosterone-musky white truffle (here, you're close enough to both Alba and the Périgord to benefit from both).

As we were eating, a dripping sea bass the size of a three-year-old was brought to the table for inspection. It returned appropriately *niçoise* and I made a promise to my stomach that only in extremis would I ever again order those flabby, farmed, mucoidal midget jobs we get served ad nauseam. Then came thick blocks of fillet with black and peppery skins and bloody red middles. And finally, five puddings that included poached peaches and white-chocolate mousse that tasted like puréed cherubim.

This was simply head, shoulders and genitals above any other dinner I've eaten all year. It was an impeccably, confidently French benchmark of what food can aspire to. It's easy for a critic to lose his sense of proportion in a world of mediocrity, flannel, fad and fusion. I begin to mistrust my memory: perhaps this one wasn't that bad? perhaps I'm losing a sense of proportion? But then a place like this turns up and it's a Plimsoll line of hospitality and appetite. So, sated and with renewed vigour, I again pick up the trusty fork of taste and the broad spoon of greed to fight the good food fight.

Which is tough on the restaurants to come. I'm back. Mr Nice Guy.

Gascon food

If I were forced by Desert Island Dinners to choose a single cuisine to eat for the rest of my life, it would be a tough choice. Much as I love Scots home cooking, that wouldn't be it, and although I'm passionate about the food of northern India, I couldn't face Asian breakfast. Amid much wailing and gnashing of teeth, it would be a close-run thing between northern Italy and Gascony. Perhaps because I don't drink and because the company's better, northern Italy wins by a short skirt. But nowhere has ever produced a canon of cookery as sybaritically lascivious, as Frenchly snoggable, as the Gascons. At its best, their food is like being massaged by a troupe of naked can-can dancers smeared in duck fat. It's a board that manages simultaneously to be rigorously erudite and nuptially comforting.

Generally, I don't reckon anything is a substitute for sex, but if anything might make you moan 'Not tonight, Josephine', it would be cassoulet, and perhaps *foie gras* in all its inexhaustible wonder, not forgetting *confit* and chestnuts and prunes and the uniqueness of spice (Gascony was on the old spice route from North Africa through Italy).

But I love Gascony most because the Gascons understand – truly, fundamentally understand – the velvety, seductive, opalescent brilliance of that most misunderstood and maligned of ingredients: fat. Fat is venerated and adored. They breed Sumo ducks and geese that ought to appear on Jerry Springer. I'm also fond of Gascony because it's home to my favourite character in literature, Cyrano de Bergerac: a bellicose pamphleteer who lampooned hypocrisy with panache until they dropped a log on his head. In France, a Gasconard is a byword for a braggart and a boaster.

Given that the food of this region is one of the greatest ornaments of civilisation, why, you may ask, aren't there Gascon restaurants on every street corner in the country? Why isn't cassoulet and chips vying with pizza and burgers? The reason, sadly, is fashion. This is big food. I mean big, Cinemascope food.

Once you're lunched, you stay lunched for the rest of the day. It's not food for the fiddly, frenetic way you live now. The grub of Gascony is an endangered culture. Its natural habitat, the space and time it needs, have been eroded and exploited by the 'I can't believe it's food' society.

There is a Gascon restaurant in London. The menu is what St Peter orders for lunch. It's as close to heaven as we, or at least I, am ever going to get. Five sorts of *foie gras* for starters: a terrine, with artichokes, *bordelaise*, in a warm flan, carpaccio in a Xipister sauce. If you want something a little lighter, there's *rillettes* (pig bits in lard), or *piperade* with beans (not essentially Gascon, but wholly welcome). There's smoked eel in filo pastry, like a spring roll. And for main course, there is, naturally, an old-fashioned Toulouse cassoulet, roast *confit* of duck with cream, pigeon with more *foie gras* and a maize waffle, carpaccio of duck magret with anchovy sauce, and a kebab of duck hearts.

How utterly, utterly splendid.

'Vegetables?' I hear the paler of you whimper. Well, you can have grapes with your grilled *foie gras*. Or there's a *galette* of ceps or mushrooms *bordelaise*. And then there are chips for the vegetarian: big, fat, duck-fried *frites*. Ha ha! We pretty much ate the card. I particularly recommend everything, but especially the kebab of duck hearts. So romantic to offer someone you love a duck heart on a stick.

The Blonde smiled weakly.

For pudding, we had a definitive *crème catalane*, prunes in armagnac and an almond cake with a thimbleful of fresh, crisp apple juice that was so moreish I had it twice. Oh, and some fantastically thinly sliced Pyrenean cheese with perfect bread.

It all goes a long way to making amends for the theft of Bordeaux, which by right is a part of Plantagenet England (my private prosecution at the International Court of Justice in The Hague is still pending). I could make a very good case for claiming that Gascon food, with its animal fat and spices and fruit, is far more English than French. But I'm feeling too replete to make it now.

I left the restaurant with that rare, soaring sense of having been given a truly memorable lunch that was culturally rooted, cooked with honesty and élan, and presented with a relaxed pride. Frankly, I can't think of a higher recommendation.

St Tropez

The rich are different. Scott Fitzgerald said that after a couple of weeks in the South of France. He was wrong, of course, it's the poor who are different. Actually, down here both the rich and the poor are different, and they're different in almost exactly the same way.

We're staying just above St Tropez, and one of the great pleasures is to walk along the harbour at dinner time, where the overweight pleasure boats bob their bottoms at the world.

Here you can see just how like the very poor the very rich can be when they set their minds and their wallets to it. Nobody could have conceived of a better or more expensive imitation of a makeshift Third World shantytown than the harbour at St Tropez. The boats wallow huggermugger, like fibreglass townships, a collection of smelly, waterborne favelas, horizontal Portakabin tenements, cramped and damp, with the sort of plumbing that would be condemned on dry land. They're smelly, uncomfortable and dangerous, and everybody on them has broken toes and purple lumps on their heads. If you dumped a £1 million cabin cruiser in a suburban cul-de-sac, not even tramps would live in it. The rich all have to eat out on their porches or patios or poops or whatever they call them at sea, being gawped at by me and a few thousand others. They have to put up with each other's smells and CDs and jostling.

Now, the different thing is what they eat. Think about it. You pay upwards of four grand a day to bring the family on a fortnight's holiday in the South of France, the place that gave the salivating world bouillabaisse, *bourride* and a thousand other incomparable dishes. What do you eat? I'll tell you what you eat: you slowly masticate frozen hamburger and oven chips and tinned sweetcorn, or face-flannel fried chicken with oven chips and ketchup and a side order of taco chips with bottled guacamole followed by muesli ice cream and Diet Coke.

In the early evening there are dozens of little dinner parties serving the most expensive junk food in the world. This is the weird and different truth about the very rich: they love and crave to eat like the very poor. Nothing bores a rich man like a langoustine and caviar bore him. Ask a rich man what he wants for dinner and he'll say something bland and blonde and boneless with thousand island dressing.

I have a theory about why the rich hanker after cheap food. They want the one thing the poor have that they never can: hunger. The rich are never, ever, hungry. Once in a while they can rise to peckish, but the rich man yearns for the savour of a poor man's ravenous appetite, and that the rich man can't manage, even if he does dress up like a cabin boy from the *Bounty*.

Now, down here, when the bobbing flotsam rich want to go out and eat on dryish land, likely as not they'll go to a beach restaurant. The coast here is parcelled up into little private stretches, and each has a slightly different nuance and style. Some are tasteless, naff and common and some are tasteless, naff and chic. The one we chose is the *chien's rognons blancs*.

The cool way to arrive is by huge white ship. The maître d' sends out a tender to bring you to your table. And the flotsam rich can sit and admire the floating car park. We came in the back way. John, Sarah, the Blonde and I bounced through the dunes in a white Bentley with sunstroke vermilion upholstery. A Bentley driven over sand has all the dubious regurgitatory pleasure of being at sea without the concomitant fear of drowning.

This wasn't so much a restaurant as two dozen tables in search of a restaurant. The shanty town motif was skilfully reworked in a sort of Blue Peter sticky-back-plastic-and-old-loo-roll way. There was a collection of huts that served as a loo, kitchen and I-wouldn't-wear-that-for-a-bet swimsuit shop. There was a nailed-together plank bar of the type that's so popular with rum advertisements and a couple of sickly palms in buckets and a lot of umbrellas pretending to be a roof. The poor would never put up with this, they would think it shoddy and tacky and *prenant le pipi*, but the rich love it.

We sat down and were approached by a man wearing Lycra shorts, Hamlet's shirt and a footballer's wedding waistcoat.

"Ow many balls you think I have in my 'and?"

I don't know, I don't care and if any of them are mine you'll be fundamentally sorry.

It doesn't allow children, but it has a table-hopping magician. What does that tell you about the mental age of the customers? He was, without a shadow of doubt, the worst magician in the world, not so much sleight of hand as cack of hand.

'Thank you. Enjoy your meal. I will enjoy any tip you give me.'

Then the waitress. The waitresses are obviously employed to distract you from the ghastliness of the food. They wear flowers behind their ears and little bits of Tahitian tablecloth. Ours leant so far over my shoulder that my plate was piled high before I'd even ordered. We had squid swimming in what smelt like lukewarm baby oil, then sardines that tasted as if they had been thoughtfully brushed with factor 15 sunblock, a tuna steak that belonged in a council refuge for abused fish and ice cream that was sweet, chilled facepack. The waitress was under the delusion that with servants, as with lovers, absence makes the heart grow fonder. The bottles and plates arrived randomly at hourly intervals. The food wasn't for eating, it was just the price of entry.

The point of the place is lubricated, lubricious lust, which was fine by me. Frankly, a *tableau vivant* of incredibly pneumatic, sexually provocative women pandering to world-class hideola men is always a pleasant way to while away an afternoon. Between the tables, semi-professional models paraded, wearing the you've-got-to-be-joking beach kit and holding large boards with their names on, in case they forgot or you wanted to remember. Tickets with figures fluttered from their tiny pants – they might have been the price or their mobile telephone number. They flashed huge yacht-catching smiles of breathtaking insincerity and then reverted to chewing gum.

The bar hots up as the afternoon grinds on: hard-bodied girls with wiry, sunstriped hair do the lambada and giggle maniacally for stool-lounging, stateless, mongrel geezers whose breasts and bellies melt over their Day-Glo tanga briefs. Bottles of Krug wrapped in Lucozade-yellow cellophane are left in baskets for them to shake and squirt over perky brown chicks younger than their daughters. The onanistic irony of this happily doesn't translate to the flotsam rich.

By three o'clock, the beach is a crowded, throbbing, pump-ing, greasy swagger of poiseless poise. Every body is minutely aware that it is continuously auditioning. Stomachs twitch with the exhausting effort of being permanently sucked in. A wallet-skinned cod-eyed girl spends fifteen minutes trying to arrange her arms and legs seductively on a sun lounger. Faces become glassy with the rigour of fun. But it's all a libido cul-de-sac, one huge inarticulate mime flirt, all pay and display but no overnight parking. It's a eunuch's dry dream.

Just before we left, I noticed two British girls. They were whip thin and undercoat white, with the curved shoulders and myopic fringes of the lower sixth. They sidled in and hung around the edges of the bar, trying to look cool and edible in napkin triangle bikinis with an inconspicuous alert lethargy. You just knew they didn't have 10 francs between them and they'd hitched from Dover. They were achingly attractive ingenues from some subtitled 1960s art movie with a harmonica soundtrack. A hairy, wrinkled brown arm offered a glass and a fag and stayed to rest on a slender shoulder. I was glad I wasn't their father. I suppose one day I will be.

Two days afterwards, I sat at the bar and took a two-quid sip and there, swaying in a swarthy group like an hour-old giraffe, came one of the British girls, shoulders back, chin up, chest out, relaxed, motoring and high as a kite. On her head she jauntily sported a cap embroidered with a yacht's name. She'd scored. Phew. Summer on the Côte, welcome aboard, chicken and chaps.

Lipp

There is a French proverb: 'In Paris, life passes as a dream.' I'm always aware that I don't visit Paris so much as revisit it. It's the memories that are so pervasive and powerful; they overlay and edit the real-time city. I keep thinking I'm about to catch sight of myself as a teenager just crossing the road, or sitting at a table, holding hands with someone whose name I've forgotten. Paris is an intermittent fever, a déjà vu, one big tea-dipped madeleine.

I first came in 1969, a few months after the year of Europe behaving badly. The streets were still full of CRS, with their fore-and-aft caps named after ladies' parts. The ripped-up cobbles lay in piles and the city had a great naughty grin on its face. This was what Paris had been designed for: forlorn romantic gestures; grand, elegant tits-out-pour-les-garçons exhibitionism.

Each time I've been back – and that's probably about once a year ever since – I notice the things that have gone. Paris is a palimpsest of vanishing. The pissoirs, the smell of Gitanes, the 2CV vans, the Nicolas bottles, the clochards in Prussian-blue cotton suits, the concierges with Colette-red hair, gendarmes in capes and kepis, sculptured poodles, shops on the Left Bank selling pale, yellow-boarded books. In fact, the whole Left Bank has all but gone, overrun with international brands and universal labels. The pensions and bistros, 10F menus, *tripes à la mode de Caen*, coffee with chicory in bowls and 9am pastis have vanished.

That's not to say there aren't still places to be seen and stylish people to see. And one of the best places to play with your food is Brasserie Lipp. Lipp is one of the few things that has remained exactly as I remember it: the long little bistro in the 6th, with the central stairwell and a nicotine-glazed mural of an Amazonian parrot hunt on the ceiling. These arty nouveau 1920s restaurants and bars seem quintessentially French, but they owe most of their style to America, to jazz and cocktails, Josephine Baker and the glamour of dollars. It was American women wanting to look like French women who paid for and invented the French fashion houses. The special relationship between America and Paris is far deeper than the one between the Yanks and the Brits. We share only a few words. They share mutual jealousy.

At lunchtime, Lipp is packed and the queues reach out the door. You can't book.

The French invented the restaurant to be fraternal and egalitarian, so that the best food wasn't just the province of the aristocratic dining-room. Then they instantly went about contriving ways of keeping out the wrong sort of people, or at least letting them in so that they could be humiliated by being put in the wrong place. There are a pair of Richelieus on the door who deftly divide diners into 'pukka Lipp' and 'none of your Lipp'. Upstairs is a place (I'm told) that makes Siberia feel like Provence, a limbo of broken egos and the lunch of losers. Lipp can give you indigestion even before you've eaten. It is the final queue of shame available to grown-ups. The last time I went, I took Hugh Grant and Jemima Goldsmith as table insurance. I managed to get them in.

The food is not exactly the thing at Lipp. It would be a lie to say it was great. It would be generous to say it was good. It's probably fair to say it's adequate, gusting fine. For two decades, I've only ever had *oeuf en gelée* and sauerkraut with boiled porky bits. I've yet to finish either. The roast chicken is probably the top of the kitchen's game. You go to Lipp to be part of it, and, despite the swarms of Sartre-sated students, Gide-guided Germans and lost, illiterate English, Lipp still manages to be an authentically French performance.

Here are the characters who are ghosts in the rest of the city: the fat cabinet minister with the drooling lip, eating oysters with one hand and fingering a lady of belles-lettres with the other; the French pop star dressed entirely in leather, with leonine hair and dark glasses the size of satellite dishes; the old glamour model with her dog; the father with his daughter, or perhaps a friend of his daughter. But the character I keep coming back to see, who fills me with the greatest expectation, is the waiter. In Lipp, you can still bask in couture rudeness that is as authentically Parisian as a tumbrel and scent instead of soap.

Happily, we got my favourite – a chap who I'm sure has served me reluctantly for twenty years. His face has been melted into a gargoyle of resigned despair by the heat of his internal ire. He takes every order with a mournful shrug, serves every dish with a disgusted clatter.

And when, finally, I said a supercilious 'Merci', he regarded me with a withering, world-weary, watery eye and said slowly, as if in great pain: 'You see, you can speak French if you try.'

Italy

Tuscany

All professions incubate myths about themselves. It's part of the *esprit de corps* that mitigates the fact that you're actually only replaceable moving parts. In my line, the legend is 'the lost ark of the perfect little restaurant'. I'm asked about it continuously. People write to tell me they think they've found it, always in the most unlikely places: off a lay-by outside Scarborough; in a back room on the spine of the Pennines, only approachable for two weeks of the year with the help of satellite navigation.

The mythological 'perfect restaurant' has to have a number of things to fit the Arthurian bill of fare. First, of course, nobody else must know about it. It must be simple, unpretentious and run by a family who, uniquely, have no thought of profit. Ideally, it should have one megalithic, totemic dish; simple ingredients elevated to ambrosia with manna *jus*, in a recipe that has escaped the collective wisdom of every chef and writer for three hundred years.

This isn't a modern obsession. For as long as there have been restaurants and epicureans, there have been reports. Brillat-Savarin wrote of auberges found by accident in the night, where a dozen geese revolved on the spit above crackling vine logs, so that only the most delicious morsels could be served to a single diner. Elizabeth David can be read as an endless pilgrimage in search of fugitive love on a plate: the impossibly light and unctuous omelette, the quintessential Dionysian fig.

For the English, the likely home of the perfect restaurant has always been 'over there'. As an American said: 'Everyone has two countries: his own and France.' France is inhabited by the French, but only as gardiens. Gastronomically, it's ours. And up some dusty track, on a dappled terrace, is the auberge of Saxon dreams. The rough but refreshing local wine, the plump olives, the deep white sarcophagi of duck liver and shredded pig, the black-legged hen seeping syrupy sauce, the weeping cheese and the steaming *tatin*. Oh, lordy, lordy, how many fortunes have been made peddling this sort of titillating dribble?

I only mention it now because – strictly between you and me – I've actually found it. Yup, the perfect restaurant. And it's not in France. It's in Italy – which, as you know, is this year's France. We came across it quite by accident, just looking for lunch in Chiantishire. Driving up a dirt track, my palms started pricking. Could this be the fabled dirt track? And then, hidden on top of the hill, just as the kitchen sibyls predicted, was the lone restaurant. Father cooking. Mother and son serving. Terrace tables glowing with crisp linen. (Why is linen always crisp, and how come nobody ever points out that crisps are all too often like linen?) And all around, in the searing, clear sunlight, a high Renaissance landscape that was just too, too purely Uffizi glitzy. And then, the menu … oh, staunch my cataracts of spit.

Most of you make the forgivable mistake of imagining there's a thing called Italian food. But for all day-to-day purposes, Italy is still a collection of republics and city states, each with its own plateful of identity. In the north, they laugh at the poverty of southern bruschetta and cook with butter, not olive oil. Sicily's palate is closer to Tunisia than to mainland Italy, and the food of Tuscany is not what you've been led to believe by the supermarket advertisements. It's heavy and fattening, made for ravenous peasants. Its signature dish is a Florentine steak that would shock a Texan, hacked from bulls that could sexually molest elephants without using a stepladder.

Tuscan food is also long on game: pheasant, boar and hare. In the perfect restaurant, I started with *lardone marinato* – that's white pig fat on toast. (Look, if you don't like the sound of it, what on earth are you doing reading a food column?) And then *lepre in umido*, served all on its own. I adore hare, but I've had so many bad jugments that I'm wary of it in restaurants. This being the perfect restaurant, of course, it was perfect: a complicated, deeply Machiavellian concoction, whose constituent essences I couldn't begin to deconstruct.

You'll have noticed I haven't passed on the address. You'd only go and find fault and then it wouldn't be the perfect restaurant any more; it would be full of *Sunday Times* readers complaining about the service, and they'd start serving pizza.

Venice

The Venice Marathon sounds like a joke. Of all the cities in all the world that you'd lay money didn't run a marathon, this one would be a safe bet (indeed, 'You look like you've just run the Venice Marathon' might be something you'd say to someone who'd just got out of bed). But, like so many things that sound like jokes, it's not. It's real. It happens. They have to build extra roads over the canals. Twats.

Venice is a funny old place. I'm always in two minds about it. Of course, it's transcendentally beautiful: round every corner, the eye is professionally massaged by vistas that know a trick or two. But there's something else here, too. Something frightful. Something amoral. It's like the sergeant always says: 'There's something not quite right here, sir. Aaaaagh!' There's something not quite right about Venice.

It's not just that it was built out of polished exploitation on a swamp of fiscal misery – after all, almost everywhere with a dash of architecture was. Despite what the Bible says, the wages of sin is tourism. Venice's rise to glory, riches and sophistication was as megalomaniacally culpable as any place on earth, an empire based solely and wholly on cash. They didn't even bother with the fig leaf pretence of taking religion, law or democracy to the heathen – Venetians were in it for the lucre.

Back home, they had official league tables of hookers, from international Premiership courtesans, who were transferred for fortunes, right down to Endsleigh League semi-professionals who'd head a ball in the street for a couple of groats and a half-time orange. Assassin was a registered occupation.

Venice's redeeming quality is sublime beauty – proof that pulchritude isn't inevitably the product of goodness and love. Venice's beauty is an offertory candle, lit by greed to propitiate guilt. Venice is a Dorian Gray city. Somewhere up there in the world's attic, there's another place with the haggard, poxed and ravaged face of unspeakable evil. And I suspect it's Cardiff.

Uniquely, in all of Italy, Venice's food is decidedly so-so. You'd have thought that, with its money, its exotic trade, its sybaritic tastes and fondness for indulgence, it would have some pretty bonzer tucker. But in fact they do quite ordinary things with fish and liver. It's proof of Gill's picture-window law of catering – the better the view, the worse the food.

Bread

There is a thin, crisp bread called music paper because it makes a noise when you eat it.

It looks like any of a dozen crisp breads made in Europe and the Middle East but it's quite different, baked two or three times a year in Sardinia in an exhausting and time-consuming fashion. It is the most versatile bread ever: it keeps for months, it can be broken up in milk to make cornflakes, it can be wetted and magically turned back into a sort of soft pancake, it can be filled with cheese and ham and then grilled back to a toasted sandwich. I eat it with bresaola and olive oil, but the point is that it's a product of a poor place that treats all ingredients, however modest, with infinite respect and time-consuming love, and you can taste it.

Puttanesca

Puttanesca is prostitutes' spaghetti – hot and, I suppose, cheap and fast. This one was finely chopped black olives, flat-leaf parsley and a touch of chilli on spaghetti. The pasta was dried, not home-made. Far better. The sauce was about 10 per cent of the dish, a little black mound that sat on the steaming palely opalescent pasta. It was sexually pungent, gratification without complications. They laid it on the table, I ate, I paid, everyone satisfied. There are a lot of recipes for *puttanesca* – they grow more complex the farther north you travel from Italy. They get capers and tomatoes and garlic and cheese and then some fool is bound to add basil ("cos it's Italian, ain't it?'). And by the time it reaches Fulham it's no longer a La Strada tart, it's your blooming fiancée.

Carluccio's Caffe

Let's get one thing straight. I stand behind no man in my admiration of Eyeties. To be born a slinky-hipped, oleaginously quiffed, chaffering little Latin is to have drawn first prize in the lottery of life. Spiritually, the closer a country gets to Italy, the nicer. The further, the worser. But it's the obligation of true friends to point out the flea in the ravioli. And it has to be said – the Italians have no sense of humour.

Now before you start, let me tell you the funniest Italian joke ever. It was considered so dangerously amusing that the Vatican kept it locked in the heretics' library, until the Pope (who, being a Pole, couldn't find a punch line in his underpants, even if it glowed in the dark and sang 'How Much is that Doge in the Window?') let it out for restricted educational use in Jesuit training camps.

Here goes. A man walks into a trattoria and says: 'I'll have a pound of one-inch flat-headed nails and three yards of knicker elastic, please.'

'This is a trattoria,' says the waiter.

And the man replies: 'I'm a Venetian.'

Funny? It turns Italians into screeching epileptics. (There is a shorter version that works just as well. A man says: 'I'm a Venetian.') Now I know you're aching to point out that Italians are possibly the happiest people on earth, that to be in Italy is to be in the land of smiles. Quite so. This is because Italians have a sense of fun.

But fun and humour are not the same thing. Humour is structured, demands planning, a sense of plot, drama and timing and, mostly, it's a reaction to predictability and order. So, obviously, they can't manage it. There is no word in Italian for structure, planning, plot or order. Which is one of the reasons I love the old boot so much. If you spend your life grinding out quippy wit for the most humorously epicurean nation on earth, then Italy – where the very height of Wildean aperçu is to throw a plastic bag full of water over a girl with big breasts from the back of a speeding Vespa – comes as a blessed relief.

The one thing that no Italian has a sense of humour about – or indeed much fun with – is food. For a nation that has managed to squeeze such inventive variety out of three squares a day, the Italians are surprisingly picky and pedantic eaters – and, for the most part, indissolubly wedded to the food of their childhood.

Now some government minister wants to copyright Italian food worldwide, because, he says, we don't do it properly and that it's a joke and therefore unfunny. To which, one must say: 'Hey, Giuseppe, lighten up.' Throw a plastic bag of water over that man. Bad food doesn't detract from good food. Indeed, it makes it more memorable. Try drinking a cup of English tea in Rome. But it's true that most Italian food abroad is not as mother made. To get Italian Italian dinner in England you have to pay London London prices, which really aren't authentic. We just don't do good cheap Italian food.

Carluccio, the avuncular man with fungi off the telly, has a chain of cheap Italian cafés, which he claims will fill the gap. There's one in the basement of Fenwick on Bond Street, so I went for lunch with Dino, Faggionato and Giovanna, three Italian art dealers living under duress in London, who are more fernickety, pernickety and capricious than a bag full of Siamese cats with diarrhoea. It was packed with women sitting in a tundra of shopping bags. If you're in the market for an afternoon mistress (and I imagine many of you are), then the basement of Fenwick might be a good place to shop.

The room is as noisy as a room full of bored women who have been massaging their shopping glands can be. It's utilitarian, a canteen rather than a café, with a long takeout deli counter and waitress service. The menu comes in sections: bread, soup, antipasti, salads, main courses, puddings and cheese, and there's a children's menu and a blackboard of daily specials. The Italians sat gingerly composing their faces into the polite rictus that you put on for children's plays.

We ordered a bit of everything to come all at once, because another Italian trait is to be fanatically prudent with your own time, while being capriciously profligate with everyone else's. An Italian will turn up three hours late without a mutter of apology, then fly into a hissy fit when the wine comes out of the bottle too slowly.

The food was a mixed smorgasbord. For me, the basics were good, nudging excellent. Good bread, good olives, excellent parma ham. The more complicated things showed the limitations of the concept. Lamb chops with tomato sauce and lemon risotto was not a success. The rice was a claggy pudding, the sauce an acidic single note that buried the rather fine cutlets. Spaghetti *vongole* was a castanet of dud shells that smelt of uncooked wine and had a chemical, metallic taste. The star was a mushroom soup: intense and dark and mossy. *Affogato* for pudding was simple and elegant, the coffee served separately from the ice cream.

But what did the Italians think? They shuffled. They minutely regarded their fingernails. They brushed imaginary motes from their Milanese tailoring. 'Carluccio. That's a good name, isn't it?' Yes, but did you like it? 'Well, the *vongole* was ...' Wave of hand. Apart from the *vongole*? 'Goodish. The mozzarella was good, the parma ham maybe wonderful. Better than the slimy gristle the English usually eat. The mushroom soup, she was beautiful, but she wasn't Italian.'

'The coffee,' blurted Faggionato, 'is the best I've ever had in London.' The other two regarded him with a wild surmise, as if he'd let the side down. 'Of course, the service is slow,' added Dino, trying to retrieve the decorum of patronage. 'And I liked very much that lady over there. She is very fit for an English. She has beautiful eyes with, I think, a touch of sadness. Perhaps I should wink at her.'

I think perhaps you should.

Truffles

Within a ten-year-old's living memory, white alba truffles were almost unknown in London. The only place that was famous for them was in Pimlico. After the unctuous nastiness of truffle oil poured over everything, the real thing is happily now erotically endemic. I've managed to eat truffles every day for the past week and never repeat a dish. They are best treated very simply, on something bland and oily: pasta with melted butter; blond risotto; or my favourite, fried eggs.

Truffles are unequivocally a good thing. The season is short, the pleasure intense. And while I don't, as a rule, believe you can have too much of a good thing, you can have too many varieties of a good thing. A five-course truffle menu is showing off. It detracts from the star. So we dipped in and out. The Blonde had mozzarella wrapped in warm ham and then truffle risotto; I had the bunny and beans and then a gilthead bream, which is a wonderful fish that this month I prefer to the over-familiar farmed sea bass. We also tried a salad of sweetbreads, all presented with a stuffy elegance and made with a clenched-buttocked care. Personally, I like Italian food to come a little more Italian, a bit more *La Strada* and Verrocchio and Puccini. This was like Italian food made by liberal Belgians.

But it's pudding that sticks in the mind and lingers on the palate. What do you put on a truffle menu for pudding? You and I might have thought of a creamy warm cheese with grated truffle. But spiritually, we're liberal Belgians. They, with an uncontrollable burst of Latin tumescence, made truffle ice cream. I saw it on the menu and did a double take, like a character in a Bateman cartoon. Truffle ice cream! Is there no decency left? Has the natural order of civilisation collapsed? Is God dead? The reality was even more distressingly bizarre than the imagination: a ball of truffled ice cream wallowing in a glass of running zabaglione. Some tastes (truffle is one) teeter on the edge of being disgusting, but are actually fabulous, their sheer knife-edge daring making them even more attractive. But then there are some flavours that are almost delicious, but fall the other way, into utter repulsiveness. Truffle ice cream is like that. It almost makes it: the eggs and cream are fine, but the sugar and marsala ... no, no, thrice no.

The Blonde got really quite upset. She shook her head and pruned her face like a colobus monkey that has swallowed a hornet. 'Yeuch, yeuch, that's horrible, horrible. No, more than that, it's deeply discombobulating. I'm all upset and confused.' She remained upset and confused for some hours. Late that night, she hugged me and said, all of a quiver in a small voice: 'You know what it was like? It was like slipping into bed in the dark and finding a familiar warm body there, then switching on the light and discovering it's your grandfather, naked and aroused. You know what I mean?' Not precisely specifically, but generally.

By all means, go and try it, if you need the gastronomic furniture rearranging.

Rome

You know the Piazza Navona? Of course you do, world-weary, über-Eurotrash that you are. Well, I was there last week. And perhaps, because you know it so well and could find your way across it blindfold, you may have forgotten – or perhaps failed to notice – that it is staggeringly fabulous.

If you stop for just the briefest moment for a gander, you can feel your soul ripping off its workaday overalls to dance and ululate naked, ten feet above your head. In the middle of the square, there's a fountain, made by Bernini. It represents the four great rivers of the Renaissance world.

Now, what I like about Bernini is that he thinks big. In fact, he probably never had a small idea in his life. He never said: 'Oh no, just half a slice for me.' He never learnt to fold a napkin into the shape of a peacock. His figures are all heroic-ally solid, not just larger than life. They contain supralife, with massive feet and massive hands, spatulate thumbs, vast ears and colossal thoughts. Everything about them relishes and adores bigness – except their willies, of course.

If Michelangelo seemed to release figures from inside the stone, and Donatello made ones that looked as if they had been turned to stone just the moment before you entered the room, then Bernini conjures figures that could only exist in stone. Flesh and bone couldn't support them. These aren't people realised in marble, they are stone compressed into humans.

There's a gap in the fountain where one of the idealised rivers spouts, and I imagine the engineer asking Bernini: 'E, maestro, whatta you gonna put here?' 'I make the horse's arse,' the old genius bellows. 'The horse's arse? You think this a good idea? You think Innocent X is going to want a horse's arse in de Nile?' 'I don't give a monkey. It will be a magnifico horse's arse.' And it is. It's still there, galloping through the spume, a major, historic horse's arse.

Anyway, this isn't a lecture on Bernini, it's just scene-setting.

In a dilatory, amateur way, I like to collect pointless occupations – and here, in the 32 degrees of a perfectly clear and sunny
Roman day, there is also a human statue. Now, obviously, all
forms of street mime are utterly ghastly, ugly road furniture,
clockwork dog-do, but none is more depressingly pointless
than the mime statue. And, let me tell you, a mime statue
competing with a Bernini statue plumbs the very depths of
human shallowness.

This one was a green Egyptian mummy, effortlessly hideous,
a capital crime against culture. But, in its irredeemable stupid-
ity, it made a small fable. There was the Bernini, an image of
man's aspiration to achieve and think and feel things that are
bigger, more permanent and profound than his own corporeal
life, a sculpture that expresses that our reach may yet exceed
our grasp. And, in front of it, there was a man whose only
aspiration was to imitate a dead thing in nylon, the measure
of his talent being the ability to do absolutely nothing for as
long as possible.

Here, in one frame, was art that transcended nature alongside
nature that belittled and humiliated both art and itself. One
beggared belief, the other just begged. You can go on drawing
the metaphors, similes and parables from this at your leisure,
because they are legion. Indeed, I can feel a whole *South Bank
Show* coming on. Anyway, it was just a thought.

One of the smartest decisions I ever made was to cut Rome
dead until I was forty. If you scoff all of Europe on a student
railcard before you're out of rucksacks, then everywhere comes
glazed with the bodily functions of youth and the jagged
memories of cheap booze. But Rome for me is the shock of
the new to the newly old.

Someone arranged a private view of the Sistine Chapel. It
was my first time; I was a Sistine virgin. I looked up and burst
into tears. You see, I hadn't seen it before it was cleaned. I
don't have that 'well, of course, they've ruined it' conservation-
versus-restoration baggage. It just landed on my head like a

thunderclap, with all the poleaxing astonishment of the utterly familiar. When I collected myself, I said to Mariella (for it was she): Oh look, there's God creating Melvyn.

However manipulated, purloined, twisted, clichéd and desecrated great art is, it never ceases to be great. Nothing can detract or damage the imprint of genius. Later that evening, there were fireworks set to Vivaldi's *Four Seasons*, and it was the same again: no amount of sarcophagal lift music and easy-listening compilations can drown out the fact that, even through a dodgy PA with accompanying detonations, it's still a brilliantly, spiritually vertiginous piece of music.

And it's the same with the food. No amount of flabby, stewed pizza or boiled-knitting pasta can prevent the real thing being gobsmacking. And Roman food is the Sistine Chapel of Italian grub. Endlessly reproduced, plagiarised, cheapened and daubed on T-shirts, it just makes the real thing that much better. I developed a manic addiction to *abaccio*, the tiny, milk-fed lamb, either roast or stewed in white sauce. Utterly beyond words. And proper mozzarella. You eat so many rubbery balls that you forget. Oh, and little Roman artichokes, puréed and stuffed in ravioli. And the first white truffles scraped over hot cheese sauce.

Considering that Rome must be one of the most visited cities in the world, it's Italianly unprepared for tourists. There are no package-tour diners, and they've never really got their heads around visitors' need for hotels – though we did stay in Sir Rocco Forte's newly opened Hotel de Russie, which was exceedingly comfortable and chic.

My abiding memory of the weekend will be the Communist Party rally in the Piazza della Repubblica: hammers and sickles, Cuban flags and thousands of excited falsetto-voiced Garibaldis wearing natty red neckerchiefs. And there, through the middle of it all, tottering like a marabou stork on precipitous heels, was Ivana Trump. Isn't that just so *La Dolce Vita*? If, like me, you only really know Rome through art books and

1960s films, then everything looks fabulously like clips from Visconti or Fellini. And who, in this life or the next, could possibly ask for more?

Rome is the rest of the world's second home town. If they could only connect a telephone and were just a smidgen less corrupt, we'd all live there, and that would rather ruin it.

Toast (the chef has a particular affinity for bread and this wasn't just toast – it was Toast) with finely chopped onion and anchovy. It was one of those robust, earthy, working-class combinations that links arms and marches in step. The crisp, warm texture of the bread, the sweet acidity of the onion and the soft sea-saltiness of the anchovy made you want to sing the 'Internationale' at the top of your voice, wear a red bandanna and join the International Brigade, pausing only to steal a pocket edition of Homage to Catalonia. *All that for £3.70 – not bad.*

There was this bar in New York on the Upper West Side. Years ago I lived there. In New York, not the bar; well, not this particular bar. In the daytime, the place was perfectly ordinary – a long brass bar, art posters, small tables and: 'Hi, I'm Shane. The special's blue fish, the clams are off and, hey, you're from England. I'm going up for Edmund in King Lear. *Would you say, "Now God stand up for bastards" for me, and have you made a beverage decision?'*

The dishes melted into a wasabi-fume dream. I think some kimchi was poignant and properly aggressive, like eating wrinkly old Korean swearwords, and the udon noodles were noodly and wormish. But the speciality of hotpot rice with crab was too foreign for everyone except me – I liked it because it was like risotto that was being held to ransom by yakuza shellfish.

The chicken and bits, which came as a terrine, was a pixie's packed lunch: pretty, but not really worth the bother. I went for the farmed snails, frogs' legs and bacon with pine nuts. This description, which frankly sounds like various parts of a heraldic beast, doesn't do justice to what arrived: a large green ball, with a pair of frogs' legs. Inside was a mélange of snails and guck. The whole was utterly delicious, if unusual. The Spanish have a way with snails. I'm told they still have organised snail hunts where the sports men chase helter-skelter, shouting 'Arriba, arriba!'

The Blonde's green curry should have come with a life-jacket. She ate for a bit and was oddly silent – cogitating, I imagined, Voltaire's great truth that everything is for the best in the best of all possible worlds. But then, in a voice not unlike Chewbacca's, she said 'try this'. And, trustingly, I did. And nothing was ever the same again. My mouth turned into a Serbian old folk's home. I must have passed out briefly. Coming round, I found I was numb from nipples to bald patch. Why do people do this? Why do they imagine that eating things this hot is fun? Or clever? Or enjoyable? How can anyone imagine that it has anything to do with dinner, when, in fact, it's a puritan test for witchcraft? What did the green curry taste like? God alone knows. What does molten steel feel like?

I don't know what it is with Spanish restaurants, but they're invariably decorated in vibratingly hot and insistent colours. Someone comes in and says: 'The only thing the Brits know about Spain is that it's hot. I want the walls to radiate the warmth of our native soil, the passion of Lorca, the emotion of the corrida, the all-consuming sensuality of flamenco and the barking madness of Quixote.' And so they do. The walls are a visual brass-band muzak.

It's Australian gourmet backpacker tucker – except that this menu is written in pidgin jabberwocky. And why do they do this? Is it insecure showing off, or do they really think their customers are so internationally sophisticated that they're fluent in three or four Asian languages? I no longer ask. I just amuse myself by casting Japanese porn films from the menu. This one stars Shank Musoman doing it with Jasmine Rice. And grab your crotches for the nymphet Miso twins, Akadashi and Shichimi, entertaining the massively endowed Lon Guppie. Also featuring Honey Popcorn, Futo Maki and Babycorn Panang. It's the only diverting thing to do with this menu. Eating the stuff was nothing like as much fun as imagining it having sex.

Afterword

Expense

'Dear Mr Gill, don't you ever get blasé about your job?' is one of the most common letters I get. I don't mean it's written by common people. It's one of the most frequent. And, in truth, it doesn't usually start 'Dear Mr Gill', it usually starts Dear Mr something more fundamental, and goes on to imply that I've reached saturation point: a point where I stopped being an aesthetic epicurean and morphed into Mr Creosote.

Nobody ever writes this to book reviewers. 'Hey Bud, ain't you sick of literature yet? You've got enough books for a Nazi winter solstice.' Or ballet critics (and there are only five ballets). Or, even closer to home, wine critics. You don't get people writing: 'Aren't you bored with wood shavings, marmalade, starched linen and a top note of stripper's handbag?'

Drink is the more the merrier, but food is for special occasions – the sort of food I write about, napkin food. You see, a lot of you don't associate food with eating. You've got to eat, you eat every day. But that's just taking on ballast, replacing wastage. Restaurants are different. What they sell is a treat, and you can have too many treats.

You can work out roughly how many restaurant dinners you've got left. Take what's left of your life expectancy, multiply the years by birthdays and anniversaries, add a few holidays, an occasional apology, and that's pretty much your lot. Now look at that figure and ask yourself: what's it worth? If I could buy them all off you, what would it cost me? Remember, you're not going to pass this way again. It's worth more than you thought, isn't it – all those dishes, all those sauces and flavours, all that skill and pleasure, and you're not going to get round to all of them. You're not even going to get round to 1 per cent. I do it seven days a week and my spoon isn't anywhere near the bottom of the bowl yet. So many dishes, so few dinners.

I want you to bear this in mind as you read the rest of this review. My editor asked me to go and find the most expensive dinner in Britain. Must I? As if I didn't have enough on my plate. This is one of those moments when you thank heaven you work for the *Sunday Times*. If it had been the *Guardian*, they'd have asked me to go and find the most disgustingly esoteric minority ethnic food in Britain. The *Telegraph* would have wanted the most inaccessible rural restaurant that accepts dogs. The *Independent* would have wanted a list of late-night takeaways for the munchies; the *Daily Mail*, the one where the chef had the most illegitimate children. And the *Sun* would have said: 'Sod the food. Find a platinum-blonde sixteen-year-old waitress who has trouble carrying a tray.'

Finding the most expensive meal in the country is more difficult than you would imagine. First of all, I excluded the wine list. You could spend fifty grand on a wine list without visiting the loo, no problem. Those expense-account lunches we read so much about are made up entirely of first growths. Eaten by first growths, too.

I took an executive decision to exclude single expensive ingredients. I could have starved myself for a week, walked into Caviar Kaspia and said: 'Keep the beluga coming until I slide under the table.' Or I could have gone to a Japanese restaurant and said: 'Roast me a whole fatted Kobe calf.' Kobe beef is the histrionically expensive and delicious Japanese bullock that's fed beer and given massages and a key to the minibar and geisha hooker heifers and God knows what else, and is served in Barbie-lite slivers. That would have set the expenses back a bob or two. No, this had to be a proper meal without gold leaf or *premier cru* or blindfolded string quartets.

So I called Marco Pierre White. I'm sorry, I know that's predictable and I've written about White more than is decorous, but he does have the priciest carte in the country. Give me dinner and money's no object. 'Six courses?' Lovely. 'Okay, that will come to …' Now what do you think? How much is the most expensive meal Marco could come up with? No, no, you're way off. It's £190.

That was surprising. £190 is a lot for dinner – it's a lot of money – but as the most expensive, it was a lot less than I had imagined. It's Wagon Wheels for two, if you eat them in the estate agent's stand at Chelsea. It's the price of a chicken breast, if you eat it on a bucket flight to Malaga. It's a mouthful of champagne, if you drink it out of a Russell & Bromley patent pump. Marco, are you really concentrating? Can't you try a bit harder? No, that was it.

If you think of other things you buy – say, a frock – the range in price from high street to couture is huge. The same with a car or, indeed, a bottle of wine. It's rather heartening that food falls into such a reasonable spectrum.

The Blonde and I took Nick Allott because it was his birthday and he's two months older than me. And fatter. And balder. Marco gave him a bottle of 1942 Romanée-Conti La Tâche, which, at the list price, would have cost more than all our dinners put together.

The first course was a mouthful of oyster on a smear of cream cheese, with watercress set in champagne aspic. Oysters aren't easy to improve on, but this one glided provocatively onto the palate dressed in the skimpiest, silkiest underwear. Next, the starter proper: *foie gras en surprise*, a perfect ball of smooth *foie*, wrapped in black truffle, glazed with port jelly. It looked stunningly minimal, more like a vet's advertisement. Eaten with brioche toast it's an unimpeachable classic.

Then half a Cornish blue lobster, grilled with black-truffle butter. Truffles were the theme of the evening. Taking one ingredient and weaving it through a whole dinner can be problematic. Dishes come with more déjà vu than Proust. I've had a white-truffle menu gourmand where, by the end, I felt I was being force-fed rugby socks. But black Périgord truffles have an infinitely complex and fugitive flavour. Like Lon Chaney, they fit into a thousand disguises. The lobster was sweet and trusting, yet firm, with a whiff of outdoorsy ozone. The truffle added an earthy, roué's nuttiness. It's Lolita on a plate, a sophisticate's surf'n'turf.

Then a Bresse pigeon breast – try saying that with your teeth out – wrapped in savoy cabbage, secretly stuffed with more *foie gras* and served with *pommes purées*. Then, a whole *brie de meaux*, with the lid sliced off, some of the inside scooped out and mixed with a couple of spoons of mascarpone and whole shaved truffle, then stuffed back in and the lid replaced; a sybarite's victoria sponge left to ripen in the warm kitchen. This is the most fearsomely erotic thing you can do with a cheese – with food. Girls who don't want to go all the way on a first date shouldn't toy with the truffled brie. It is a taste and texture that creeps up behind you in riding boots and undoes your buttons with a violinist's fingers in cream kid gloves, then slides a velvet cushion under your hips.

Pudding. A huge, priapic prune and armagnac soufflé, the prunes cunningly looking like little sweet truffles. Then coffee and sweet things. Then cigars.

So that's how you puff 200 quid on dinner. The food was a perfect pleasure, but apart from that, Mrs Lincoln, was it worth it? For me, unquestionably, but the best thing didn't come from the kitchen. The best thing was Nick's reaction. He was overwhelmed, beyond the nicety of guestly thanks, beyond birthday gratitude and hyperbole, beyond the sum of the parts.

He's taken away the menu and, in an act of ultimate naffness, had it framed. That's how overwhelmed he was. That was worth it: to be able to offer hospitality as good as this and to pass it off as my own.

On a technical note, the meal was beautifully balanced, so that each course rose and fell naturally into the next. You'll have noticed that nothing was terribly complicated, and often what you ask from a good chef is that he be great enough, and confident enough, to leave the ingredients be. The art of cooking is knowing what not to add.

And if you're still miserably thinking about the number of dinners you have left, consider the worth of a meal where the memory of every course is so happy and sparkling that it can be used to rub out all the really disgusting, cynically unloved plates that are going to be put in front of you between now and your wake. There's a lot more of them to come. We have to ask ourselves, can we afford not to eat like this?

Dates

Appetite

Ramadan	4 December 2005
Concert	6 July 2003
Politics	20 April 2003
The yak	4 March 2001
Vegetarians	2 April 2000 and 24 December 2005
Army	16 April 2006
Organic	27 March 2005 and 22 July 2001
Dinner parties *(1)*	6 June 1993
(2)	21 November 2004
Picnics	20 June 1993 and 4 June 1995
Pubs: *Gastropub*	16 March 2003
Pub food	29 February 2004
Hoxton	3 December 2006
Ex-pub	14 July 1996
Nouvelle cuisine: *the case for*	26 November 1995
and against	13 April 2003

Ingredients

Cabbage	*Tatler* October 1994
Rice	2 December 2001 and 15 June 2003
Fish: *Fish and Chips*	28 January 2007
Fishing	2 May 2004
Bouillabaisse	29 August 2004
Oysters	8 September 1996
Whale	19 March 2000

Durian   27 January 2002
Blood and beluga   7 November 1999
Pomegranate   *Tatler* February 1998
Fondue   28 October 2001
Almonds   2 March 2003
Roses   *Tatler* August 1995

Restaurants

Pizza Express   21 March 1999
Country pubs   11 June 2006
Chefs   28 June 1998
Waiters   24 September 1995
Bills   9 March 2003
Rainforest Café   26 October 1997
The Dome   23 January 2000
Health   3 January 1999
Jabberwocky   7 February 1999
   Jabberwocky's revenge   13 February 2000
Egyptian   3 August 1997
Nostalgia   7 May 2000
Starbucks   9 February 2003

Home

Countryside   26 June 2003, 29 September
                                2002 and 23 November
                                1997
Stow-on-the-Wold   30 July 2000
Yorkshire   1 July 2001
Leeds   3 September 2000
Isle of Man   22 January 2006
Scotland   13 October 2002 and 10
                                October 2004
Cornwall   31 August 1997 and 13
                                September 1998

Elizabeth David   3 April 1994

Away

America: *Tex Mex*	3 May 1998
Colorado	20 August 1996
Breakfast	15 August 2004
Arizona	25 February 2001
Fat	7 July 2002
California	18 July 1999
Hamburgers	11 March 2001
Corn	*Tatler* May 1996
Miami	18 April 1999
Las Vegas	27 July 2003
Argentina	7 January 2001
Germany	6 December 1998
Peshawar	18 November 2001
Japan: *Market*	27 May 2001
Manners	3 September 2006
Vietnam	8 December 2002, 15 December 2002 and 17 February 2002
Chinese: *Chinese restaurant*	3 November 1996
Shark's fin soup	2 August 1998
Sichuan	21 May 2006
Indian: *Butter*	12 December 2004
Curry	2 April 2000
South Africa: *Game park*	4 February 1996
Ostrich	1 September 1996
Johannesburg	3 April 2005
Ethiopia	3 December 2000
Morocco *(1)*	5 November 2000
(2)	24 April 2005
Greece	7 March 1999 and 8 September 2002
Lebanese	12 May 1996
Jewish food: *Jerusalem*	14 November 1999

Dates refer to *Sunday Times* unless otherwise indicated.

Index